# BLACK NIGHT
# FOR BOMBER
# COMMAND

For Arthur and Joseph

# BLACK NIGHT
# FOR BOMBER
# COMMAND

## The Tragedy of 16 December 1943

RICHARD KNOTT

Pen & Sword
**AVIATION**

First published in 2007 and reprinted in paperback format in 2014 by
PEN & SWORD AVIATION
An imprint of
Pen & Sword Books Ltd
47 Church Street
Barnsley, South Yorkshire
S70 2AS

ISBN 978 1 47382 295 5

A CIP catalogue record for this book is
available from the British Library

Printed and bound in England
By CPI Group (UK) Ltd, Croydon, CR0 4YY

Pen & Sword Books Ltd incorporates the Imprints of Aviation, Atlas,
Family History, Fiction, Maritime, Military, Discovery, Politics, History,
Archaeology, Select, Wharncliffe Local History, Wharncliffe True Crime,
Military Classics, Wharncliffe Transport, Leo Cooper, The Praetorian Press,
Remember When, Seaforth Publishing and Frontline Publishing

For a complete list of Pen & Sword titles please contact
PEN & SWORD BOOKS LIMITED
47 Church Street, Barnsley, South Yorkshire, S70 2AS, England
E-mail: enquiries@pen-and-sword.co.uk
Website: www.pen-and-sword.co.uk

# CONTENTS

# INTRODUCTION

It is a scene familiar from dozens of black and white war films, and it chimes with so many family memories across Europe: lone serviceman on a station platform, kitbag at his feet, going back to active service, in this case flying over Germany on dark nights, often in cruel weather. This is Donald Penfold, a rear gunner with 97 Squadron. It is 1943. On the platform edge is a small boy for whom this airman is his Uncle Donald. The boy, Peter, is nine years old and will never forget this moment, although he was never to see his Uncle Donald again. Soon after returning to the war, Penfold, along with many other RAF aircrew, died when the Lancaster in which he was flying crashed as it attempted to land in thick fog in the dead of night.

During a lunch party sixty-three years later, close to the point where this book was finished, a chance conversation revealed that I was talking to Donald Penfold's nephew, someone whom I had known for fifteen years or more without ever touching on this link with the past. Later, his wife wrote to me: 'Peter's main memory is of the two uncles Don and Len, in 1943, standing with him ... on the station at West Worthing, about to return to their home in Surrey before Uncle Donald went back to the War. They looked at each other and said: 'What shall we give him?' – and to Peter's delight and amazement they each gave him a *florin* (i.e. 2/– 10 new pence).' I could see the three of them, suspended in time, on a day of bright summer sun, long ago.

For me, having spent three years of my life researching the events of one grim night in RAF history – Black Thursday – it was one of those moments when the people caught up in that drama emerged from the shadows, the more so when I realised that Uncle Don had died in Lancaster 'P' for Peter. The connection between the two Peters hints at the story this book seeks to tell. *Black Night for Bomber Command* has been written with an eye to people's history, rather than the detail of aerial combat and bomb loads. Necessarily it describes the raid on Berlin that began the tragedy, but the emphasis thereafter is on the struggle between airmen and the elements, and what makes the former worthy of memory and record.

# ACKNOWLEDGEMENTS

A book of this kind relies hugely on the good will – and memories – of many people. I am enormously grateful to all of them. Without exception, where I have asked for help and advice it has been freely given. My father-in-law, Arthur Spencer, has been a constant source of information, a critical friend, and a great encouragement throughout this enterprise. All writers should have such a companion on the way. One of my oldest and best friends, Thain Hatherly, read the manuscript at a critical stage and was a wise counsellor on matters great and small. He gave hugely of his time in commenting on the draft and I am extremely grateful to him.

Of the survivors of Black Thursday, Roger Coulombe was a most willing and encouraging witness to the events of 16 December 1943. Our continuing e-mail correspondence across the Atlantic never fails to warm my heart. Other survivors who provided me with information and insights included J Peter Green, Henry Horscroft, E Hedley, Len Whitehead, Ken Duddell, Mike Hedgeland, Bill Kilmurray, Ted Mercer, Charles Clarke, Ronald Low, John H Ward, Bill Pearson and Sandy Sandison.

I am particularly grateful to Bob Wilson for permission to quote from his autobiography *Behind the Network* and to include photographs of his brother Billy; to Jennie Gray for the initial inspiration; 'Dick' Barton for information about the crash at Eastrington; Rich Allenby; Roger Stephenson; Robin Lingard; Dave Cheetham; Ron Parker; Des Evans; Ian McGregor at the National Meteorological Archive; Brian Boulton for information, research and photographs relating to the crash at Iken; Angela and Peter Awbery White; Bob Adams for information about Malcolm Western; John Whiteley; Ray Barker; Pauleen Balls; Julian Hendy; Max Liddle; Ian Reid and Ian Walker, for the loan of photographs of his father Arthur Walker, together with his log book.

I would also like to thank the following for help and advice at various points in the research: my wife, Vanessa; Chris Thomas; John Thorp; Tom Gatfield; John Rees; Bill Napier; James Heneage; Dr Gerald Rolph at Allerton Castle; Vern White; Peter Parnham; Alex Wedderburn; Horace Bennett; Arthur White; David Fell; I D Golder and Graham Pitchfork.

The following organisations have been invaluable resources: the Yorkshire Air Museum; the National Meteorological Archive; the National Archives; National Defence Headquarters, Ottawa, Canada; the Memorial Room at RAF Linton-on-Ouse; the RAF Museum; the Imperial War Museum; Lincolnshire County Archives; the Second World War Experience Centre; the Yorkshire Evening Press; City of York Libraries; York City Archives and Ipswich Record Office.

I have sought to acknowledge in the text and footnotes the provenance of my sources. I am very grateful to those on whom I have drawn. Every effort has been made to seek permission to quote wherever practicable. I am conscious, however, that I have failed to track down the family of Sergeant Bernard Clark whose diary I draw on in chapter three. I hope that this recognition of his heroism and humanity compensates for the unsanctioned use of his diary, found on the BBC's 'People's War' website.

Finally I apologise for any errors I may have inadvertently made, or sources I have not fully recognised or thanked. This book could not have been written without the diligence of others who put pen to paper before me.

'I am not pressing you to fight the weather as well as the Germans, never forget that.'

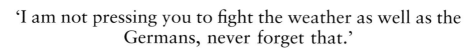

Sir Winston Churchill

'I also decided that the book I'd write would not be a novel, but simply a true tale cut from the cloth of reality, concocted out of true events and characters.'

'Soldiers of Salamis', Javier Cercas

# CHAPTER ONE

# COLD DECEMBER NIGHT, 1943

They watched the gathering mist slowly roll across the airfields as the afternoon faded, expecting the raid to be scrubbed. It was mid-winter and mid-war – 16 December 1943 – and the target was Berlin. Across eastern England thousands of young men readied themselves, periodically pausing to gauge the developing weather on that sombre winter afternoon. The anticipated cancellation never came.

At dusk, nearly five hundred aircraft – almost entirely Lancaster bombers – began to trundle down the runways. They resembled 'enormous black birds going off into the night.'[1] The journey was a long one – more than seven hours[2] – and meant penetrating deep into enemy territory. The crews lifted off from dozens of airfields in eastern England, from north Yorkshire to southern Cambridgeshire, soon after 4 pm. Bombs began to fall on the German capital some four hours later. They were expected back around midnight, maybe earlier if luck was with them. Luck however was to prove capricious. In the event, more than 300 RAF men died that night, almost half of them when the raid should have been over. They were victims of foul weather, not the Germans.

Once the decision had been taken to fly, the false comfort of routine took over. The crews ate an 'operational meal' in the mess – real eggs and bacon. The more cynical airmen reflected that they were being fattened up for the kill. There were three priorities: food (sandwiches to be stowed aboard, and a thermos of coffee); warmth (long johns, a heavy submariner's sweater, fur-lined Irvine suit); and safety (the checking of vital equipment, Mae West and parachute). Then the drive by bus, or in the back of a three-ton lorry, to the waiting aircraft, a black, brooding presence in the darkness. Desultory chat with the ground crew, final fag and ceremonial pee against the wheel – for luck.

Soon the aircraft began the slow trundle along the tarmac, each pilot intent on the one in front – observing the impact of the wind at the point of take-off – and mind racing with thoughts of darkness, bomb and fuel load, home and destiny. The light on the runway controller's caravan flashes green through the mist ... Once airborne, it isn't long

*'Enormous black birds going off into the night.'* – *the Lancaster dwarfing its crew.*
From the Museum of Lincolnshire Life, by courtesy of Lincolnshire County Council

before the fleet heads out over the North Sea, past Flamborough Head or Southwold, and on towards the German mainland and, deep in its heart, the distant capital. So began this bleakest of nights for Bomber Command in its onslaught against Berlin.

The Battle of Berlin had begun with the advent of long hours of darkness as the winter of 1943 unfolded. Arthur Harris, Commander-in-Chief of Bomber Command, saw it as a crucial battle. He wrote to Churchill on 3 November 1943: 'We can wreck Berlin from end to end if the USAAF will come in on it. It will cost between us 400–500 aircraft. It will cost Germany the war.'[3] The RAF had long since lost its taste for daylight raids, however, and recent night attacks on Berlin did not augur well: the most recent raid, on the night of 2 and 3 December, had been hindered by an inaccurate weather forecast, so that the Pathfinders struggled to pinpoint locations in the murky confusion over the German capital. It was a particularly challenging target: the end point of a four hour outward journey, and if they got there, it was prodigiously defended by flak, while the city itself sprawled, rather than having its key buildings grouped in close, readily-combustible

*Air and ground crew, 100 Squadron.* From the Museum of Lincolnshire Life, by courtesy of Lincolnshire County Council

proximity.[4] Its sheer size presented particular difficulties for navigators whose H2S sets were too primitive. One navigator commented: 'It was just too big!'[5]

The winter brought further problems. Harris later wrote: 'The whole battle was fought in appalling weather ... Scarcely a single crew caught a glimpse of the objective they were attacking (and) ... scarcely any photographs taken during the bombing showed anything except clouds.'[6] Morale was eroded by the Command's stubborn, bulldog insistence on attacking Berlin again and again: novice crews were required to set off for midwinter flights for the city within days of arriving at the squadron base fresh from training. Many passed through base invisibly on a rapid journey from training to death. They scarcely had time to unpack. As one survivor put it: 'Sadly the new ones got the chop. It was like Russian roulette.'[7]

Inexperienced pilots were far more likely to crash on returning to base. Work by the Operational Research Section[8] clearly showed the vulnerability of tyro pilots: 'The investigation confirms the higher missing rate, crash rate, early return rate and combat rate among inexperienced crews.' The Section's report went on to point to increased vulnerability just after the middle of the first operational tour. Then, it noted, 'the only significant point is the higher crash rate among beginners. The corrective for this would be an increased number of practice landings under all sorts of conditions.' Fog was not mentioned specifically, but it might well have been ...

Morale was affected by key operational decisions at Bomber Command HQ. For example, crews were tempted to jettison bombs in an effort to improve manoeuvrability; they were often sceptical of the decision to increase bomb tonnage with consequent adverse effects on the ability of pilots to throw the aircraft around the sky in determined evasive tactics[9].

Berlin became – for the survivors anyway – an all too familiar objective: one pilot's diary entry for 16 December 1943 reads: 'This is our fourth trip to Berlin in succession. It's become a "milk run" for us.'[10] A navigator in 97 Squadron, Flying Officer Jim Logan, looking back on those days, commented that 'it was easier to get to Berlin than Nottingham, our favourite retreat.' The vast distance tested the crews' stamina and, once they finally got there, the city's defences were fierce and unrelenting. To get there and back under the cover of darkness meant flying in the middle of winter when the sun set early and rose late. The weather, in consequence, was usually bad – cloud and rain, frost and snow, and often fog that refused to break, drifting for days over dank, mournful aerodromes. George Barrett, a Flight Engineer with 158 Squadron[11], caught the Yorkshire weather perfectly: '... 1943's cruel, bitterly cold winter was a nightmare, with coke-fired stoves providing us with scant warmth in Nissen huts strategically placed in the middle of mud-filled fields ...'[12]

The weather was grim in London too: Australian Cliff Halsall (460 Squadron) wrote in his diary for 11 December: '... It has now rained on 71 of the last 97 days. Tonight is a typical winter's night in London – wet and misty, dark and cold, dreary and uninviting ...'[13] Fellow Australian Ken McIntyre 'faced fogs so thick that he could not see the motorcycle he was riding on.'[14]

Despite the determination to take the war right to the heart of Germany, attacks on Berlin had been heavily restricted in early December, in marked contrast to late November when raids had been launched on the nights of 18th, 22nd, 23rd, and 26th. Thereafter, there had only been one raid – on the 2nd – then a long gap when the weather had closed in. Time was killed with conventional airforce – and pre-Christmas – activities. 426 Squadron based at Linton-on-Ouse, to the north of York, was typical: on 4 December a squadron band entertained at Hull's New Theatre and raised over £100 for the Orphans' Fund. Two days later, the Joe Loss Orchestra played at the NAAFI. There was flying training on the 8th and two successive full moons, as unwelcome to bomber crews as thick cloud, but for different reasons: it was as bad to be easily seen at night as to blunder on blindly in the cloud-thick darkness. A raid on the 11th was cancelled just after midnight because of bad weather. All flying was cancelled on the 15th – a day of unremitting fog. Thirteen days without a flight in anger. It was a time for mending socks and playing poker.

At Skellingthorpe, near Lincoln, Sergeant Bernard Clark, a wireless operator with 61 Squadron, wrote feelingly in his diary[15] of the grim weather on the 14th: 'Awful morning, fog and frost.' He killed the time writing letters, and no doubt his diary, while his Australian air gunner wrestled with the problem of how to skin and cook the rabbit he had snared in the wintry fields. At Gransden Lodge, Cambridgeshire, 405 Squadron's gunners went clay pigeon shooting on the 15th, while the bomb-aimers made do with a quiz and the navigators sat through a lecture. For two weeks Berliners had slept at night undisturbed.

By Thursday the 16th, there was great pressure on to get crews airborne and thundering east towards the 'Big City'. Much rested on the weathermen ... 'We had to take what the Met told us ... the Met bloke would come on with the weather expected. Always wrong. That was one of the things, the tragedy of the war ... Lots of crews were lost due to weather on return. We were diverted often because your base was under fog. It depended what petrol load you had left. A lot of fellows went for a burton that way.'[16] 'On many raids,' 61 Squadron gunner Len Whitehead[17] recalled, 'the planning was suspect, poor meteorological reports being one of the chief reasons ... at one briefing the met officer stated the skies would be clear for take-off. This was greeted with wild laughter as it was lashing with rain outside with little hope of it stopping before flying was due to start.'

Not all aircrew would share that bitter judgement about those working hard at an imprecise science in a world where life or death might rest on the outcome of informed guesswork. There were, after all, no weather satellites in 1943, nor even the weather ships in the Atlantic which had informed forecasts in peacetime. While weather forecasting in that harsh winter of 1943 was always uncertain, the weather itself was an unforgiving, unremitting enemy. Aircrew were beset by flak and fighters; physical exhaustion; biting cold; cacophonous noise; fear – and deteriorating weather conditions that could place their lives in jeopardy. Even over England and close to home ... The night of 16 December 1943 – deep and bitter midwinter – proved the point. The death toll – victims of the night's cruel weather – earned it the name 'Black Thursday'.[18]

CHAPTER TWO

# BEGINNINGS – YOUR BRIEFING

Six decades on, you can't drive far in Yorkshire – at least the flat bits of it – without seeing the remains of a derelict airfield: rubble from disused runways; a control tower with its windows boarded up and weeds high up the walls; huts with scraps of flowered curtain at the moss-streaked windows. Each time I drive past, or stop and look across the spread of it, I am aware of ghosts from sixty years ago: those young men, that night sky, those early deaths. It is a recent obsession, born not of a fascination with combat – the tonnage of bombs or even the cut and thrust of mid-air jousting – but more to do with trying to understand how it felt, what enabled some to survive and consigned others to die all too soon. And you were more likely to die, the fewer trips you had flown. The most dangerous time was during the first five raids. I think of them each time I drive past; despite the dereliction and decay of the runways and buildings, I can sense some lingering imprint that these fields had once been dense with aircraft and the lanes peopled with long-lost airmen cycling shakily back from a night out in Betty's Bar in York, weaving across the road in beer-fuddled darkness. Now there are shabby industrial estates where the bombers flew, and post-war houses in roads called Halifax Way or Blenheim Close.

They were so young too, for the most part. Arthur Spencer, a navigator with 97 Squadron (and my father-in-law), writes about his Canadian pilot Jimmy Munro: 'There was no transport about to take us to dispersal, so we trooped into the Flight Commander's office ... The Wingco said at once, "My van's outside; I shan't be needing it for an hour or two. Take that." Jimmy at once responded that he couldn't drive. W/C Alabaster turned to me and commented, "It makes you realise how long the war's been on, doesn't it? Here's this chap who's done nearly forty trips in a Lancaster, and can't drive a car!" '[1]

Arthur was lucky enough to miss Black Thursday by less than three months. He had completed forty-five operations by the time he was in his early twenties. His non-driving pilot, Jimmy Munro, was shot down over Berlin during the night of 22/23 November, 1943. He and his crew have no known grave. It was Jimmy's fifty-seventh operation.

During 1999, Arthur was contacted by Jennie Gray, the daughter of a 97 Squadron survivor from Black Thursday, who was writing a book about the experience of her father's crew on their ill-fated return from Berlin on the 16 December 1943. The book – a moving and compelling picture of the events of that night as they affected one Pathfinder crew – was published in 2000[2]. It is that book which has triggered my further investigation: why was it that so many men died trying to land their aircraft? 97 Squadron lost eight[3] aircraft that night, but the losses extended to a string of other squadrons flying from airfields as far apart as Wyton in Cambridgeshire, Grimsby and Elsham Wolds in Lincolnshire, East Moor and Linton-on-Ouse in north Yorkshire, and so on. There were forty-three crashes in all.[4] As well as the losses amongst Lancaster crews, others died on their return from

Special Operations Executive (SOE) trips to northern France. The skies were full of confused and befogged pilots: 13 per cent of them were diverted to alternative airfields[5]. Four crews even crashed on training flights, two of them in the broad area from which the bombers charged with bombing Berlin that night came. For example, a Halifax hit a low hill between Harrogate and York late at night on the 16th and a second careered into two straw stacks and a large chicken coop near Cottingham, Lincolnshire. Quite why inexperienced crews were flying that night when, within the hour, the skies would be full of tired, disorientated pilots struggling to find base in such grim flying conditions beggars belief.[6]

*Jimmy Munro and Arthur Spencer – then both sergeants, but subsequently Flight Lieutenants – photographed in the latter's garden at Southampton. Munro – too young to drive a car – flew fifty-seven operations.* Arthur Spencer

*The certificate awarded to the Munro crew for its commendable accuracy over the target, in this case, Milan.* Arthur Spencer

Early in the exercise, I made a list of the questions that I wanted to investigate:

- How was it that so many men could die, not by enemy fire, but by deteriorating weather conditions?
- Why did 97 Squadron lose so many more than the other squadrons?
- Who was to blame?
- What happened afterwards?
- What kind of investigation took place afterwards and what did it reveal?
- What was learned as a result?
- Was it all kept under wraps? Or did the country at large know about what happened?
- When did it become apparent that the night was to be of such disastrous proportions?
- Why did some crews run out of fuel?
- Why were there marked differences in the times the planes crashed?
- Was there ever a near repetition of these events?
- What happened to the survivors?
- Finally: what were these young men like?

I started by writing letters to squadron associations, wondering if the search for survivors – of age, not war – would be in time. How effective and reliable is memory after sixty years? It was, after all, a long time ago.

CHAPTER THREE

# FIRE IN THE BELLY

The curtain is pulled back. A red ribbon – apt colour – stretches across a familiar map. There is a collective groan. Berlin. Again. Between November 1943 and March 1944, this pattern was to be repeated sixteen times[1]. But on Black Thursday it had been two weeks since crews had seen the red ribbon reaching for the German capital. At RAF Wyton in Huntingdonshire, the squadron commander, Group Captain 'Honest John' Searby read out a signal from the Commander-in-Chief: 'Butch wants you all to know that the only reason you haven't been going to the Big City of late is that he's been waiting for a night when the weather is so bad that all the German fighters are grounded and so give you all an easy trip.' Perversely, given the treadmill that Berlin had become, the crews burst out laughing – a combination perhaps of nervous tension and shock at Harris's insouciance.[2] The raid two weeks before Christmas 1943 was the sixth in the series. Months before, Harris had sent another signal to his crews that left little to the imagination: 'You have the opportunity to light a fire in the belly of the enemy and burn his Black Heart out.' In the five raids from mid-November, over four weeks, an estimated 4,536 Germans, foreign workers and prisoners of war were killed. RAF deaths attacking Berlin over the same period totalled 766.

Bad weather and Berlin were synonymous: the city was completely cloud-covered on each of the first three raids. On 26/27 November it was clear over the capital, but the marking of the targets was inaccurate. The Berlin Zoo was hit,[3] freeing the inmates: liberated wild animals – leopards, panthers, apes – roamed the city streets until they were shot. The early December raid was not hindered by cloud – or the wind that played havoc with the raid on the 26th – but the damage was scattered and haphazard.

The raid launched on the 16 December was one that the survivors would never forget. Canadian gunner Warrant Officer Doug Curtis[4] spoke for many: 'There is no doubt that the one op that stands out in my mind was the trip we did with No.97 Squadron to Berlin on the night of 16/17 December 1943 ...'

\*    \*    \*    \*

An optimist waking early on the 16 December would have taken one look at the weather, turned over and dreamt of peace. It was cold, dark and damp and when the light finally came, there was no glimpse even of wintry sun. It was England at its most dank. Clouds lay heavy over the airfield. Everything dripped. Elsewhere, decisions had already been taken: Harris's finger had settled on the German capital; reports from weather reconnaissance aircraft[5] had been scrutinised; qualms suppressed; and orders teleprinted. ('The first wave is to be manned by specially selected experienced crews.')[6] At each airfield, there was intense activity: the towing of bomb loads, rattle of loading cartridges, rumbling petrol bowsers, painstaking ground crew with oily rags, reliant in their tiredness on checklists and systems. Airmen shivered, looked at the sky and wondered what the night would bring.

There was no break in the weather by mid-morning. The test flights went ahead and the crews speculated on the night's target, perturbed by the fuel and bomb load whose capacity and tonnage was enough to narrow down the options. The prospect was not reassuring: it was a distant target and that was enough to set rumours flying and stomachs turning. 'I knew it when they put 1850 gallons in the tanks. I thought it'd be Berlin'[7]. Time dragged despite the preoccupied games of cards or shove ha'penny.

Briefing conformed to the familiar pattern: the top brass's brisk centre aisle entry through a haze of cigarette smoke; roll call (not the only echo of school routines); intelligence officer with his well-worn preamble ('Well, gentlemen, your target tonight is – Berlin'); and then the met man, with the room darkened, screen illuminated by a slice of light – 'This is the estimated synoptic situation for 2300 hours ...' At Wyton, there was little attempt to disguise the prevalence of fog: 'The met officer ... painted a gloomy picture of fog obscuring the country, and with no diversion airfields available by the time of our return, the general attitude was one of 'If we're going, let's get on with it – we might even get back before the fog really clamps down ...'[8]

\*     \*     \*     \*

At Skellingthorpe, near Lincoln, 61 Squadron's Flying Officer Bob West is preparing for his crew's first operation; he alone knows what to expect following his 'second dickey' trip to Leipzig nearly a fortnight before.[9] The preceding days have been shrouded in fog and the crew has killed time as best they can: tramps in the dark to the nearest phone box to ring girl friends; cinema in Lincoln ('Five Graves to Cairo'); cards, table tennis and snooker; haircuts; rissoles and chips, bread and butter at Boots in the city; and setting rabbit snares in the wood behind the hut. Suddenly it is 'ops tonight' and 'the Big City': a rapid change into long underwear and an 'ops meal' – egg and bacon, bread and butter and coffee. When they take off, they are touched by the line of figures waving them off into the twilight. Then things begin to go wrong: *Monica*, a device for locating enemy aircraft, develops a fault; next wireless operator Clark finds the fuselage door open and struggles against a fierce wind to close it. Eventually he and Flight Engineer Bill Warburton manage to tie it shut with a length of rope. All this and they haven't reached Holland yet ...

\*    \*    \*    \*

They took off in the late afternoon, in cloud and darkness, heading inexorably for Holland and then northern Germany, carrying nearly 7,000 pounds of explosives and incendiaries[10]. Apart from fifteen Mosquitoes, the aircraft were all Lancaster bombers: the RAF's principal four-engined bomber, rather than Halifaxes which were no longer relied upon for raids on Berlin. Ironically, given the events of the night, the reason for preferring the Lancaster, it seems, was its ability to cope better with bad weather: '... owing to weather conditions, only Lancasters were able to operate ...'[11] Back at Bomber Command HQ in Buckinghamshire, Arthur Harris had serious reservations about the Halifax. On 20 January 1943 he had written to the Secretary of State for Air about the aircraft, characteristically pulling no punches: 'This is to acquaint you fully of the situation regarding the Halifax ... it is unacceptable for operational use in this Command now, and unless greatly improved, it will be impossible to use it on operations within a few months.'[12] It didn't stop seventy-five Halifaxes bombing Lorient three days later, or indeed Berlin on 20 January 1944, when 264 Halifaxes were despatched, or 15 February when 314 were sent to Berlin (plus three other attacks on Berlin in January and February).

On 16 December the take-off time was suddenly brought forward twenty minutes and aircraft took off with less than a full bomb load.[13] Inevitably this change of time caused what pilot 'Skip' Lloyd called 'a bit of panic' at RAF Linton-on-Ouse. Two of Linton's aircraft turned back, its crews torn between relief and an awareness that their early return would not count towards completing their tour. Turning for home they had ditched their bombs into the North Sea. The rest pressed on, peering into the darkness, checking the gauges or the maps, waiting for the rattle of bullets against the fuselage. It took just over an hour to fly across the North Sea. Thereafter, it was enemy territory with Berlin still hours ahead. Moreover, the Germans knew they were coming. . . .

\*    \*    \*    \*

Enemy coast at 21,000 feet; heavy cloud and bursts of flak. Despite the problems, 61 Squadron's Bob West[14] is on time, neatly wedged in the stream of bombers on the pre-set path between Bremen and Hannover. Then it is Berlin and there is a flurry of activity: bombs gone at almost the same time as rear gunner Frank Langley is heard whimpering in his lonely turret: his oxygen is failing. As the aircraft shudders with the release of the bombs, Sergeant Clark thinks: 'Take that one. And those. Share that lot between you!' Then there is a faint cry of help from Langley and throaty gurgles down the intercom. West's eyes remain fixed on the fire-lit night in front of him: 'See if you can give him a hand.' Clark carries a spare oxygen bottle and a torch to the rear of the plane. It is bitingly cold here, not least because the rear door is slightly ajar, and it takes a moment or two to open the doors of the rear turret. There is ice around Langley's oxygen mask which Clark breaks off, acutely conscious as he does so of the lights all around them and the tracer flying past. Moments later, Clark finds his arm pinioned between the turret and the rear of the fuselage and feels a wave of panic: he only has two minutes supply of oxygen in his own bottle. He struggles with increasing intensity and drops the torch, before freeing himself. Below them the land changes to Denmark, and then ocean, and at that point where one gives way to the other, there is heavy flak reaching up at them.

Langley is hauled from his turret and stretched out along the tail cross member and attached to a new bottle of oxygen. He starts to recover, although the electric heating in his flying suit is not working and he is unbearably cold. Bob West loses some height to ease Langley's discomfort and blasts headlong through the flak barrage. First trip nearly over, they head out over the North Sea.

\*     \*     \*     \*

Pilot Officer F E McLean of 83 Squadron took off from Wyton a minute before Bob West at 4.39 pm. They would have been close together in the steady stream of bomb-laden aircraft. An Australian, flying with a fellow Australian and a New Zealander in the crew, he described his experience in Lancaster JB344 that night in a letter to his mother:

'We had flown over Holland, Belgium, France, Denmark and Germany[15] and arrived over Berlin's defences a couple of minutes before our bombing time, and seeing that we were the first aircraft to arrive over the city we had to take all the flak that Berlin's five hundred guns had to offer for a few moments ...' McLean killed time in the darkness, turning away from the aiming point and circling apprehensively while the guns blazed away below him. One Intelligence

Officer soon after this raid told his squadron's crews that Berlin's flak guns were fired by schoolboys and loaded by Russian prisoners of war.[16] But this blasé advice wasn't borne out by the intensity of that night's barrage. A stray shell exploded directly under the aircraft's nose, reducing the wireless to silence and damaging some other instrumentation.

Flight Engineer W Kilmurray, 115 Squadron, was flying with Pilot Officer E H Boutilier for the first time: ' "Boots" believed in weaving over enemy territory ... I stood by the flare chute, dropping "Window" every minute whilst the aircraft was going up and down like a roller coaster. I was violently sick!'[17]

The cloud over the city – as it was all the way from England and, crucially, for the entire return – was impenetrable. In a hundred log books, the surviving pilots echoed Flight Lieutenant Charles Owen's entry, (97 Squadron), 'ten tenths cloud over target'. The fleet of Lancasters had been trapped in continuous cloud from take-off. Cloud exacerbated the risk of aircraft collisions in the confusion over Berlin: the official view was to expect as inevitable one or two collisions over the target on a big raid.[18] The bombs when they fell seemed to the Germans to have no obvious aiming point: they tumbled from the sky unforgivingly, black and bulbous and caught in their plunging path by the flickering light of flame and gunfire. Berliners, according to Christabel Bielenburg, an Englishwoman married to a German, were phlegmatic rather than consumed with fear: '(the) barrage from the air ... (bred) a certain fatalistic cussedness, a dogged determination to survive.'[19]

Most of the damage occurred in the central and eastern parts of the city: rows of burning houses, disrupted railway links, but little impact on factories or industrial sites. Later, in the confusion, with the air heavy with the smell of destruction, the Germans estimated a thousand deaths, including 279 'foreign workers', the majority of them women. More than a quarter of those workers (seventy-nine) were killed in a train at Hallensee station. In the centre of the city, the National Theatre was blown apart and nearby a building which housed military and political archives was gutted. Photographs taken on 20/21 December by two Spitfires from 541 PRU Squadron revealed damage to legations, embassies and the main income tax office – with some eight square miles being devastated.[20] The most significant damage was to the railway system, the result of which was delays of supplies to the beleaguered Russian front (Kiev had fallen to the Russians in November and the Red Army was everywhere relentlessly driving forward).

The raid had begun with 482 Lancasters heading east in weather that was forecast to be cloudy, breaking up near the enemy coast to become thinner and patchier over the continent. Low cloud was predicted over Berlin. The weather was not enough to deter night fighter activity over Holland en route to the German capital. 409 aircraft actually attacked the city (ten had diverted to alternative targets); over thirty had aborted or failed to take off; others had been shot down. Seventeen returned damaged by flak. The raid was characterised, like most others, by mid-air collisions, aircraft damaged by incendiaries dropped by their own side; and aircraft shot down by the significant fighter response.

With the job done, the remaining crews turned and headed west towards the North Sea, flying on instruments because of the weather that continued to worsen, but oblivious to the danger into which they were flying.

\*      \*      \*      \*

Bob West and his crew struggled on until they reached the coast near Cromer. The cloud hung low at just 700 feet and West chose to keep above it until they reached base. Landing was 'wizard' according to Bernard Clark, recapturing a memorable night in his diary. It was twenty minutes to one on the morning of the 17th. Eating the post-interrogation breakfast, Clark reflected on how the ground crew had cheered their return. It was approaching 3 am before they fell into bed. West's luck, and the rest of his crew's, was to hold for a while longer, but others that night were not so fortunate ...

CHAPTER FOUR

# THE LIE OF THE LAND

One Wednesday in March 2004 – a day of brisk westerly winds and distant views – I drove to each of the four crash sites in North Yorkshire. To me the places seemed connected somehow, and they were all just a few moments' flying time from Linton's runways. I half expected – certainly wanted anyway – some evidence of the crashes: if not deep craters, and farmland periodically revealing fragments of metal, then maybe a memorial, or someone with a long memory and a tale to tell. But for the most part there was no sign. High on the moors, I found thin rusted fragments of metal amongst the rubble from a collapsed wall that a Lancaster had hit, but in truth, they could have been decaying tractor parts or broken farm fencing.

The first three sites all involved Lancasters flying out of Linton-on-Ouse. Hunsingore is a tranquil village clustered around the church of St John the Baptist – daffodils, mossy graveyard and stone flecked with pink. The village stands on a paltry ridge about 150 feet above sea level, dividing the River Nidd from the A1. To the west, on this day of breezy clarity, I could see the Pennines. At 11.31 pm on the night of 16 December, the pilot, Flight Sergeant R D Stewart (426 Squadron) from Cochrane, Ontario, could have seen nothing beyond his perspex screen other than thick proliferating fog. The ridge, little more than a wrinkle above a floodplain, would have been hit before he could see it, peering as he was into the darkness, searching for the Linton runway just six miles away. Even closer is RAF Marston Moor, under three miles away to the east. Stewart was relatively inexperienced – he had flown just sixty-four hours at night and only twenty-two in a Lancaster. He hit the ground while desperately searching for the lowest point of the cloud base.[1] The two survivors – both gunners – 'escaped with slight injuries.'[2] Sergeant D S Jamieson, from Winnipeg, Manitoba, had a particularly eventful war, but not one with a happy ending. He crashed again at sea on 5 March 1944, and then was shot down in a Halifax in the early hours of 29 June 1944 over Metz. Don Jamieson had left his turret, stepped through billowing flames, and baled out through the main hatch. He and his colleague Pilot Officer Birnie, the aircraft's navigator, evaded capture for a while, heading west for the Allied lines. They were captured near Pont l'Eveque in Normandy. Both are presumed shot by the Gestapo.[3]

*Sgt Don Jamieson, a gunner with 426 Squadron, who survived the crash at Hunsingore. He was to die at the hands of the Gestapo in the summer of 1944. The photograph is from his personnel file.*
Julian Hendy

There is no monument here, and at that time I had no grid reference for the actual site. In truth, I did not feel close – the village was too neat and tranquil somehow. It is the sort of cautious place where a stranger's parked car makes the curtains twitch: a sign on a gate illustrates a slavering hound and the words 'I can reach the gate in three seconds. Can you?' Above me I could hear the roar of jets from Linton. I headed north, past Allerton Park and over the wooden Aldwark bridge (a fifteen pence toll for a slow crossing over the River Ouse) and then skirted around the edge of Linton aerodrome while single-engined trainers practised their circuits and bumps in a sky half blue, half cloud.

Yearsley is another small village: a few houses and farm buildings astride a crossroads in the Hambleton hills. It is ten miles from Linton, but high above it. Beyond the market town of Easingwold, the road starts to rise and fall and Yearsley is on the first green shoulder of hill standing proud above the Vale of York. At 550 feet above sea level it presented a brooding threat to the Lancaster of Squadron Leader Thomas Kneale (RCAF). The fog was sufficiently thick to negate Kneale's experience: aged twenty-nine, he had flown sixteen operations and was commander of 426 Squadron's B flight. He had fulfilled that role for just nineteen days. A Canadian from Woodstock, Ontario, he was 'a very nice person, rather quiet and respectful of the men of his Flight ... he was liked and respected by all of us.'[4] At a quarter to midnight he thundered into the hillside. According to one resident, the Lancaster took the roof off one of the buildings and came to rest close to the crossing of the two minor roads at the head of the village. He was emerging from the cloud base when he hit the ground. The subsequent Accident Report Form – Form 1180 – raised the possibility of an error in setting the altimeter correctly. In a rare moment of bureaucratic hyperbole, the form continues: 'the slightest E of J meant disaster'. 'E of J' stands for 'Error of Judgement'.

As with all such accidents, the debris was cleared as soon after the event as possible, with recycling of any surviving parts being a prime motive. A search of the internet revealed a photograph of something they missed – a fire extinguisher bottle, since metamorphosed into a vase and sitting somewhere on some anonymous window sill. I was told that no one was left alive in the village who had lived there when the Lancaster erupted from the night sky killing all but one of its crew. Later, I came across details of an auction held at The Golden Fleece Hotel in Thirsk on 19 June 1944 which included a property (Lot 20) situated next to Chestnut Cottage whose outbuildings had 'been damaged by a recent bomber crash.' The damage apparently extended (Lot 11 – the 'Valued Licensed Property known as The Wombwell Arms') to the wall surrounding a nearby field.[5]

To the east of Yearsley the hills soon turn to high moorland. A Lancaster from 408 Squadron – again flying from Linton-on-Ouse – crashed into Silver Hill farm, near Hawnby. It is windswept and bleak

*The reference to the crash at Yearsley in the sale of the Wombwell Arms in 1944: 'the wall running around the field nearest the House has suffered damage through a bomber crash'.* Max Liddle

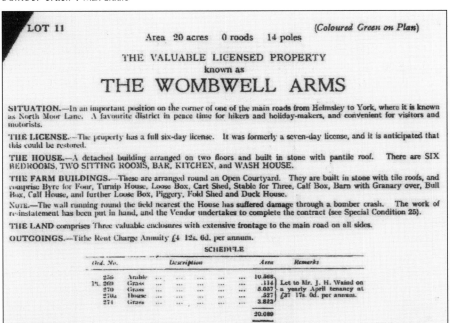

*'The Lancaster took the roof off one of the buildings and came to rest close to the crossing of the two minor roads', Yearsley, Yorkshire.*

up here, even on a day in early spring, and the farm building has largely subsided into crumbling ruin. The crash site here is well documented: it is set just over the road from the farm in a shallow indentation in this rugged landscape about a thousand feet above sea level. The views are spectacular on a fine day but the wind cuts sharp: it is a tough place to farm, and harder still if you're at the controls of a returning bomber in the dark and irrevocably lost. The nearest airfield must be Linton but it seems quite distant. Flying Officer Russell S Clark, the Canadian pilot, survived the impact: his aircraft clipped the skyline above the farm, marked now by a thin screen of trees capping a field of close-cropped wind-streaked grass. It came to rest in a welter of branches, bricks and churned mud and metal. It was seven minutes short of seven hours since he had taken off. He died on 21 December, but two other crew members survived. They were both gunners. It was the dead navigator who was blamed by administrators back at Linton: '(The pilot) tried to land, but due to poor visibility and low cloud base a landing was attempted with a GEE fix ... the navigator misjudged the location.'[6] I combed the site for debris, found none, had a discreet pee standing on a mound of crumbling stones and headed further east, to the last site at Danby, ten miles from the coast at Whitby.

*Silver Hill Farm, a thousand feet up on the North York Moors: the lonely spot where Flying Officer Clark (408 Squadron) and his crew crashed.*

The circumstances here were different: the crew of 432 Squadron's Lancaster, faced with being lost and out of fuel, had baled out close to the northern edge of the moors. They had taken off from East Moor, near York, at three minutes to five in the afternoon, survived the trip to Berlin and returned to an England shrouded in ten-tenths cloud. They circled around looking for some glimpse of an aerodrome but when the decision was taken to abandon ship they were well adrift from any potential landing place. The Operations Record Book (ORB) notes: '... the aircraft was abandoned over English territory due to technical failures ...' It had been unable to land 'because of the poor visibility' and had been diverted to Leeming.

The crew came down on the heathery slopes of Danby Beacon while the aircraft plunged into Black Beck Swang, near Clitherbeck, an area of boggy ground on high land to the north of the moors village of Danby. For once, this was a lucky crew: what could have been a desperate jump into a chaos of rocks or worse turned out to be a soft descent into a carpet of heather on a broad plateau. Villagers in the subsequent years have searched the site for aircraft remains, despite the best efforts of 60 Mechanised Unit from Tollerton who cleared the area soon after the crash, being forced to use sleds to cope with the engulfing marsh. One villager commented to me: 'We went up there in that hot summer – was it 1976? – found nothing, but some kids went up there later and found bullets! The bog still occasionally regurgitates bits of aircraft when it's very dry.'[7]

Driving home, I thought, almost for the first time, of what it meant to be one of these young men – late teens or early twenties, cold December, eight hours in the darkness, through the hellish turmoil of the raid, full of relief at surviving the night, increasingly panic-stricken as England refused to shed its blanket of thick grey cloud – and after all that, to die – most of them – on a bleak hillside far, too far, from home.

*'The bog still regurgitates bits of aircraft when it's very dry!' Clitherbeck, near Danby, high on the North York Moors.*

CHAPTER FIVE

# HOME TO WHERE WE THOUGHT ENGLAND WAS . . .

A storm cloud of Lancasters then, thundering east towards Germany in the late afternoon of the 16 December[1]. This was the largest force of Lancasters sent to Berlin thus far. With take-off time being brought forward by twenty minutes, the sun was still setting as the first aircraft took to the skies. The bombs began to rain down on the city around 8 pm and in the following hour the return journeys of those who had survived (significantly fewer now) began, following the pre-arranged route over Denmark. Once the fighters had been evaded and the flak faded away behind them, the remaining battle was with fatigue as eyes strained to see through the darkness and the gathering mist.

Back at the English airfields, the ground crews waited, not expecting the first distant rumblings of returning aircraft before 11 pm. Those who looked outside shivered at the deteriorating weather: WAAF Joan Beech, a meteorological assistant at RAF Bourn, the home of 97 Squadron, wrote later: 'A real pea-soup fog descended on eastern England while the squadrons were out, so that they came back to find every airfield shrouded in gloom.'[2] The implications of that gloom would have been clear to her and everyone else on each base, and most of all to the crews droning west through the night. This had become a night where you wouldn't want to drive the car, let alone fly. Oddly, just as the crews were returning, the Prime Minister was taking off for Gibraltar[3]. The fog had come down over RAF Lyneham in Wiltshire and had threatened to ground Churchill's aircraft. The Prime Minister's entourage had struggled west along roads darkened by mist and blackout and it was 11.30 pm before the Liberator took off in the fog, eventually flying above the cloud at 5,000 feet. Churchill then was airborne, his aircraft nosing its way through layers of dense cloud, at the very moment when that winter Thursday began its decline to black.

'After we bombed,' wrote Pilot Officer McLean (83 Squadron) to his mother, 'we had to fly (for) nine hundred miles above cloud without getting a glimpse of anything to position ourselves, and then when we got to where we thought England was, there was thick cloud down to a couple of hundred feet. Not being sure of our position to within twenty miles, we had a few trying moments hoping not to hit a hill (while) flying low without being able to see the ground.'[4] In the hours that followed the raid itself, in the darkness over a wintry and uninviting North Sea, each member of each crew had time to reflect on the fragility of where they were, and what yet might be in store ...

\*     \*     \*     \*

A Lancaster normally had a crew of seven: pilot, navigator, flight engineer, bomb aimer, wireless operator and two gunners, cooped up in perspex turrets, one in the middle of the aircraft and one at the rear. Sometimes, a second pilot went along for the experience, prior to taking his own aircraft and aircrew on his first full operation. Perhaps the unluckiest men of all were those airmen who died on a 'second dickey' trip of this kind.

The journey home was long and arduous: 'You weren't supposed to smoke in the aeroplane, but on the long road home over the North Sea the temptation was usually too strong for me. When we had descended below oxygen height, I would ... loosen my straps, engage the automatic pilot, sit back and really enjoy that cigarette ...' So Jack Currie, a 12 Squadron pilot who bombed Berlin that night, wrote.[5] That black, bleak mid-winter, however, was not one that encouraged such insouciance. Most pilots felt a debilitating blend of exhaustion and growing anxiety about what awaited them once the time came for bad weather landings.

\*     \*     \*     \*

Imagine that you are there, an unseen observer on this grim winter night, less than an hour from a fog-bound airfield. There is a luminous glow from the instrument panel that hints at the extent of the cockpit. In front of you, you can just make out the broad shoulders of two men ignoring you and staring deep beyond the perspex canopy: your pilot and his flight engineer. The number of instruments is daunting – there are, you would guess, more than eighty: ignition and landing light switches, rudder panel, bomb jettison control and throttle levers. Behind the pilot's seat is one of the parachutes. You wonder where yours is and whether there are enough to go round. There is something reassuring about the still calm of the pilot and flight engineer as they sit beside each other in that faintest glimmer of light, the pilot presiding over a sweeping view from port quarter to starboard beam ... 'The glass house. Soft moonlight. Two silent figures ...'[6] They sit enthroned, at the apex of the aircraft, tight with concentration, as if it is their collective willpower alone that keeps them aloft.

You would like to squeeze past the flight engineer's pull-down seat, push aside his foot rest, and step down to where the bomb aimer alternates between lying on the padded door of the nose-hatch to work the bomb sight, and standing to control the gun in the front turret. He seems to fill the space, and he, together with the aching vulnerability of the position at the plane's prow, makes you hold back. There is now nothing to see but the impenetrable night from the perspex blister in the nose, but you can all too easily imagine the carpet of fire and light below you not so long ago. Burning Berlin. There is no room for you in this cramped confine – you're in the bloody way! – so turn towards the rear of the plane. Immediately behind the pilot is a metal desk facing to port, with a curtain drawn to prevent spillage from the light of the navigator's angle-poise lamp: he is there, surrounded by charts, pencils and rulers, juggling with landfall. It is a closed world here of artificial light, angles and calculation. Arthur Spencer, 97 Squadron navigator, described that sense of isolation[7] thus: 'I was working over the charts and maps behind a black-out curtain.' He asked the pilot (Jimmy Munro) '... if I could move up to the front to have a look.' He duly did so and 'moved forward to be absolutely horrified; there seemed to be searchlights and flak all over the sky, and I just couldn't comprehend how an aircraft could survive in such a maelstrom of fire.' With the benefit of rational hindsight – he was describing after all his first trip to Germany – he realised that the pyrotechnics were caused in large measure by shells that had already burst before the aircraft had entered that troubled patch of sky: 'Eventually, I even got used to it!'[8]

Above your head, through the astrodome, on a clearer night than this one, you can see the stars. You can linger here since the navigator is absorbed in edgy prediction, poring over maps, head in hands, while the wireless operator is also seated in his compartment. It is warm here: the hot air outlet breathes heat and fug, and the inescapable smell of the aircraft – fuel, hydraulic oil, rubber, cordite, the chemical toilet and body odour – is thickest here. In the darkness, you find the heat and smell comforting. The noise however is unrelenting. In front of the wireless operator are wall-mounted radio sets that promise human contact when times get hard and remind you of those waiting in the early hours back home.

This is the heart of the plane – a thick metal door separates off the front five crew members from those in the tail. The main spar holds the

*The Navigator at work: Flying Officer P Ingleby in a Lancaster, 1944.* Photograph courtesy of the Imperial War Museum, London. Negative: CH 12288

plane together, but acts as a barrier for someone like you, floundering in the darkness. There is no one to tell you to duck and you crack your head against an escape hatch near the rest bed in the long dark fuselage. Below your feet, the bomb bay is empty. You are startled by the pigeons cooped up in the darkness – and it dawns on you that a ditched crew might rely on a homing pigeon's instincts.[9] Let me pause to tell you more about pigeons: their use was officially discontinued on 3 August 1943, although some aircrew recall their use extending beyond that date. Their potential for facilitating rescue had been sufficient for there to be a 'Senior Pigeon Officer' at the Air Ministry, but others had been scathing about their actual value: '(They are) a complete waste of time and effort … (They have) never contributed so far to any rescue, and are never likely to because (a) they will not fly in bad visibility, and (b) they will not fly if they get wet, and (c) they don't fly at night …'[10] Predictably, they made no contribution on Black Thursday, a dark, dank night of minimal visibility.

You take a tentative step down, and cautiously experiment with standing upright. Briefly, before the fuselage tapers away, you can stand unhindered. You might be comfortable, but those nearest you certainly aren't. . . .

The gunners – one in the mid-upper turret, and the other at the rear – seem to be half-in and half-out of the plane. The former's legs dangle down into the body of the aircraft, but his head and shoulders are out in the cold air: he has removed the middle panel of the perspex, preferring unhindered vision and wind-reddened eyes to a German night fighter unseen and firing first. What he sees is far more important than what he shoots.[11] A squashed fly on perspex looks much like a plane in the dark at 18,000 feet. Scouring the pitch-blackness, he doesn't see you and you reach the rear of the aircraft, past the intricate skeins of ammunition and the slopping Elsan toilet (drop **that** on Jerry!), and finally, a cricket pitch away from the pilot, is the rear gunner's turret, a cramped and chilled metal eyrie too tight to fit both man and parachute. Of the crew through whose space you have prowled, you envy that lonely, contorted figure least. Despite yourself, you imagine the moment when, with the plane tumbling towards the ground, and two of the engines on fire, the rear gunner fights to free himself from the grasp of that metal and perspex straitjacket, scrabbling for his parachute in the choking smoke-filled darkness. You shiver in sympathy, unaware that on the night of the 16th, the most likely to survive a crash were the gunners. Worse, by far, when an aircraft is tumbling into the ground, to be the bomb aimer, wedged in the Lancaster's nose.

Rear gunner Ernie Reynolds flew in Lancasters with 195 Squadron[12]: 'Every so often I'd snap the icicle that was hanging off my oxygen mask and chuck it out. I had electric suits. One time ... my foot started burning and the electric suit had short-circuited on my foot so I turned the heating off straightaway and after a bit I was shivering so I turned the heating back on and my foot burned again ... I had a bloody great burn on my foot when we got back. Those at the top end of the Lanc, they had heating from the engine ...'

*　　*　　*　　*

The surviving aircraft roared west, while in the final hours of 16 December, the mist over eastern England settled, denser by the hour. A journey time of seven and a half hours[13] – the average that night – meant that the first aircraft would be expected sometime after 23.15. In fact, first back was Flying Officer A W Wales (460 Squadron) whose landing time at Binbrook was 23.09. He landed safely, but elsewhere the crashes would soon begin.

## CHAPTER SIX

# AN IDEAL NIGHT

It was nearly half past midnight on the 17 December. More than an hour had elapsed from the time of the first crash when Lancaster LM 389 came unceremoniously to earth at Eastrington, near Howden in East Yorkshire. Its pilot, Sergeant N M Cooper of 101 Squadron, had taken off from Ludford Magna in Lincolnshire in the twilight of the previous day. Eight hours later, the plane came down, killing all on board: 'Crashed 00.27 on a hillside near Eastrington, ten miles ESE of Selby.'[1]

So I expected another hillside when I drove there, a week or so after locating the crash sites on the moors, but, confusingly, I found a featureless agricultural landscape – more Dutch polder than Yorkshire upland. What dominates is the sky, since it stretches to each horizon, punctuated by a few trees and the occasional thorn-like church spire. The exception is the view to the east, where the scarp of the wolds runs north to south, reaching the estuary of the River Humber at Hull. These heights are about ten miles away – too far to have brought the aircraft down in flat Eastrington. The plough rules here, deep furrows across ditch-drained fields. A couple of miles away, I can see the green roof of Howden Minster, while nearer, lorries trundle to and fro along the M62. The village is a jumble of houses and cottages, added on over centuries with scant regard for planning, the newer buildings constructed in a cheerless blood-red brick. At the centre of the village is the church – new kissing gate, locked door, and a grubby sheep lying amongst the weathered gravestones. A curtain twitches in the window of a house overlooking my uncertain stroll through the churchyard. There is nobody here to ask about the crash, though I am close to confiding in a builder unloading his lorry – too young, too pre-occupied. The village shop is staffed by a young girl in a peaked cap who looks as if she should be in school. Disappointed, I drive away, stopping in a field entrance to look again for the hillside: inescapably flat. There are planes overhead – jets from Lincolnshire racing north. But no hill at all: this has to be the wrong place.

A few days later, I spend some hours at York library, staring at microfiche editions of the *Yorkshire Evening Press* for December 1943, looking for coverage of the raid and, more particularly, of the crashes with which the raid ended. The papers mix news of the war with the unexpectedly normal: Anna Neagle and Herbert Wilcox are star guests at the York City versus Bradford football match on 13 December. Each day's headlines include reference to Christmas getting closer: *Shops' Yuletide Glitter* and the surprisingly inappropriate *The Christmas Postal Blitz*. Churchill is ill, apparently with pneumonia: 'The Prime Minister has been in bed for some days with a cold. A patch of pneumonia has now developed in the left lung. His general condition is as satisfactory as can be expected.'[2] In fact, as we know, he was out of the country, flying south on the 16th itself. Wartime news is carefully spun: there is no reference to the weather – no weather report, only the news of the extent of the blackout (5.13 pm to 8.47 am on the 16th) and the state of the moon (in its last quarter on the 19th). Weather reporting only resumed, it seems, in April 1945.[3] There is nothing to help an enemy lurking in deepest North Yorkshire. There is, though, news of the raid:

---

**CENTRE OF CAPITAL SMASHED AGAIN**

Berlin's respite from large-scale RAF raids has lasted just a fortnight. Last night – a few hours after the daylight raid on north west Germany – more than 1,500 tons of bombs were poured on the German capital by a strong force of Lancasters.

According to a Swiss report, the centre of the city, where most of the important Government offices are situated, received another heavy pounding.

Bomber Command made attacks on Northern France and Western Germany last night, as well as minelaying flights, and from all the operations 30 bombers are missing.

Foreign journalists in Berlin have been forbidden to report last night's raid ...

'... There was thick cloud practically the whole way,' the pilot of a Lancaster said. 'There were one or two breaks in it when we were crossing the enemy coast, and I saw the German beacon flashing below us. That was the last thing we saw of any ground until we began to get near the capital ...'

Squadron-Leader D. Miller[4], of Auckland, New Zealand, who was one of the first of the main force to arrive, said that the fighters were active along the route. 'The cloud was keeping the searchlights down, and they did not bother us at all as we made our bombing run, although we were so early in the attack. The fires had got going even then. It was an ideal night from our point of view ...'[5]

---

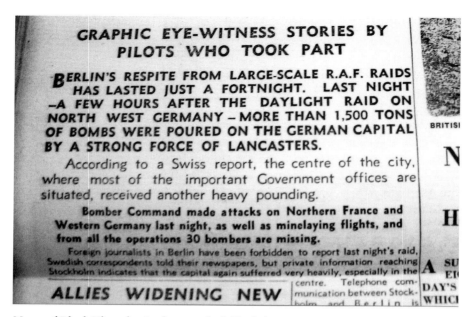

## GRAPHIC EYE-WITNESS STORIES BY PILOTS WHO TOOK PART

**B**ERLIN'S RESPITE FROM LARGE-SCALE R.A.F. RAIDS HAS LASTED JUST A FORTNIGHT. LAST NIGHT —A FEW HOURS AFTER THE DAYLIGHT RAID ON NORTH WEST GERMANY – MORE THAN 1,500 TONS OF BOMBS WERE POURED ON THE GERMAN CAPITAL BY A STRONG FORCE OF LANCASTERS.

According to a Swiss report, the centre of the city, where most of the important Government offices are situated, received another heavy pounding.

Bomber Command made attacks on Northern France and Western Germany last night, as well as minelaying flights, and from all the operations 30 bombers are missing.

Foreign journalists in Berlin have been forbidden to report last night's raid, Swedish correspondents told their newspapers, but private information reaching Stockholm indicates that the capital again suffered very heavily, especially in the centre. Telephone communication between Stockholm and Berlin is

**ALLIES WIDENING NEW**

*News of Black Thursday in the next day's Yorkshire Evening Press.* Yorkshire Evening Press

I expected a guarded account, but not the absence of any reference at all to the confusion as the aircraft returned, those young men cocooned in fog and darkness as the petrol dwindled. I had thought the local paper would have made some mention of the night's crashes in the county – after all, it is hard to keep the events of such a night secret: the skies must have reverberated with the droning roar of circling bombers. Word would have spread, prompted by those waiting and watching, the rescuers and salvage teams, the hospital staff and cemetery staff. The '30 missing bombers' was a serious understatement too – in fact the losses overall were fifty-five, a total casualty rate of 9.3 per cent. But the official line stressed the night was 'ideal'; the sub-editor of the *Press* may not even have baulked at the irony contained in his headline *'Germans' Bid to Stifle News of the Raid'*.

\*     \*     \*     \*

Around the same time, I got an e-mail about the crash site at Eastrington. Led to expect hills, I had found the landscape flat and scarcely above sea level: floodplain separated by dykes; the nearest high ground, the scarp of the wolds running down towards Hull, ten miles to the east. A stricken aircraft might plough into trees, but there was no other potential hazard. The writer of the e-mail took the same view: 'The aircraft did indeed crash at Eastrington, near Selby. A local group

I am in contact with tracked the crash site down last year. My thoughts exactly regarding the high ground description!!'[6] My correspondent told me that there were *two* crashes in Eastrington: a Halifax on another night and Lancaster LM389 piloted by Sergeant Cooper of 101 Squadron. 'The crash site is right against the edge of the field and around a small pond – it was not established whether ... the crash made the pond ...'[7] What was even less certain was what an aircraft based in North Lincolnshire was doing north of the Humber. Was it looking for a fog-free runway at Holme-on-Spalding-Moor or Breighton – both within five minutes' flying time? Which bearing was it on when it came down? What went wrong if there was no hill to hit? Was an answer possible all these years later?

Later, armed with fresh information, I revisited Eastrington. I now knew[8] the exact location, however, for the site had been combed with metal detectors in 2003 – hard work I was told in heavy 'ankle-breaking' soil – and small pieces of wreckage had been found. In fact the aircraft had come down in farmland two miles north-east of the village of Eastrington, in a deep corner of a field close to a pond. Sergeant Cooper had taken off some eight hours before from his base at Ludford Magna and had been diverted to Holme-on-Spalding-Moor, about six miles to the north. He had radioed for assistance, asking for the QFE – barometric pressure – to allow him to set his altimeter prior to landing. This was not given and he was never heard from again. His Commanding Officer – form-filling in the aftermath, and numbed by unrelenting loss – noted bleakly that Cooper was 'lost and (had) apparently panicked'.[9] At all events, he had run out of fuel and then, in a last, desperate descent, had blundered into a copse of trees before coming to rest in heavy clay, close to a farm track.

I crossed and re-crossed the River Foul Ness looking for the track and eventually found it, leading away between rain-swept hedges. Nearby was a high water-tower and the thought crossed my mind that an exhausted pilot searching for aerodrome landmarks might well have breathed a momentary sigh of relief on seeing the tower – typical airfield 'furniture' – thinking that the ordeal might soon be over, wheels kissing runway tarmac within minutes. Sergeant Cooper may well have thought he was minutes away from safety: warm drink and bed, not the cold embrace of the Humber floodplain and sudden death.

CHAPTER SEVEN

# ENGLISH COAST AHEAD

The engines droned, some pilots smoked despite the risk – the nature of risk had, after all, been redefined for these young men – and the instruments threw a thin light across hundreds of Lancaster cockpits. There was little other light, not from this tired moon[1] in its last quarter on a mid-December night. Battle-strained eyes scanned the darkness. Sometime in the next few hours nearly three thousand men anticipated cocoa and rum, predictable questions, then bed. Ahead of them across eastern England, station Met Officers were being nudged awake in time for the ritual reassessment of the weather conditions prior to landing. The onus fell on WAAFs like Joan Beech: 'I used to think that we Met girls were the only ones awake and having to brave the elements. The worst thing was having to climb that damned ladder to the roof of Flying Control in a howling gale and lashing rain to see how far I couldn't see across the airfield …'[2]

The process of landing followed a long established pattern: crossing the English coast left you ten minutes or so from base. Almost there. With luck, you might have pinpointed the exact spot where you left the North Sea by recognising, say, the searchlights at Mablethorpe, Lincolnshire. At all events, you like the thought of having dry land beneath you, rather than the treacherous ocean. You join a patient circuit of returning aircraft rumbling over your airfield. The Lancasters should be 'stacked', waiting their turn, ideally under the cloud base. You exchange the starkest of information with the disembodied female voice in the Control Tower and then you dutifully circle at the prescribed height. It is like a very slow descent of the stairs in the dark, as you systematically drop earthwards while the crews before you in the queue take their turns. You acknowledge each instruction, remembering the voice from training days: '… so we know you're not flying up someone else's tail.' There is a perceptible change in the aircraft's slipstream noise as the wheels come down. Eventually you get the invitation to land, and the altimeter is logging around 1,000 feet.

Now it's time to switch on the downward light that identifies you as J-Johnnie, or U-Uncle. Ahead you can see the aircraft immediately preceding you and you need to judge the distance carefully and the direction of the wind. As you line up for landing, your predecessor should be down and close to clearing the runway. Your turn. You make one last call to Control, saying your aircraft letter and wait for the impassive 'Clear to Land'. The engines roar. Ahead of you are the runway lights and, for a moment, you grimace at how narrow the strip of concrete looks, the darkness pressing in on both sides. Eventually, the wheels touch the ground, tentatively at first, and then with a reassuring thump; the crew starts to unbrace – you have no seat belts – and somewhere beyond the runway lights someone – loved one, anxious padre or station commander – counts you in.

There was so much that could go wrong with landing a heavy bomber: pilots returned with aircraft shot up, on three engines or worse. Pat Burnett, a Lancaster pilot and commander of 9 Squadron, once returned from a raid on Hannover (27/28 September 1943) spluttering across the North Sea on two engines, only for a third engine to peter out as he approached Bardney, Lincolnshire. Despite a crosswind, he landed successfully on his one remaining engine[3]. Pilot Dave Leicester, 158 Squadron, returning to Lissett on another occasion, with petrol dwindling, found it fog-bound. In his anxiety to get the aircraft down, he forgot to lower the wheels. He had to abort the landing and continue circling the airfield.[4] Planes skidded on grass runways; bombs destined for Germany got fouled up in the aircraft's release mechanism and were reluctantly taken back home in a state of precarious suspension; petrol dwindled and the weather closed in ...

That night, there was some variation in the density and height of the cloud base: 83 Squadron's Pilot Officer F E McLean, at the controls of Lancaster JB344 for the past eight hours, caught momentary sight of his own base, RAF Wyton. Visibility was nil, according to the squadron's ORB.[5] 'Luckily,' he wrote later in a letter home[6], 'we got one slight glimpse of our own 'drome so we had to have a go at landing seeing that we only had enough fuel for a few minutes flying.' Feeling his way down through the cloud, with the airfield barely half a mile away, he suddenly saw a large tree at the top of a rise. It caused a sharp intake of breath and moments of heart-stopping calculation, though he guessed the aircraft was travelling too fast to avoid what lay ahead ...

The night reverberated and thundered with the noise of aircraft circling. As McLean seized the moment, tempted by a fleeting glimpse of runway and aerodrome buildings, another Lancaster (JB453) was slowly, methodically descending through the fog. McLean's Flight Commander, Wing Commander Joe Northrop was on his final approach, flying at around 200 feet and seconds from touchdown. Northrop was lucky enough to have sufficient fuel remaining and he had begun his approach on SBA[7] well above the layer of fog which he judged to be at 1,200 feet.

Patiently, Northrop circled until he was next to land. Then Control warned him to watch out for an unidentified aircraft which was in the circuit and attempting to land visually.[8] The unidentified aircraft was McLean's. Northrop gingerly edged the aircraft down ... 600 feet registered on the altimeter. 200 feet ... then, suddenly, McLean's aircraft appeared above them, blundering through the darkness, its slipstream close enough to rock the aircraft and its wheels and fuselage threatening the decapitation of the mid-upper turret, and its terrified gunner. It brushed past, crossing from the port side in a steep turn. Northrop's Lancaster plummeted towards the ground, sweeping through the branches of some trees as he fought to pull the aircraft into a desperate climb. He slammed the throttles fully open knowing that failure to do so would be catastrophic. It was a close run thing, but in the end he was successful, levelling out and repeating his descent, landing 'blind' on instruments alone. Coming in for his final approach he could see the glow from a burning aircraft through the gloom. He estimated later that he was probably the last aircraft in the Pathfinder Group to touch down safely. It was seventeen minutes short of 1 am.

Moments before, a wing of McLean's aircraft clipped the tree that he had seen on the rise – it was a more substantial meeting of wood and metal than his commander's plane had suffered – and McLean had a brief and forlorn struggle with the controls to get the aircraft flying on an even keel. He had just broken cloud, but both his radio and SBA were out of action, making landing the aircraft particularly testing.[9] It eventually came down in a ploughed field and careered towards a brick wall with a ditch in front of it. The ensuing collision sent the aircraft's four engines spinning in all directions, shattered the fuselage in three parts and ripped the wings away from the bodywork. McLean later commented that the aircraft's biggest remaining piece could fit snugly within the confines of a billiard table.

Then the wreck caught fire, triggering explosions of ammunition, signal cartridges and petrol. 'We had a busy time getting the Flight Engineer and Bomb Aimer out of the fire, especially as the Flight Engineer had a broken leg and arm. Tony Lindsay, our New Zealand Navigator, also had a broken leg and arm, and in spite of that was trying to help the others ...'[10] Lindsay won the British Empire Medal for his courage. It was his third operation and he had been thrown fifty feet clear of the aircraft. Suffering from facial burns, in addition to his broken limbs, he pulled two comrades out of the fire.[11]

McLean survived, along with five of his crew.[12] The bomb aimer, Flight Sergeant Greg Tankard, in that most vulnerable of places in a crash landing, the nose of the aircraft, died during the morning of the 17th in Ely hospital of the injuries to his head. An Australian, he was due to marry his English girlfriend later that week. McLean survived, albeit with two sprained wrists, a deep cut to the head, and much bruising. In his Log Book he meticulously logged his 'Grand Total' of flying hours (529 hours and 40 minutes) and the remaining fuel in the petrol tanks – 30–50 gallons, less than 2 per cent of the Lancaster's fuel capacity. This would have given between nine and fifteen minutes more flying time at most.[13] 'Aircraft completely wrecked and burning,' he wrote, in capital letters. McLean had survived that night; time was to tell if he would survive the war.

## CHAPTER EIGHT

# CANADIANS

The airfield at Linton-on-Ouse lies just north of the River Ouse, twenty miles from York. To the north east, about fifteen miles away, is the scarp of the North York Moors, bleak heather moorland stretching away to the North Sea coast. The airfield's runways stretch north east/south west so aircraft tend to take off into the prevailing south westerly with the green ridge dark behind them. The road nudges up to the airfield perimeter and, heading west, describes a series of sharp bends to accommodate both a serpentine river and the Ministry of Defence. It is flat river-bed country, still achingly rural: rustic pubs, church spires and a wooden toll bridge to the west of the airfield making the road journey towards where 6 Group had its HQ at Allerton Park considerably shorter. The Canadians who flew from Linton called HQ Castle Dismal and you can see why: now it looms above the motorway but it retains an air of mystery and grandeur. Those turrets and high windows must have seemed a lifetime from Ontario and Manitoba.

Not so far away is Beningbrough Hall, now National Trust with a garden designed for family picnics; sixty years ago, it was aircrew accommodation, providing an interesting contrast between staid English mansion and transatlantic high spirits typified by the Canadian airman who rode a motor bike up a flight of stone steps before entering the faded grandeur of the house itself. Many years later – in 1995 – as a returning veteran, he expressed a wish to repeat the prank. 'What was the guy like?' I asked, on a visit to the house and expecting a description of an embarrassed, rather diffident, senior citizen. With a smile, Beningbrough's National Trust property manager, Ray Barker, said, 'Well, a bit of a delinquent!' At that same veterans' return, Ray had made a light-hearted plea for the return of the house's missing brass door knobs. We shook our heads, laughed and reflected on the difference between rural north Yorkshire and where they had come from. 'A cornfield in Canada,' Ray said, 'and you end up here!' He told me about the airman who had arrived late at night, fresh from training school. There was no available bed so he slept on a paliasse in the great hall of the house. Leaving before it got light, he was taken to the airfield at Linton, a mile or so away. He was sent on his first operation that night, was shot down and spent the rest of the war as

*The steps at Beningbrough Hall, Yorkshire, offered a challenge to a Canadian flier on his motorcycle which he was only too pleased to accept.*

a POW. He too came back to Beningbrough in 1995: 'I kind of wondered what it looked like in daylight ...'

Linton was opened in May 1937 and welcomed its RCAF squadrons (408 and 426) in the summer of 1943. The two squadrons supplied thirty aircraft for the raid on Berlin on 16 December. By the following morning, twenty-eight airmen from five of its crews were killed, thirteen over enemy territory, many in the mayhem above the German capital, or lost without trace; while the remaining fifteen were strewn amongst twisted metal across fog-bound northern and eastern England. A further seven were interned in Sweden after the crew baled out from their damaged and fuel-starved aircraft. Eighteen were Canadians, from Ontario, and Moose Jaw, Saskatchewan and Quebec amongst others. They were very young and a long way from home.

Twelve of the aircrew that had died in Yorkshire were buried in the Stonefall Cemetery in Harrogate: while British fliers were ferried back to graveyards in their hometowns, the Canadians were exiled forever in northern England. I went there in early May, a day of fierce scudding showers from clouds heavy with rain, interspersed with blue sky destined not to last. I wasn't sure what I expected: words on headstones that added to what I already knew; perhaps a brief encounter with a Canadian with a long memory. It felt right anyway that, having seen where these men died – most of them on bleak boggy moorland high above sea level, I should pay my respects to them in their final resting place. I was beginning to feel I knew them.

The war graves are regimented in a quiet corner of the cemetery. Where the late citizens of Harrogate are buried beneath headstones of all shapes, sizes and colours, the Canadians are lined up in rows, by date of death. The headstones look new still, white stone and no divergence from the war graves template: the stones are identical and even the wording follows the same pattern. The borders are neat and well tended; the grass is velvety. There is no one here but a gardener, bent double until the rain comes again. He has gone once the shower passes away to the south. A rabbit scuttles across the greensward. It isn't hard to find the line I am looking for: I recognise the names and mentally place them in crews and squadrons. The ages range from twenty-nine (Squadron Leader Thomas Kneale who died at Yearsley, and Flying Officer M E Marynowski whose Lancaster crashed into Silver Hill farm above Hawnby) to nineteen – Sergeant R K Rye. His epitaph reads: 'In loving memory of our dear son Bob. We the many salute you the few.' The epitaphs in general are poignant, emphasising sacrifice, patriotism and family. One – for Flight Sergeant Boily – has the date of death in French, but the concluding words are in English: 'To my beloved son who died for the freedom of his country.'[1] There is a Star of David on the grave of Pilot Officer Marks. Mac Jones lies below a stone that proudly speaks of comradeship: 'In death they were not divided. He met

'They are lined up now, more than sixty years later – still together.' Canadian graves at Stonefall cemetery.

The gravestone of Squadron Leader Tom Kneale (426 Squadron); the words below the cross say 'Greater love hath no man than to lay down his life for his country.'

his death with six members of his crew.' They are lined up now, more than sixty years later in an English rainstorm, still together.

A few weeks previously I had posted several letters to Canada seeking contact with survivors of the raid. Returning home from my rain-swept visit to the Harrogate cemetery, I received a lengthy e-mail from Roger Coulombe – ex-426 Squadron pilot and known at Linton as the 'Berlin Kid' – whose Lancaster (DS711 OW – B) had returned from Berlin that night on three engines. Later, in 1944, he was presented with a gold watch for dropping more bombs on Berlin than any other pilot. He made the long trip twelve times.[2] Coulombe's account was entitled 'Memories of my Raid on Berlin on the 16/17 December 1943.' He had served in Squadron Leader Kneale's flight, the same Tom Kneale at whose sombre graveside I had stood just hours before. Coulombe's flight to and from the German capital had taken ten minutes over seven hours. 'The weather,' he wrote, ' was fine for take-off, but totally closed in by thick fog on return.'

He told me about his scrap over Nordhausen, east of Hannover, with a Junkers 88 ... He is flying at 18,000 feet. Nothing but the roar of engines, until in a flurry of light and fire, tracer sweeps past and, soon after, bullets tear into metal. Within moments, the starboard inner engine is destroyed, its cowling blown away, the entrance door is plucked out, together with the dinghy that is normally stowed in the starboard wing. It batters insistently against the fuselage and finally, fully inflated, breaks free and drifts down into fields far below. There is an exchange of fire and the Junkers 88 peels away, with sparks flowing from its port engine ... So, the Lancaster drones on, one engine down but its crew stubbornly intent on getting there ...

Coulombe described the damage: 'We lost our entrance door which was knocked right off the aircraft and the dinghy was knocked out of its storage and kept floating in the air trailing behind the starboard wing and flapping along the fuselage until it finally separated and fell off somewhere.'

He flew on despite the damage, acutely conscious of the fact that he was losing height and having to reduce speed. The consequence was that DS711 bombed Berlin later than the rest: '... Fortunately, we had taken off with the first wave of bombers. So, the delay ... put us back only a short time after the third and last wave ... We were alone over the target area when we did our bombing run.' Phase one was due to bomb between 20.00 and 20.04; while the final third phase was scheduled to end at 20.12.[3] The Germans, he noted, were too busy struggling to contain the proliferating fires caused by the raid to offer much more than token resistance to the lone Lancaster lingering overhead. Job done, they turned ponderously back towards England.

'We eventually made it back to England,' Coulombe wrote, '... to find our base airport closed in because of very thick fog so thick that it gave the impression that we were floating in milk ... The visibility was zero ... The atmospheric pressure had changed so much in seven hours that our altimeters functioning on atmospheric pressure gave false height readings ...' Altimeters were critical in bad weather since they measured the aircraft's height above sea level. Critical they might be, but they were also relatively unsophisticated, dependent as they were on the vagaries of atmospheric pressure.[4] Necessarily therefore on nights like this one, when the pressure had changed significantly in the course of the seven or eight hours the crews were away, the altimeters could not be relied on for true readings without being amended to take account of the changed circumstances. The procedure essentially was to alter the equipment in the light of data about the revised pressure – the QFE – transmitted over the R/T.

Coulombe's wireless operator received a message from RAF Headquarters giving the code number to adjust the altimeters to the correct height – in other words registering the change of atmospheric pressure after seven hours of flying. 'Unfortunately,' Coulombe wrote, 'the number which was sent to us was erroneous.' It meant the reading was dangerously inaccurate: about 1,000 feet out.

The consequences of this were brought home in startling fashion: Coulombe's Lancaster circled closer to the runway at Linton and turned for its final approach at what he thought was a safe height of about 1,000 feet. Suddenly, looming out of the milky fog, he saw something which would have made him shake to his boots: 'I suddenly saw the black tower water tank of the station appearing right off my left wing tip.' It must have been a terrifying moment, at eye level with a feature of the aerodrome that he had seen a hundred times, knew to be about thirty-five to forty feet above the ground, and could have described with his eyes shut. To all intents and purposes of course, they were.

He knew then that his altimeter was registering almost 1,000 feet out. He put the aircraft into a steep climb and then asked his navigator, Gerard Tremblay, to find him a precise fix using GEE.[5] He wanted a precise course to steer to line up the aircraft with the runway, and an accurate assessment of the likely flying time. On three engines, in this situation, Coulombe's aircraft was dangerously vulnerable.

He knew too that he was running out of petrol and guessed that the chances of finding an alternative landing field were virtually nil.

'It was foggy all over the area around York all the way North and God knows how far down South ... So, my navigator who was extremely competent and knowledgeable gave me a course to steer at a given speed and for how long to take us right over the beginning of the runway. So, not seeing anything in that thick fog as thick as milk, I put all my trust in my navigator's professional competence and decided to prepare to land totally in the blind and follow his instructions in every detail ...

'I think that the time to fly was around 60 or 70 seconds. After flying just about the indicated number of seconds and seeing that I had too much height, I decided to side-slip[6] my Lancaster on its left wing tip to lose height very quickly (like going down in an elevator) which is not a recommended manoeuvre with a four-engine bomber ...'

The aircraft plummeted towards the ground ('like a rock'). Then at about fifty feet, the runway emerged from the mist. Coulombe managed to touch down about half way up the runway. His speed was too high, so he used as much brake as he could with the intention of sinking the wheels in the mud to slow him down. To his immense relief, he was able to stop the aircraft just a few feet from the nose of another Lancaster parked in one of the dispersal areas. It was four minutes short of midnight.[7]

His e-mail concluded: '... So, it was that kind (of) a miracle which saved us that night after having made a completely blind approach without any sort of approach lights indicators, totally on the indications of the navigator ... this experience demonstrated to me how important and precious was the presence of a proficient navigator who was very competent in operating a Gee Box machine on board of a bomber carrying a crew of seven men. I shall never forget the name of Gerard Tremblay of Quebec City who was my navigator during my entire tour of operations. At the end of our tour of operations I suggested to the Squadron Adjutant that my navigator be awarded a DFC.... And indeed the King himself pinned the DFC on his chest when visiting the flying base where Gerry Tremblay had been posted after the crew separated.' Tremblay survived the war. There was another minor miracle that night: Coulombe's aircraft had been unable to release all its bombs. Four incendiaries had got caught up in the mechanism, making a crash landing even more hazardous.[8]

Roger Coulombe was in no doubt as to the cause of the crashes that night: '... The error in the sending of the adjustment of altimeters cost our base the loss of three aircraft crashing all over the place around our airport that night: two aircraft from my squadron 426 and one from 408 Squadron which was based at the same station. My flight

*Roger Coulombe and crew take off for Berlin aboard Lancaster DS 841 on 24 March 1944.* Roger Coulombe

*Roger Coulombe – the 'Berlin Kid' – on his twelfth trip to the German capital, 24 March 1944.* Roger Coulombe

*Roger Coulombe photographed at Harrods in London.* Roger Coulombe

*The Coulombe crew: from the left: Joe Jankun (rear gunner); Gerry Tremblay (navigator); Ed Titheridge (flight engineer); Roger Coulombe; John Bradbury (wireless operator); Stan McKenzie (mid-upper gunner), and (kneeling) George Daymond (bomb aimer).* Roger Coulombe

commander S/L Tom Kneale and his entire crew died that night when they crashed at Yearsley, Yorkshire, ten miles North East of Linton.'

I thought again of Tom Kneale, deep in the ground, soft Yorkshire rain falling from the sky on his grave and a long line of white stone crosses.

# CHAPTER NINE

# THE THEORY OF THE FAULTY ALTIMETERS

R oger Coulombe was not the only one persuaded by the altimeter
theory. The Lancaster of Pilot Officer Pete Drane (207 Squadron)
was one of a number of pilots who found themselves similarly confused
about their aircraft's height. Trying to land at Spilsby in Lincolnshire,
he had banked and straightened for the final approach, then reacted fast
when his rear gunner, Ron Buck, had suddenly bellowed a warning.
Drane, unhesitatingly, had lifted the aircraft's nose and climbed.
Moments later, there was a fraught discussion about the difference
between what the altimeter said – 300 feet still to go – and what Buck
could see – the ground up close. Buck was sure they had been given the
wrong QFE with the result that the aircraft's altimeter was dangerously
inaccurate. His aircraft was not alone in this regard he felt.[1]

Altimeters may have been primitive in those days, but the basic
principle, it seems, still applies. Look up 'QFE' on the internet and it
tells you that it is '... a Q code used by pilots and air traffic control to
refer to the current air pressure which will calibrate the pilot's altimeter
to give actual height above the ground at a particular airfield. This
setting is used during take-off and landing ...'[2] It should then be
straightforward: 'the barometric pressure here now is x, so the altitude
is y' – and the protocol too is uncomplicated: pilot identifies his aircraft
to the control tower; WAAF responds with the necessary figure ('QFE
niner niner eight millibars'); pilot repeats and begins the approach. So
what could go wrong? If it did go wrong, was it enough to bring down
thirty or more aircraft? How much difference to the altimeter setting
would a rapidly falling barometric pressure make? And, if it was a
widespread problem, why did more aircraft not crash?

\* \* \* \*

The Yorkshire crashes were usually on high ground[3] and, unlike other
areas of the country, no aircraft crashed as they began their final
approach. Most came down some distance from base, either redirected
to another aerodrome in the hope that the weather was better there, or
presumably floundering and lost in the ubiquitous milky fog. There is a
clear connection between the potential problem with altimeters and the

hilly terrain that is characteristic of the county, particularly that over which the returning bombers had to fly. While most airfields north of York lie in a line either side of the A1 as it arrows north through the Vale of York, the land to the east towards the North Sea is high moorland or rolling wolds. A fault in the altimeter setting which led the pilot to think that he was flying at a safe height when in fact he was, say, 500 feet below that height would inevitably prove catastrophic in such an unforgiving landscape. I wondered then whether the same could be said of the crashes further south, in Lincolnshire and Cambridgeshire.

The Lincolnshire Squadrons were more seriously affected than any other by the events of the night.[4] It was time to turn my attention there. On the very day I was reflecting on the altimeter issue, the postman delivered a letter with details of the last moments of Lancaster JB596 piloted by Flying Officer Robert Proudfoot of 100 Squadron. His aircraft had been one of thirty-two Lancasters flying out of RAF Waltham, near Grimsby, to bomb Berlin that night. He returned to a wall of fog which, for the Grimsby-based pilots, obscured the usual landmarks – the most notable being the tower in Grimsby docks. He was the first of the returning pilots to crash (at 11 pm) at Park Farm, Hatcliffe, five miles or so southwest of Waltham. Judging by the location of the crash site – on the edge of the Lincolnshire Wolds – Proudfoot had striven to swing the aircraft to the south of Waltham aerodrome and search for a gap in the banks of cloud to bring his bomber down to earth. Height, it seems, was again an issue. The letter[5] goes on:

'... Eye witness accounts say that ... just prior to the crash, they heard the sound of an aircraft flying low overhead coming from the direction of Waltham, the pilot probably ... doing a left hand circuit to line up with one of the runways. Following the crash it was thought that the altimeter might have been faulty, for had it been flying thirty feet higher at the point of impact it would have cleared the trees ...' His commanding officer took the view that the altimeter was faulty, noting that there was 'no evidence why a/c flew into the ground when the altimeter read 600 feet.'[6] Instead of coasting through clear sky, the aircraft plunged into the ground some three hundred yards from the road and ploughed through earth and trees for over a quarter of a mile. Its starboard wing scraped the roof off a farm cottage, while the other wing carved a path through a stand of pine trees. There was damage to part of a wash-house, lavatory, bedroom and roof of the farm foreman's house which was partly demolished. There were no civilian casualties. The burning aircraft set fire to a stack of barley.[7] Eventually it stopped alongside an ash tree. The aircraft's nose section was separated from the main structure and landed some distance away. The air was filled with debris, earth and tumbling branches. A silence began to settle. Then, suddenly, a fire started, triggered by canisters of incendiary bombs. Some malfunction in the bomb bay had spared the citizens of Berlin that element of fire; instead it was a hillside in rural Lincolnshire that burned in the night.

Air Ministry files, as well as pilots' accounts, are full of doubts as to the accuracy of altimeters. Sergeant 'Nick' Knilans, a Lancaster pilot with 619 Squadron, returned from a raid on Hamburg in July 1943: 'With the instruments showing 1,000 feet, the bomb aimer suddenly yelled "there's the ground"'. When the aircraft finally rolled to a standstill, the altimeter read 960 feet.[8] In late November, 12 Squadron's Wing Commander Richard Wood was returning from Berlin on his thirtieth operation. He encountered fog on return to Wickenby and crashed, colliding with muddy ditches when the altimeter read 500 feet.[9] Their experience was typical. A minute to the Deputy Chief of the Air Staff in January 1944[10] observed that there was 'a possibility that some unexplained instances of experienced pilots flying into the ground at night might be due to inaccuracies in the standard altimeter.' The file also reveals that checks on altimeter accuracy were not always completed properly. Moreover, even when properly maintained, altimeters had a 'permissible error' of sixty feet, and readings lagged behind the *actual* height of the aircraft in the same way that a modern GPS system takes time to arrive at a 'final' reading. Such a time lag 'depends largely on the rate of descent'.[11] Older altimeters were demonstrably less accurate than newer ones. All of which could mean disaster: 'Careless pilots may not regularly check the altimeter and consequently it is possible, although not very probable, that (such) ... causes may lead to an error of as much as 200 feet.'[12] Without frequent checking and careful reading, it seems that altimeters could not be relied upon when operating in low cloud base, at say 400 feet. 'A *further* (my italics) error of up to 300 feet may take place when the forecasted barometric pressure is faulty.'[13] With the worst of luck it would appear that a crew might be cursed with an altimeter reading some 600 feet out – the height of a small hill, or as some pilots called them, with withering sang-froid, 'hard clouds'.

At the Command Accident Investigators' Conference held on Tuesday 4 January 1944 – with the memory of Black Thursday still painfully sharp – 'several investigators were of the opinion that accidents had recently happened due to pilots not adjusting their altimeters to a changed barometric pressure before landing.'[14] More pilot forgetfulness, it seems, than 'error of judgement'. But aircrew were all too aware of what a faulty, or neglected, altimeter could mean: Bill Pearson, a Canadian from 9 Squadron, is just one airman whose altimeter nearly killed him. 'Our altimeter setting was a way off (and) we were descending through cloud on GEE and, as bomb aimer, I was in the nose ... I saw the tops of trees and yelled to our skipper to climb which he did ... we still had several hundred feet on the altimeter ...'[15]

Something else then to worry about as you feel your way through the darkness: not only might the petrol run out, some rogue returner swing into your path, or you realise with a jolt that this base doesn't feel like home at all – 'Where the hell is this?' – but you cannot even trust to being at the height your instruments say you are. At any moment, there might be a coming together of aircraft with trees, a water tower, church steeples or dark unforeseen hills.

# CHAPTER TEN
# 100 SQUADRON

K ate Reid was a radio/telephone (R/T) operator in the control tower at Waltham (Grimsby) aerodrome and, as such, one of those calm women's voices charged with the placatory conveying of instructions and information to tired pilots as they prepared to land. She was close to the wireless operator on Proudfoot's aircraft, Sergeant Bernard Heaton, and would have been only too aware of the growing chaos in the skies above the airfield and the dangers threatening each crew – and him in particular. There were to be just three survivors from Proudfoot's crew, all of whom suffered severe burns.

Kate was not the only one waiting for news: the wife of the squadron's commanding officer, Wing Commander David Holford, was staying the night at a local pub (the Ship Inn, Grimsby). They had been married a matter of a few weeks. There were only two survivors from the crash that followed his attempt to land at nearby Kelstern airfield, high above the Humber floodplain. David Holford had been appointed Wing Commander on 17 February 1943 and, at that time, was the youngest man in Bomber Command to achieve that rank. He was twenty-two on 21 February.

Only 97 Squadron fared worse in the Black Thursday raid on Berlin than 100 Squadron. The latter lost four aircraft on return (and none on the raid itself). The first aircraft to land safely was the Lancaster of Flight Lieutenant Major (at 11.19 pm) while above him the aircraft circled in mounting anxiety, desperate for a break in the cloud base (the QBB). That was reported to be at 800 feet, with a swirling mist in impenetrable patches below that.

Flight Sergeant Alastair Smith was running short of petrol and had taken his aircraft as low as he dared, hoping for a sight of the runway.[1] He called up control to ask if any help in terms of pyrotechnics was likely. He got no reply. Circling anxiously, he suddenly saw a light below him and, conscious that petrol was getting very low, he headed straight for it. He got down, but not at Waltham. The saving lights had been at Binbrook, six miles away to the south west.

Others were not so lucky. At 12.40 am the brand new Lancasters of Flight Sergeants Allen Kevis and Gilbert Denman collided head-on at the southern end of Waltham airfield. The wrecked aircraft tumbled to the ground, one near the church at Grainsby, the other close to Waithe

*RAF Kelstern, high on the Lincolnshire wolds, on a summer's day with the runways long since covered over.*

House farm, a quarter of a mile away on the other side of the A16, the main Grimsby-Louth turnpike. There were no survivors here. In little over an hour and a half, twenty-three crewmen from this squadron died.

*    *    *    *

Kelstern airfield has reverted to farmland and, on a May day in 2004, there is little sign of what happened just over sixty years ago: the country lane leading up to the plateau is broader than you might expect, suggesting wartime road widening for military transport, and there is a memorial to 625 Squadron at a road junction near some bulldozed airfield rubble. There are occasional glimpses of frost-eaten runway between the crops. It is 400 feet above sea level here and there is a stiff breeze from the north west buffeting green crops where once aircraft taxied and took off. The sky seems vast in this remote landscape: scarcely a farm cottage, just telegraph poles and wind-stunted trees. As at other airfields, I can hear the distant drone of a single aircraft, like a ghost from long ago. Driving around what once was airfield, the lanes are edged with shepherd's beard, as white as snow. This is a land of chalk and lapwings.

Wing Commander Holford's aircraft crashed here, while his wife waited for him, unable to sleep, conscious no doubt of the roar of returning engines and the fog pressing against the bedroom windows. Australian navigator, Don Charlwood, met Holford earlier in the war when 'he was the personification of all that was best in the RAF.' Charlwood '... reported to a pale, boyish Squadron Leader ... of his words I remember very little but his dark staring eyes I have never forgotten.'[2] Like other pilots on this grim night, Holford fell just short of the airfield, clipping a hillside that suddenly loomed from out of nowhere. The sudden glare of landing lights dazzled him and the aircraft hit the ground nose first.[3] His Lancaster exploded on impact and Holford was blown clear of the cockpit, breaking both ankles in the process. The two gunners were also thrown clear and survived. The pilot was not so lucky. Holford's frozen corpse was found the following morning in a snowdrift. It was left to Wing Commander Jimmy Bennett, a friend of Holford, to break the news to the dead pilot's wife.[4]

It was a difficult night for Kelstern's 625 Squadron: of seventeen aircraft which set off for Berlin, four were 'early returns', while one (Warrant Officer Baker) was lost over Germany. The return to base was chaotic: an American, Flying Officer A E Woolley crashed at Gayton-le-Wold, about a mile from the airfield. Two of the crew died. The ORB[5] lists the misadventures of the remaining squadron members: Warrant Officer Ellis 'overshot at base, turned low and slow, hit ground with inner wing and belly-landed'; Pilot Officer R G Bowden 'was hit during the bombing run' and an engine caught fire. The pilot lost control of the aircraft briefly, but bombed successfully and limped home, finding sanctuary at RAF Blyton. Five other aircraft were diverted to Blyton; three to Ludford Magna, one of which landed on three engines. Seventeen aircraft were 'bombed up' that night; nine were diverted, two crashed, one was shot down, and three returned early, leaving just two which landed back at the appointed base.

I did not expect to find the actual sites where the two colliding planes of Kevis and Denman came to earth: Grainsby church nestles behind yew trees, its back turned to the airfield at whose perimeter it sits. Waithe House Farm is circled by flat agricultural land, oddly untouched by the proximity of Grimsby, while Grainsby has a Rupert Brooke quality about it: an unchanging English village. I didn't stay long, but drove instead to Hatcliffe Top where Proudfoot's plane, with its young wireless operator Bernard Heaton, came down. There's a monument to the crew here at the point where the aircraft finally stopped its careering path through the woods. The 100 Squadron crest on the monument has been crafted using the roof flashing from the farm cottage that lay in the path of JB596's starboard wing. It is some 170 feet above the Humber estuary here and surprisingly bleak despite the early summer sun. It is a tree-lined ridge of trees falling away via farmland to the road below. There is a high wind here again, and pheasants pecking in the dust.

The wonder is, looking at where these aircraft plunged from the night sky, that anyone survived at all. Bernard Heaton was not one of those who did. Kate Reid remembered him as a special friend, and mourned the fact that he was only nineteen when he died. Sixty years later, on 7 June 2003, she stood at Hatcliffe Top on the place where his aircraft died, a tree-shrouded spot now marked by a monument to those who did not survive. Those standing at the simple ceremony ('They shall not grow old . . .'), held to commemorate the dead crew, could still see the scars of the aircraft's tumultuous final moments on the surrounding pine trees.

Wing Commander Jimmy Bennett had completed two tours and arrived at Waltham in November 1943 to form the new 550 Squadron. He flew that night with 'Bluey' Graham and his crew: 'Bluey decided to come down through the cloud over the North Sea. In conditions like these it was always wise practice . . . we dropped down into the mist but Bluey picked up the outer circle of sodium lights at Waltham, stuck his port wing on them and followed them round until he found the funnel and put her down.' Bennett, Graham and the latter's crew decided that it was safer to walk away from their aircraft as soon as possible since 'planes were coming down all around us, landing at the first opportunity.' Shortly afterwards they saw a Lancaster's starboard wing-tip light – evidently the aircraft was circling contrary to accepted practice. Moments later, in a crescendo of sound and fire, the aircraft hit the ground. Later, Bennett accompanied Nick Carter, the station commander at Waltham, to a village just outside Louth. 'When we arrived we found one of those wartime wooden buildings which was in the charge of an Irish nursing sister and she had turned it into a temporary mortuary . . . . The bodies of 40 or 50 lads (were) laid out in there, down both sides of the room, all covered in service blankets.' Bennett was profoundly shaken: 'It was a terrible sight, a sight I will never forget. It was impossible to recognise some of them. All we had to go by was their identity discs.'[6] They were made from asbestos and hence immune to flame.

The survivors girded themselves for the next operation and reflected on what they were going through. Sergeant Dick Tapper , a bomb aimer with 100 Squadron,[7] wrote in the immediate aftermath: 'Berlin, 7 hours duration. Ten bombers seen to crash in flames from enemy coast to Hanover . . . flak very heavy . . . visibility on return very bad, clouds down to 500 feet at base. This caused collisions and crashes. Two bombers collided over their base ... It is all over ...' The writing is laconic and you expect a tired, bitter conclusion to the paragraph; instead, in a phrase that speaks volumes for Tapper's wide-eyed resilience, he writes: '... I would not have missed it for anything ...'

A new squadron commander for 100 Squadron, to replace David Holford, arrived at Waltham on 20 December. Wing Commander John Dilworth took over on the night of the next operation (Frankfurt) and presided over further operations to Berlin either side of Christmas. He was to die just two months later.[8]

# CHAPTER ELEVEN
# DITCHED

The aircraft broke cloud and plunged nose-first into the freezing depths of the North Sea almost simultaneously. This was the last tortured moment of 57 Squadron's Lancaster JB373[1] which had left East Kirkby in Lincolnshire at 4.25 pm the previous afternoon. It was now ten minutes after midnight on the cold morning of 17 December. The sea was calm with no significant swell. Mist swirled above the waves. There was no moon and the darkness was total. As the aircraft hit the water, there was no time to brace against the impact, and not much more to escape from the fuselage: maybe four minutes before the sea finally consumed them. They had taken a normal fix about thirty minutes before, but the aircraft's flight subsequently had been erratic. Later, dutifully desk-bound on Christmas Day 1943, the Air Vice Marshal commanding 5 Group noted, in a memorandum to Bomber Command, High Wycombe: 'the aircraft must have been 'wandering' considerably.'[2] They had found Berlin well enough, but returning to the English east coast was beyond them.

Flight Sergeant Hurley[3] was the aircraft's wireless operator. His cubby-hole amidships protected him somewhat from the effects of the crash: momentarily knocked out, he came to and began a frantic scramble to get out of the aircraft, a process hindered by the growing pressure of sea water against the hatches. Moments before, he had registered in his mind where everyone else in the aircraft was. Things had a veneer of normality: Sergeant J Hinde, the pilot, strapped into his seat; flight engineer standing next to the pilot; navigator at his table; gunners marooned in their turrets; while the bomb aimer – the one officer on board – was in the nose and was, by a fleeting, horrific second, the first to realise what the aircraft's fate was to be. Eventually, Hurley opened the exit hatch in the middle of the aircraft and found himself in the darkest of nights, with the sea slapping against the Lancaster's skin. The dinghy was floating alongside the aircraft, but Hurley chose to scramble back on board, conscious that he was alone in the ocean. In the darkness, and with the water slowly filling the space, he made a desperate attempt to free the navigator, but the man's weight and the diminishing air forced him back outside before he could release him. Alone, and conscious that he would remain so, he heaved himself into the dinghy and then, belatedly, inflated his Mae West.[4] He saw the aircraft sink beneath the waves and lay there propped against the dinghy's side, hope fading as he drifted, lost and alone.

The dawn was a muted affair: fog drifting across the wave tops and no sound bar the movement of the sea. Hurley took stock of his situation: decided not to eat for twenty-four hours, and to preserve his limited stock of water until he could wait no longer. He stared into the mist and knew that finding him in these conditions was unlikely. He began to calculate how long he could survive. The sea's rise and fall became mesmerising and soon the light began to fade, the shortened day truncated even further by the gloomy weather. The night of the 17th was long, however, and bitterly cold. When the dawn came again, he knew that time was running out.

At 11.11 am on the morning of the 18th, the dinghy was spotted by a pilot from 106 Squadron, and two hours later, Hurley was picked up by the minesweeper HMS '*Typhoon*'. He had been drifting at sea for thirty-eight hours and had only had his first drink when he saw that he, in turn, had been sighted. He was the sole survivor from the crew of Lancaster JB373.

# CHAPTER TWELVE
# NOT MUCH CHOICE

The Lancaster of Pilot Officer A C Davies (426 Squadron) is on course for Berlin, flying east amongst the inexorable stream of bombers, at 24,000 feet. This is his ninth operation. It is around 7 pm on the night of 16 December 1943. About 250 miles short of the German capital, just over the Dutch border, above Osnabruck, the aircraft is hit by flak, intense enough to damage the hydraulic system. The immediate effect of this is to render the rear turret virtually immobile, and necessarily locking the rear gunner into his plastic bubble over the fire and darkness. Things get worse: a further flak barrage rakes the port side of the aircraft: holes the port wing, empties the port petrol tanks and destroys the outer engine. It blazes until the Flight Engineer, Pilot Officer R F Richards, succeeds in dousing the flames. The Lancaster rumbles onwards under the reduced power of three engines. A second petrol tank on the port side is also not functioning properly – shrapnel having damaged a valve – and so the aircraft is heavily reliant on fuel from the starboard side of the aircraft. There is about 500 gallons[1] of fuel left, with two thirds of the trip still ahead.

Davies weighs the options – which are few and all unattractive. He knows that a return to England is impossible; they would not make it back across the North Sea, so, mentally shrugging tense shoulders, he presses on to the target, clinically drops his bombs and turns north for neutral Sweden. The solution rests with parachutes on this dark night.

Baling out, however, is not that straightforward: the aircraft is damaged, but so too is the mid-upper gunner, Sergeant George, who has badly sprained an ankle. Stoically, he ignored the pain during the passage over Berlin, concentrating instead on providing a steady stream of information – notes on evasion – to the aircraft's captain. Now, with escape beckoning through the aircraft's hatch and crewmen anxiously fiddling with parachute toggles and wondering if jumping ship in the Swedish night would be remotely akin to practice in the gym, there is the dilemma of what to do about the trapped rear gunner still pinioned in the jammed turret. George scorns subtlety, takes a fire-axe to the problem, prises open the door and releases a hugely relieved rear gunner ...

Soon after 9 pm the crew baled out over Avesta, fifty miles from the Swedish coast and perhaps seventy-five miles south west of Gothenburg, leaving the aircraft to plunge into the sea as protocol dictated. George lost a flying boot as he scrambled through the escape hatch, and hit the ground hard, breaking his leg.[2] Inevitably, the crew were scattered and the luck that had stayed with them during a torrid night began to dissipate: pilot, navigator and wireless operator were all soon arrested by Swedish police. The bomb aimer struck out across country, using a compass from his escape kit and kept on the run for nearly forty-eight hours before being captured. The concept of cloak and dagger resistance has not reached Swedish farmers whose first instinct faced with wild-eyed Canadian fliers is to call the police. Sweden was, after all, neutral throughout the war; indeed there is a view that in the early years of the war she was frankly 'pro-German.'[3] The crew eventually were repatriated to England in instalments from September to October 1944.[4]

While Pilot Officer Davies was grappling with his stricken Lancaster, and the decision – such as it was – of heading for Sweden, the pilot and crew of Lancaster DV173 (460 Squadron) were facing the same dilemma. Hit by a missile over Berlin, the aircraft's pilot, Flight Sergeant Mervyn Stafford, was virtually unable to manage the damaged aircraft's controls. He had bombed at just after 8 pm, but the return was to be fraught with difficulty. Getting home looked a long shot, but the alternatives were as unpalatable. He invited the crew to share in the decision and in the darkness they voted on a choice of making for Sweden, or taking their chance on returning safely to England, despite the challenge of flying a damaged aircraft across the freezing North Sea. The vote was close: four votes for making for England against three for Sweden. What tilted the vote was the pregnancy of the rear gunner's wife. She was the magnet that drew them home.

GEE was not working and the pilot, try as he might, could not locate his home base of Binbrook in Lincolnshire. The official view of the ensuing accident was stark: 'Unable to find base so located Grimsby again. This happened three times. Finally, owing to low cloud and possible altimeter error (the aircraft) skidded into the hilltop at Rothwell Top . . . the rear gunner was thrown out with the tail unit and killed . . .'[5] Binbrook was less than six miles away. Six of the seven crew survived, bruised and shaken. Pilot Officer Garment, the rear gunner and father-to-be, was the only man to die.

# CHAPTER THIRTEEN
# FINAL APPROACH

Thick cloud over Berlin suited edgy airmen: Johnny Bank, a young crewman with 432 Squadron, noted in his diary that '... with a 10/10ths cloud all the way to Berlin, conditions were ideal for a raid ...'[1] Being entombed in cloud gave a false sense of security: you were left staring into impenetrable murk, lulled by the drone of engines and consoling yourself with the fact that German fighter pilots were similarly blinkered. Admittedly, not everyone felt this way: Canadian pilot Warrant Officer R T 'Skip' Lloyd (408 Squadron) commented: '... We have mixed feelings about cloud cover over the enemy route. On the one hand the cloud prevents the searchlights from 'coning' us, for the guns to pick away at us; but on the other hand when the searchlights shine up on the cloud from underneath we look like flies crawling across a white tablecloth to the Jerry fighters flying above us ...'[2]

If cloud offered a spurious protection over enemy territory, it held no corresponding benefit once the crews were trying to land: that was the moment when a bright moon became the pilot's friend. Fog was anathema, and disturbingly dense all too often. An American pilot was shocked by it: '"Can you see the runway lights?" the control tower asked (him), to which he replied: "Shit, I can't even see my co-pilot!"'[3] Not everyone found the process as straightforward as Skip Lloyd whose diary has him in blasé mood: '... I reduced height[4] to just a few feet above the water all the way across the North Sea and arrived home to find our base enshrouded in a low cloud height of 400 feet. I circled above our bombing range until I got a turn to land and then neatly whipped into the circuit and landed.' He would soon be embarked on the post-flight rites: conversation with ground crew, debrief, meal and sleep. Ken Duddell, a flight engineer with 103 Squadron, returned early, his pilot having been forced to turn back with mechanical difficulties, and was tucked up in bed by 10 pm. 'We heard them coming back and just turned over.'[5]

Just a few miles away from Lloyd's base at Linton, Johnny Bank's pilot, Pilot Officer Tom Spink was having a much more difficult time trying to find East Moor, north of York: '... Arriving back over Yorkshire we found the whole area covered by a solid cloud layer ... the first thing we saw, as it loomed up in front of us, was the cooling tower at York,[6] so Tommy pushed the throttles wide open, hauled back on the stick and climbed away.' Just as Roger Coulombe had groped around the night sky above Linton and had suddenly come face to face with the airfield water tower, so Bank's aircraft, '... descending through the murk ...' for a second time, found itself '... suddenly confronted by the red warning lights on top of a hangar ...' While Coulombe got down by the skin of his teeth – he became an orthodontist after all – Bank's crew was diverted: '... By now the Air Traffic Controller was becoming a little fed up with our display, so he ordered us to divert to Leeming. We heard 'Tower' divert another of our kites ...' This was the Lancaster of Flying Officer Hatfield whose aircraft was to crash into the moors above Danby.[7] Hatfield was exercised by the critically low reserves of fuel and he and his crew were then advised to bale out. Within minutes, the occupants of Lancaster DS832 were tumbling from the sky towards the damp bracken of Danby Beacon. There must have been an interesting and apparently democratic discussion aboard Bank's aircraft: '... As our crew was too scared to bale out,' he writes, 'we decided to have another go at landing ...' They made it, with 370 gallons left in the tanks. His diary entry for the day concludes with further evidence of the secrecy surrounding the crashes on Black Thursday: '... Bomber Command was supposed to have lost thirty-one aircraft on this operation, but we heard (unofficially) that another thirty-seven had been lost over this country as a result of 'prangs' etc ...'

\*    \*    \*    \*

Getting a crew there and back again was the dual responsibility of pilot and navigator, but the science of the enterprise fell to the man tucked away behind the navigator's curtain. ' "Pilots," said Air Vice Marshall Bennett, "were merely chauffeurs to get the really important people, the navigator and bomb aimer there." '[8] You were the one with the maps, after all, and all the paraphernalia that went with them. Before the operation began you would have prepared detailed logs and charts, a flight plan, and in some cases, anticipated areas of fighter plane activity.[9] Now, despite the tight confines of the aircraft, and the six other members of the crew scattered through its length, it comes down to you. Here's what you must do to get us there – oh, and back again: make sure that all your kit is there – charts, pencils (H and HB), eraser, pencil sharpener, navigation computer[10], protractor, straight edge ruler, dividers (with spare parts), navigation watch (set at GMT), message pad, sextant (with spare bulbs etc), astronomical tables, air almanac, navigation log ... Got all that? Berlin tonight, taking off at 4.30 pm, so be at the aircraft by half three. Check the gear: compasses, air position indicator and the rest. Wait for the green Aldis light and then the thunderous struggle between Merlin engines and gravity.

For a while you can trust to pre-arrangement: prepared height and speed, the precise passage across England's last recognisable feature – Southwold lighthouse, maybe, or the dim white of the cliffs at Flamborough Head. Feed the pilot the new course and then as the aircraft goes through the 7,000 feet mark, bury your face in the oxygen mask. Note what needs noting on the navigation log. Check the course is right – oh, and the airspeed. Fiddle around with the GEE box and get a proper radar fix. What's the wind doing? And is that ... ? Yes it is! Deadpan announcement: 'Enemy Coast Ahead'.

Sod it – you miss getting a fix from the bomb aimer as you crossed the coast: too much cloud around. Let the skipper know that the fighter belt is imminent. Don't get too bothered by what the pilot's determined evading tactics does to your attempts at pinpointing where you are. Or where you think you might be at least. The closer to Berlin you get, the more you'll feel out of control: GEE jammed by the enemy, searchlights, flak. Fire and light. So much noise. The disconcerting sight of Lancasters falling away in flames.

Once the bombs have gone, it's down to you again. Set a course for home. The canny thing was to give your pilot the course for home as the bombing run started so he could turn straight into it once the run was over. Nothing to be gained by hanging around. Ideally it will be a milk run: '... Comparative calm of North Sea ... Descending, oxygen mask off, dirty mark around the face ... Our turn to land. Breathe wonderful East Anglian summer air. 'Another one tucked away, skip', shouts the rear gunner. Cigarette. Debrief. Meal. Try to sleep as the sun comes up.'[11]

Tonight, though, it's not like that. Remember what the book[12] says: 'Before descending into low cloud or fog always remember the three golden rules: check your position, check your altimeter, check your safety height.' Safety height? You need to know that tonight of all nights – the aircraft must be 1,000 feet above the highest ground which is within twenty miles either side of the proposed track ... got that? So, given that the North York moors reach about 1,100 feet and you're flying into Linton, you'll need to be at over 2,000 feet. Above the cloud base, I know, and there were orders that returning crews over the North Sea should fly in **below** the cloud ...

Landing was a time of high risk:[13] you could overshoot the run-way; the wheels might stay retracted; the bomb doors could be lowered inadvertently; the flaps might cease functioning; engines could fail; or the undercarriage; you might collide with trees, high tension cables, birds, a hangar, a hut, or even other aircrew.

So how do you get down when you can see nothing but clouds thicker than bonfire smoke? What can you rely on up there as the petrol runs out and the fog rolls in ever more impenetrable?

The basic navigational principle is DR – Dead Reckoning. A phrase with unfortunate connotations on a night like this. It works by relating compass (direction) with chronometer (time), air-speed indicator (speed) and forecast wind: you fly in this direction at this speed for this length of time ... Back in May 1939, a senior RAF officer[14] in reporting to Bomber Command HQ on DR was pessimistic about its accuracy, claiming that it would do no better than bringing an aircraft to within fifty miles of its target. This was on a cloudy day and in peacetime. He did not attempt to quantify the degree of inaccuracy at night and under wartime conditions. 'The pilots and their crews tended to rely on a form of navigation popularly referred to as 'By guess and by God' ... DR was of limited use at night and in poor weather, and celestial navigation (route finding by star gazing) was too slow.'[15] It was entirely possible to get conclusively lost: for example, the middle of the war – Arnold Barker, an electrician member of the ground-crew at remote Silloth on the Cumbrian west coast is trudging outside intent on his task of lighting up the runway. He hears a bomber approaching in the darkness and hastily adds more lights. After the aircraft has landed, he notes the white-faced horror as the crew climb out to be told where they are: they have flown over most of the British mainland unknowingly and missed venturing over the Atlantic Ocean, and its thousands of miles of whitecaps, by moments.[16]

DR was not the only acronym on which harassed navigators could rely: GEE was '... an airborne radar navigational device which, when used within range of associated ground transmitting stations enables the navigator to obtain a fix of great accuracy at any instant during flight ...' The on-board receiver picked up transmissions from two transmitters, calculated the difference between the two, and then used that information to identify a position on a special GEE map. A more accurate 'fix' could be determined using two further transmissions. The *Training Notes for Air Navigators*, from which this definition is taken, notes also that it is effective 'under any weather conditions'. Don Charlwood, a navigator with 103 Squadron, describing a return from Essen, on a night of broken cloud, emphasises the security that GEE provided: '... The GEE is clarifying, making navigation easy and enjoyable ...'[17] It was neither of those things however when the weather closed in and all you could see was cloud and more cloud; with the petrol running out and the rest of the crew looking to you to get a reliable fix in a hurry.[18] You could be the difference between the reassuring thump of tyres on the runway, dull-eyed debrief and bed; or a calamitous metal-twisting descent into perimeter fence, parked aircraft or wooded hillside. GEE could not be relied upon since there were many instances when it failed to work properly. In 97 Squadron, for example, during November 1943 there was a failure with GEE on every 21.6 sorties.[19] Given the fact that twenty-one aircraft from 97 Squadron flew on operations to Berlin on Black Thursday, the likelihood, statistically, was that one crew would not be able to use GEE to land. That crew would, in effect, be blind.[20]

In addition to GEE, there was SBA (Standard Beam Approach); this was essentially a directional radio beam pulsing down the runway. After Black Thursday, some senior officers took the view that pilots' grasp of SBA was inadequate. 97 Squadron, in particular, were deemed blameworthy – each Form 1180 has a terse, tetchy comment from the squadron's CO: 'Pilots should have practised SBA.' You can sense the heads shaking in righteous disapproval. The Inspectorate-General noted in a report on RAF Waddington – interestingly dated just six days before Black Thursday – that 'safe landing in fog remains a stunt to be attempted by the expert only ... SBA is proclaimed as a means of landing in fog, a claim which justifiably scares the average pilot.'[21] The Inspectorate-General does not share the view of 97 Squadron's senior officers: it is unequivocal on SBA and fog – 'Standard Beam Approach does not enable the average pilot to make a safe landing in fog ... for the average pilot and for general operational purposes, landing in fog is not yet with us.' This is echoed by experienced pilots like Joe Northrop: 'Although every effort is taken to practise SBA ... the lengthy process ... required a high standard of skill and no little experience. Not only that, but as many as twenty or thirty aircraft might have to get down using the beam in the space of an hour or so before they ran out of fuel. On such a night, a single pilot unable to cope could play havoc with the stacking and positioning of other aircraft in the circuit.'[22] However, as we shall see, the Inspectorate-General could change its mind – and duly did so after Black Thursday.

# CHAPTER FOURTEEN
# THE MAN BEHIND THE DESK

The man behind the desk breathes concentration: there's a war on, after all. His hair gleams in the cone of light from the desk lamp: both light and hair are varying shades of yellow. His side parting is the product of decades of precise combing. His half-moon glasses convey just the right mix of a forensic eye for detail, and professorial certainty. A scrubby moustache nestles above his top lip. He has a nose down which he can stare disapprovingly, and those academic glasses add an air of quizzical wariness. You would not want to cross him, even if you were in the right. He does not look like a man who laughs a lot, and for Arthur Harris, Commander-in-Chief (Bomber Command), this war-time winter, there is not much call for humour. The room is heavily curtained against the night and the Commander-in-Chief has no eyes for anything but the weighty document on his desk. He reads, annotates and occasionally snorts with disapproval. Despite the deep concentration, he is only too aware of the armada of Lancasters flying east. He has been Commander-in-Chief since 22 February 1942 and has, ostensibly at least, got used to the nights when he knows that some of his young men will die. Inwardly, though, he is troubled: 'The whole of the responsibility, the final responsibility, for deciding whether or not to operate falls fair and square on the Commander-in-Chief's shoulders, and falls on them every twenty-four hours. For all he knows he may lose ... a very large proportion of the force by the weather alone ... It is best to leave to the imagination what such a daily strain amounts to when continued over a period of years.'[1]

Berlin, and the weather over northern Europe, had played a key role in Harris becoming head of Bomber Command. On the night of 7/8 November 1941, his predecessor, Sir Richard Peirse, had sent a force of 169 aircraft (predominantly Wellingtons) to the German capital and losses had been unacceptably high: very few bombs actually landed on the city, and only nine Germans were killed, while some 120 aircrew were lost in the process.[2] Peirse blamed the weather, and the weathermen, as well as contending that some of the pilots were insufficiently experienced. He did not point out that, with losses approaching 13 per cent on raids like this, experience was something not readily achieved –

death tended to come first. The raid foreshadowed Black Thursday: weather conditions were grim, and Berlin was covered in 10/10ths cloud. Ice forming on aircraft wings was a major hazard, the weight dragging the aircraft back, or down. For a while it looked as if Peirse had survived the debacle, but when it transpired that the weather forecasts had presaged problems, the Air Staff homed in: '... the disproportionate losses during these operations were the result of failure to appreciate fully the extent to which icing conditions might affect endurance rather than to a faulty forecast in the weather.'[3] Peirse was judged to have been reprehensible, removed and sent to the Far East, where he added the reputation of 'bounder' to his already blemished history when, faced with the Japanese threat, he eloped with the wife of the Commander-in-Chief India, General Auchinleck. Harris was seen as the new broom who would raise both morale and performance. Churchill who had taken a personal interest in the downfall of Peirse, was unequivocal in his view about future operations: 'We cannot afford losses on that scale ... there is no need to fight the weather and the enemy at the same time.'[4]

Harris was only too aware of the flaw in Churchill's argument: weather was unpredictable and could change in a matter of hours, or less. 'Meteorology is an inexact science; in fact, it is still in the condition of being rather an art than a science.'[5] Moreover there were always going to be occasions when the weather was neither ideal for bomber operations, nor wholly unfit. Often, in an island where weather relishes opportunities to tease and confound, the decision about fitness for flying was fraught with difficulty. Harris had already shown himself to be pragmatic and philosophical about the issue, taking the view that, in wartime, needs must. In the early part of the war, he had defended an experienced pilot from RAF Cottesmore who had been criticised after his fatal collision with a hillside in bad weather taking the view that accidents of that kind were unavoidable unless operations were restricted to periods of fine weather. He did not see that as an option then; faced now with the need to use the winter months to get to Berlin and back in darkness, it went without saying, if you were the Commander-in-Chief, that crews had to cope with bad weather as best they could.

## CHAPTER FIFTEEN

# SO WHAT'S THE WEATHER FOR TONIGHT?

The clock's hands pointed to one minute to nine on the morning of 16 December 1943. The occupants of the Operations Room at Bomber Command HQ in High Wycombe stood waiting for the imminent and inevitably punctual arrival of the Commander-in-Chief, Arthur Harris. The Chief Meteorological Officer, Doctor Magnus Spence[1], true to form, was standing at Harris's right hand, shuffling through his weather charts and forecasts, preparing himself for the ritual that was Harris's 'morning prayers'. As the principal 'met man', he would be in the eye of the storm: Harris had a high opinion of his own natural 'feel' for weather and invariably subjected Spence to a grilling. Typically, this 9 am meeting was relatively short, involving as it did a brief inquest into the previous night's operations (on the 16th there had not been a meaningful raid since Leipzig had been attacked nearly a fortnight before) and then decisions about which city or cities would be the target for that night.

Harris breezed in, took off his hat and reached for one of his American cigarettes which he kept in his left breast pocket. The discussion homed in on targets before he had reached the end of his smoke. Soon Spence was elaborating on the weather, not just for the target for the night – Berlin, codenamed 'Whitebait' – but also for the bases on return. As ever, Harris probed and challenged: 'He would not be put off with simple statements and occasionally endeavoured to nudge the forecast in the direction he wanted but Spence stood firm and Harris would smile faintly and give up ... he never overruled his Chief Met Officer ...'[2] Spence stood by his forecast and the decision was taken: tonight would see the first operation on the German capital since 2 December.

Those short-lived meetings where the focus was on weather, the size of the bomber force, bomb loads and the timing over the target, placed an enormous responsibility on Spence. Any error of judgement and men could die. In retrospect, Harris was able to downplay the pressure that one might assume Churchill placed upon him for unrelenting operations in dubious weather: '. . . he (Churchill) never failed in encouragement, just as he never failed to apply the spur. When a week or two of bad weather prevented us from doing anything much to get on with the offensive he would express his disappointment but conclude by saying: "I am not pressing you to fight the weather as well as the Germans, never forget that." '[3] Harris could show a similarly prudent and philosophical response to the threat of bad weather. In the absence of key senior officers, a Group Captain at HQ, Dennis Barnett, cancelled a planned operation because of the threat of fog on return. To Barnett's consternation, the weather was not so bad as he had been led to expect and he found himself carpeted in front of a querulous Harris. Barnett declared that he had not been satisfied that the aircraft could have landed on return: the visibility had been fading fast. There was an agonising moment's silence before Harris spoke. 'Quite right,' he said.[4] Spence, however, would have walked away from that mid-December meeting wondering about which way the weather would go that night, and whether he had given the right advice.

At 10.30 am the Met Office at the Air Ministry in Kingsway, London, issued a new forecast. Its overall summary was: 'A wedge of high pressure over the British Isles is almost stationary and weakening. Weather will be cloudy in most districts, with local drizzle in the north west. Visibility will be poor over England, Wales, the north east of England, and South Scotland; local fog; cold.' The word 'fog' occurs three times in the communiqué; the forecast for the northeast (Linton, East Moor and the other bases in Yorkshire and north Lincolnshire) is unequivocal – 'visibility poor, with some fog'; while eastern England (the Cambridgeshire airfields) was scarcely better: '. . . cloudy and dull, with general smoke haze and local fog; cold . . .' 'Fog' the Commander-in-Chief knew, was 'a serious hazard for night bombing operations.'[5]

I have those forecasts and associated weather data in front of me now.[6] Stamped 'SECRET' in the top right-hand corner, they provide a meticulously logged and detailed picture of the weather against which between three and four thousand RAF aircrew were fighting as the 16th of December painfully turned into the 17th. They are handwritten in a neat script that hints at inkwells, dipped pens and squinting clerks in love with numbers. The data sheet (number 29975) has forty-two columns, in each of which are figures or letters denoting weather observations at various times of the day and night. There are some forty weather stations listed, three of which are deep in bomber territory: Catterick in north Yorkshire, Cranwell in Lincolnshire and Mildenhall in Suffolk. The 1 am forecast preceded take-off times by more than three hours; by 6 pm, the aircraft would have been over continental Europe. By then any acute anxieties about deteriorating weather would have had to be pushed away. The tables below summarise the weather for each of the three stations:

### Catterick (forty-five miles north of York)

| | |
|---|---|
| *Barometric pressure* | Falling (from 27.5 at 1 pm to 24.8 at 6 pm). |
| *Wind* | Gentle winds, swinging between south west and south east. |
| *General description* | Overcast with fog; cold (38 degrees Fahrenheit). Wet ground. |
| *Visibility at 1 pm* | Moderate fog (objects not visible at 1,100 yards). |
| *Visibility at 6 pm* | Mist or haze. |
| *Height of the cloud base* | 2,000 feet at 1 pm but 1,700 feet five hours later. |

### Cranwell (Lincolnshire)

| | |
|---|---|
| *Barometric pressure* | Falling (from 25.9 at 1 pm to 24.1 at 6 pm). |
| *Wind* | Gentle winds from the south-east. |
| *General description* | Overcast/haze; cold (36 degrees Fahrenheit at 1 pm, dropping to 34). |
| *Visibility at 1 pm* | Moderate. |
| *Visibility at 6 pm* | Poor. |
| *Height of the cloud base* | 3,000 feet at 1 pm but 1,000 feet five hours later. |

### Mildenhall (Suffolk)

| | |
|---|---|
| *Barometric pressure* | Falling (from 26 at 1 pm to 24.3 at 6 pm). |
| *Wind* | Gentle winds from the south east. |
| *General description* | Overcast/haze; cold (37 degrees Fahrenheit at 1 pm, dropping to 36). |
| *Visibility at 1 pm* | Moderate. |
| *Visibility at 6 pm* | Moderate. |
| *Height of the cloud base* | 3,000 feet at 1 pm but 1,000 feet five hours later. |

Telephoned by Magnus Spence in the middle of the afternoon on the 16th for the latest picture what would you say then? 'Fairly still and misty conditions; cloud base appears to be coming down; the visibility's not brilliant, but taking off in these conditions should be okay; chilly. A bit gloomy really. Bit worried about the forecast lowering of the cloud base – if that's an over-optimistic judgement, we'll have major problems ...' The first real hint of serious trouble is in the notes describing the weather through the night of the 16th: the symbols change from 'c f'[7] – generally cloudy and fog, with visibility between 220 and 1,100 yards – early in the day; to 'c m o F' by the early hours – the capital F signifies thick fog (less than 220 yards). As the fog thickened and the aircraft nosed through it, their crews straining for a hint of light or concrete runway, waiting for a sudden catastrophic sound of tearing metal, Harris was lying awake as was his wont, waiting for – but not expecting – safe returns. In bed by 10.30 most nights, he could not sleep until his crews had returned.

\*    \*    \*    \*

Aircrew fought the weather on a daily basis – they learned an instinctive feel for the direction of the wind or the changing cloudscape, and what that meant for operations. At Bomber Command HQ there was a protracted battle over the weathermen themselves. A month before Black Thursday, there was the first meeting of an inquiry into how the RAF interacted with the meteorological service. It was chaired by Sir Edgar Ludlow-Hewitt, a former head of Bomber Command, whom Harris described as 'far and away the most brilliant officer I have ever met in any of the three services.'[8] Harris was not a man given to lavish praise where none was due. Ludlow-Hewitt was Inspector General during this period and responsible for the scrutiny of RAF practices, including, it should be noted catastrophes, like the events of 16–17 December. The inquiry into the weather service involved twenty-five meetings, with its first such gathering taking place exactly a week before Black Thursday. Ludlow-Hewitt received a formal Air Ministry letter dated 12 November 1943 on the matter. Stamped SECRET, it referred to a recent conversation with the Chief of the Air Staff (CAS): 'The CAS spoke to you the other day about a Committee which the Secretary of State proposed to appoint to enquire into the question of an RAF Weather Service'.[9] The lines between the Terms of Reference are easy enough to read, even if they are couched in Civil Service convolution: there was a struggle over the Met Office's continuing independence, with a powerful lobby arguing that met officers should be incorporated into the RAF, the better to ensure their compliance. 'To consider the suitability of the existing organisation for the provision of meteoro-logical services for the RAF; to have regard in this connection to the operational needs of the RAF on the one hand and on the other to the responsibilities of the Meteorological Office, both at home and overseas for the supply of meteorological and climatic information to other government departments and agencies, and to make recommendations.'

The Committee was small, consisting of Ludlow-Hewitt himself, Sir Edward Appleton, Head of the Department of Scientific and Industrial Research, and two retired civil servants. It took evidence and, as committees do, touched raw nerves. Harris submitted an acrimonious memorandum on 1 December in which he made his views abundantly clear. The text appears to smoulder. He argued that the meteorological service's independence had been given ample time to show its worth. Such independence, he wrote, was 'unworkable without grave prejudice to operational efficiency'.[10] He admired the work of individuals, but he regretted the fact that weathermen had no operational experience; that it was 'anomalous' to have civilians taking significant responsibility for aspects of active service; and that the weathermen were free from military constraints and shouldn't be. 'It cannot be denied,' he went on, 'that operational opportunities have been missed and avoidable casualties incurred because their knowledge had to be gained by trial and error in the course of operations ...' He wanted 'the institution of a regular RAF Meteorological Service, staffed by personnel selected for their suitability for this highly specialised and responsible branch of meteorological activity.'

A key issue was who decided whether the conditions were 'fit for flying'. It was emotive enough for the committee to be faced with an intensity of feelings that civil servants remembering more gentlemanly pre-war days might have found inappropriate. Un-committee-like words pepper the file: Appleton talks of 'antagonism towards civilians'; Shorto, one of the civil servants, commented that there was a 'degree of petulance exhibited by senior officers'; the delightfully named Mr Crotch wrote a letter in which he voiced uncertainty about his manner – 'I fear I have been a rather obstreperous secretary.' Met officers might 'know' the weather, but they didn't know, in the main, about flying, still less about operations. A witness to the inquiry, a Colonel Mustoe, was asked by Ludlow-Hewitt if forecasters expressed views about fitness for flying. Mustoe's reply was revealing: 'Not officially,' he said, 'nor in writing. They wouldn't use the word "dangerous", for example, in expressing an opinion on the amount of icing aircraft might face. Only a word like "severe". They try to take on the viewpoint of the pilot, but they must not offer advice on whether to fly or not.' This was all in accord with Kings Regulations which stated: 'The duty assigned to the meteorological staff is to describe the weather, present or future, with promptitude and accuracy, and not to pronounce upon its suitability for flying'.[11] But then Mustoe laughed, his guard temporarily dropped, and the uncomfortable truth revealed itself: 'Mind you,' he said, 'Commanders often plied forecasters with questions in the hope of getting them to "improve" the weather ...'

The inquiry duly recommended that weathermen should be put in uniform, and, where possible, should include men with operational experience. It did not address the bigger issue of ensuring that men did not fly in unfit weather, 'improved' or otherwise.

# CHAPTER SIXTEEN

# A BAD START

Unforgiving December weather at half past four on a grey, drab afternoon. As the light faded, a truck lumbered down a narrow country lane barely wide enough to take it. The driver, Marie Harris (ATS W/44133) was one of three women drivers based at the anti-aircraft site at Goxhill Haven overlooking the Humber estuary. Their job was to ferry military materials and people in jeeps and trucks around the lanes of north Lincolnshire. As the light faded and 16 December ticked towards evening, Harris was driving away from the gun battery at Goxhill, leaving the broad sweep of the Humber behind her. Outside the warmth of the truck, it was cold and the trees dripped with moisture. Conscious of the ditches on either side of the road, she was concentrating hard, coaxing the open lorry with its canvas covered back, full of stores, along a lane rutted with muddy puddles. She could see a farmhouse to her right, and hear the Lancasters taking off from the aerodrome at Elsham Wolds some three miles away across the gently rolling hills.

The cloud was very low and if she looked away from the lane in front of her, she could see aircraft searching for height, circling above the airfield, flitting in and out of the cloud. '... I looked up and raised my right arm in salute. They were so low and near I felt I could touch them ...' She was idly wondering why aircraft in such close proximity didn't collide: she knew the sky would be full of Lancasters all struggling to reach operational height. She watched one Lancaster disappear into a wall of cloud hanging low over the sodden fields. Moments later, she saw it reappear and hit another Lancaster head-on. There was '... one almighty explosion and all hell was let loose. It was awful, I couldn't believe what had happened practically over my head ...' The two aircraft had collided over the farmer's field.

The road was lit by streaks of fire, while the truck too was scorched by debris and heat. Marie stamped on the brakes and flung herself into a ditch, pulling her arms over her head in an instinctive attempt to protect herself against the fire. She lay there shaking for what seemed like five minutes and then climbed out of the ditch intending to see if she could rescue any survivors. She ran past the farmhouse, conscious that there were still pieces of metal and other debris in the air, and on past a barn. Suddenly, she was aware of someone trying to catch hold of her

*Marie Harris – front row, second from the right – with other members of the MT section at the Goxhill Marsh Anti Aircraft Gun site 1943–44.* Ron Parker

who: '... wouldn't let go, kept saying "No lass, no lass, there'll be nothing ..."' The two of them stood there watching the aircraft burn fiercely. They were still there when the fire-crews arrived.

Later, Marie stumbled back to the truck and drove uncertainly on. What had happened she could not believe. Arriving at the Guard Room, she sat in the truck unable to move, or stop crying. '... The guard called the sergeant ... took one look at my truck with all the bits and pieces, burns on the canvas and said, "She must have been under it, sarge!"' They made her strong tea and put her by the stove to stop her shaking. She had seen something she would never forget.[1]

The Lancasters whose metal fragments showered Marie Harris that night had taken off almost together: 103 Squadron's JB 670, piloted by Flight Sergeant V Richter, had lifted off at 4.37 pm; while twenty-four year old Australian Flight Sergeant, Frederick Scott, from 576 Squadron had preceded him by one minute in Lancaster LM322. By twenty to five, all fourteen crew members were dead, and both aircraft were in smouldering pieces,[2] 'falling north of the village.'[3] Houses in the village were damaged: about one hundred suffered broken windows, doors or ceilings. The police report describes the ensuing disruption: '... one

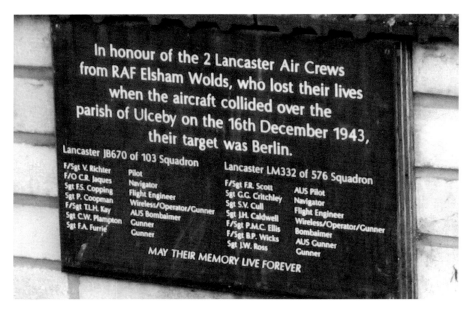

*The memorial plaque for the crews lost in the mid-air collision over Ulceby.*

civilian was injured (concussion) through being blown up against a wall by blast. An unexploded 4,000 lb bomb was found on the surface in a grass field by the side of the Wootton–Ulceby main road ... and the road has been closed. Fifty-one persons were evacuated from their homes ... The unexploded bomb is reported by the RAF authorities to be in a highly dangerous condition ... The RAF Regiment from Kirmington are guarding the wreckage and, so far, four badly mutilated bodies have been found.' An involuntary memorial to the crash lasted for the next forty years: it was 1983 before a tree harbouring metal fragments of one – or both – aircraft was felled.

This is a poignant overture to the remaining events of the night. It was the only accident during the preliminaries of the raid and it happened in difficult conditions, albeit without the acute challenges that the return from the operation provided. Once an aircraft was in the air, having hauled its heavy burden of metal, bombs and fuel above the runway, the norm was laboriously to circle over the aerodrome, in a rising spiral, to reach the height at which the flight into enemy territory would begin. Failing to do so at the outset like this would render an aircraft vulnerable to attack. Height was a prerequisite. Collision was thought unlikely, since aircraft typically kept their navigation lights on. The crash involving Scott and Richter is likely to have been the result of confusion in the poor weather conditions: made fatal perhaps by pilot error by one or both of them, or the result of a sudden malfunction in one of the aircraft. The official view was unequivocal: 'after both a/c had taken off, they circled below or just in cloud *contrary to orders* (my italics) and collided crashing in flames.' The station commander noted that while it was not possible to pin the blame on one or other of the pilots, 'both disobeyed briefing.'[4]

The weather was a remorseless and untrustworthy enemy and, whatever Arthur Harris said, there was an equally unrelenting pressure for crews to get airborne and heading east as night fell and the weather closed in. There was an inexorable sense of obligation. Australian Don Charlwood, a navigator with 103 Squadron at Elsham, commented[5] of a similar night to December 16, '... all day heavy mist had limited the horizon ... by evening it had closed in further, leaving the runway a road into nothingness ...' He describes the Wing Commander sweeping up in his car through the mist and parking close to the

*Two Lancasters – one from 103 Squadron and the other from 576 – collided over Ulceby shortly after take-off. A fragment of the crash remained in this tree until it was chopped down in 1983.* Ron Parker

Lancaster's nose while the crew waited patiently for decisions to be taken. He shouted to the pilot: '... Maddern, this weather threatens to get worse ...' and then, instead of telling them to come in from the cold and wait another day, went on: '... Will you chaps volunteer to go?' Charlwood, and the men who flew with him, were the first crew that year at Elsham to complete a tour of thirty operations. Previously, the feat had seemed impossible.

\* \* \* \*

As the rain intensified I headed east for Ulceby and the anti-aircraft site at Goxhill Haven. Approaching the Humber Bridge, in a sky of varying shades from black to dark grey, a jet barrelled overhead and swept south as if intent on flying through the bridge's arch. The Haven was misnamed, a bleak spot at the end of Ferry Road looking over the Humber towards the buildings of Hull, one dimensional somehow and strangely lit on this December morning in June. Faced with the dead end of the river, I turned around and tried to guess the route Marie Harris would have taken more than sixty years before me. The lanes were narrow and straight – no reason here for a bend in the road. The landscape was dismal seaside: a few desolate scrubby trees, grass bowing to the buffeting wind; sea and sky a uniform grey. Near a monument to the Americans who had trained at Goxhill airfield, there was a pillbox, weathered with rain and wind, choked by long grass growing to the height of its dark slits. Occasionally, in the near distance, I could see Immingham and Scunthorpe: an industrial landscape at odds with this rurality. Several times I saw a thin oil chimney from which a tongue of flame emerged, like an aircraft exhaust.

In Ulceby, the war memorial was fenced in with black iron bars. Against a wall with bricks the colour of a school sports hall was a plaque recently placed there to honour the two crews lost in the collision – 'over the parish of Ulceby' – in the murky twilight of 16 December. The wording was simple and heartfelt: 'May their memory live forever.' I drove around the parish and found a lane that matched Marie's description: ditches on either side and a farm off to the right; gentle hills, hedges and behind me the Humber close to becoming ocean.

Later, I returned to Elsham Wolds itself, high above floodplain and valley, with a view inland for miles: a windmill, villages buried in the folds of hills, dark green trees surrounded by grassland, and the weather gusting in from the west, changing by the minute. '... Beside the aerodrome rose the bulk of hangars; a glass-fronted watch office; a tall water tower and other lower buildings clustered about them ... Halifaxes dispersed about the rim of the landing field ... white windsocks swung rigidly in the strong wind ...'[6] All gone now and replaced by Anglian Water's treatment works and the unchecked sprawl of industrial estate.

Fifty-three years to the day after Black Thursday – on 16 December 1996 – an identity disc was found near the site of the sergeants' mess at Elsham Wolds. It was inscribed: 'M.G. Western RAAF'. Flight Sergeant Malcolm Western was a gunner on Lancaster DV 342 (576 Squadron) which had set off for Berlin nine minutes before fellow Australian Fred Scott. Sadly, Western's pilot and crew never had to face the daunting return to England: their aircraft was shot down over Berlin, crashing some eight kilometres east-north-east of the capital into the suburb of Lichtenberg. In the aftermath of the war this ended up in the

*A Lancaster at RAF Elsham Wolds.* From the Local Studies Collection, Lincoln Central Library, Lincolnshire County Council

*Malcolm Western of 576 Squadron photographed with his aunt Nellie Adams and cousin, Robert, while on leave in Bradford-on-Avon. Western was shot down over Berlin on his first operation on his 20th birthday.* Bob Adams

Russian sector, making investigation of the crash difficult at that time. Nonetheless, according to an eye witness – a German police chief – the aircraft was flying in an easterly direction at over 10,000 feet when it exploded, scattering debris over a wide area. It was Western's twentieth birthday. While his body was never found, astonishingly his fountain pen was – recovered from a German shop shortly after the war had ended and returned to his mother in Australia by the British Army authorities. His sister, Alison, remembers her brother's watch – 'a bit battered and beat up' – being returned to her parents. 'I remember the day it arrived back. It's the only time I saw Mum cry through the whole thing.' She also notes that Western's best friend, Don Bannister survived the war and made a point every year of visiting the Western family every 16 December.

In the summer of 2004, I received a letter from Western's sister, Alison and cousin, Robert Adams. More than sixty years had passed, and both were still anxious to know more about the events of that night. Later, Bob sent me an account of his memories: 'I remember the telegram coming and the agony my mother went through. She was too upset to tell me but I knew he had died.'

*   *   *   *

Black Thursday's route to Berlin was nothing if not direct, a no nonsense straight path just north of the 52 degree line of latitude. They breached enemy territory in the darkness over Ijmuiden, to the north west of Amsterdam, a point level with Southwold on the English east coast – and the German capital. It wasn't long before the stream of bombers ran into opposition: there were some eighteen encounters with German fighter aircraft.[7] It is evident from an analysis of the ORBs that those crews shot down were more likely to have taken off early: 55 per cent of them were aloft by 4.30 pm. The cloud base was scarcely above 100 feet[8] and one of the first casualties of the fog on Black Thursday was in fact German: Ulrich Wulff who had scrambled into the murk and crashed moments later, probably the victim of ice coating the wings. *Oberleutnant* Heinz-Wolfgang Schnaufer came out above the thick fog into a night sky heavy with stars at around 5,000 feet and soon homed in on the incoming Lancasters. He was responsible for shooting down four of them within minutes of them entering Dutch airspace.[9] Warrant Officer Wallace Watson (7 Squadron) came down in farmland near Lemmer at 6.05 pm just over ninety minutes from take-off; his crew – which included five Australians – were all killed.

*   *   *   *

Out of the blue I had a long telephone conversation with the nephew of one of the air gunners on Wallace Watson's aircraft. A retired policeman from Nottingham, Dave Cheetham had long wondered about the airman's photograph in his grandmother's lounge – 'no one knew him,' he said, and so he set out to find out who he was and what had happened to him and established that the airman was in fact Cheetham's uncle. The photograph was of Sergeant James (Jimmy)

*April 1947: an Air Ministry letter brings news to James Hurst's mother.* Dave Cheetham

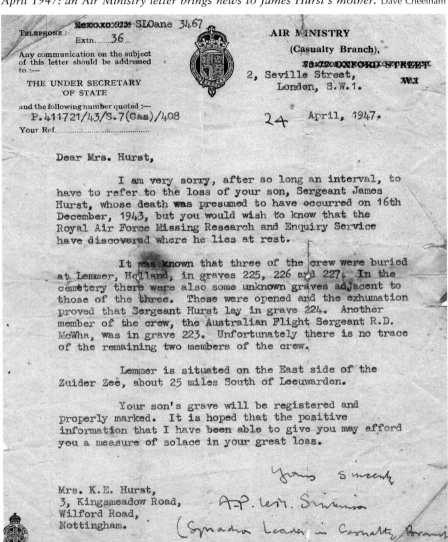

TELEPHONE : Semoxox92x SLOane 3467
Extn. 36

Any communication on the subject of this letter should be addressed to :—

THE UNDER SECRETARY OF STATE

and the following number quoted :—

P.411721/43/S.7(Cas)/408

Your Ref.

AIR MINISTRY

(Casualty Branch),

73-77 OXFORD STREET

2, Seville Street,
London, S.W.1. W1

24 April, 1947.

Dear Mrs. Hurst,

I am very sorry, after so long an interval, to have to refer to the loss of your son, Sergeant James Hurst, whose death was presumed to have occurred on 16th December, 1943, but you would wish to know that the Royal Air Force Missing Research and Enquiry Service have discovered where he lies at rest.

It was known that three of the crew were buried at Lemmer, Holland, in graves 225, 226 and 227. In the cemetery there were also some unknown graves adjacent to those of the three. These were opened and the exhumation proved that Sergeant Hurst lay in grave 224. Another member of the crew, the Australian Flight Sergeant R.D. McWha, was in grave 223. Unfortunately there is no trace of the remaining two members of the crew.

Lemmer is situated on the East side of the Zuider Zee, about 25 miles South of Leeuwarden.

Your son's grave will be registered and properly marked. It is hoped that the positive information that I have been able to give you may afford you a measure of solace in your great loss.

Yours sincerely

A.P. Wm. Simenson

(Squadron Leader in Casualty Branch)

Mrs. K.E. Hurst,
3, Kingsmeadow Road,
Wilford Road,
Nottingham.

Hurst, one of the gunners in Watson's crew. Cheetham wrote to the pilot of the fighter which had shot down his uncle's Lancaster and discovered that, although Schnaufer had survived the war, and in its aftermath built up his own wine business, he had died in France in the 1950s when his Mercedes saloon had collided with a lorry. The fighter ace died under a barrage of oxygen cylinders. Cheetham had also received a letter from Fritz Rumpelhardt, the wireless operator in Schnaufer's Messerschmitt, with a detailed account of the night of 16 December written after the war. His letter ended: 'With hindsight I am sorry to have contributed to the death of your uncle. The terrible war demanded its sacrifices. I was not untouched by it as both my brothers were killed as pilots.'[10]

The weather over Holland had been bad for days. 'At night,' Rumpelhardt wrote, 'it was impossible because of the thick fog, to get the night-fighters into the air ... on the night of December 16 ... (we) sat in the "readiness room" waiting – in vain, we thought – for action.' Schnaufer was soon in the air, however, and combing the

darkness for four-engined bombers, his eyes flickering this way and that behind the screen. The final moments of Watson's aircraft over Follega were witnessed by the teenaged son of a local farmer, Mr Bangma, and in 1994 (aged sixty-four), he told Cheetham what he had seen that night: 'I was in the kitchen when an enormous explosion lit up the field facing the kitchen window, the window was smashed and a ball of flame flew straight over the farmhouse roof ... later this was found to be one of the engines which landed in a ditch behind the farm.' Later Bangma saw four corpses 'as though they were just asleep'. One of them was wearing a half opened parachute.

*Sgt James (Jimmy) Hurst who flew with Warrant Officer Watson, 7 Squadron.*
Dave Cheetham

*Remnants of the crashed Lancaster of 7 Squadron's Wal Watson. On the right is Mr Bangma who saw the crash; on the left is Jimmy Hurst's nephew, Dave Cheetham.*
Dave Cheetham

A second 7 Squadron aircraft, piloted by another Australian, Flying Officer Rush, came down near Alkmaar. Schnaufer also accounted for Pilot Officer Ratcliffe (49 Squadron) – on his first operation – and Flight Lieutenant R E MacFarlane, a Canadian from 101 Squadron.[11] Like

*Aussies in 7 Squadron: pilot Wal Watson is in the back row, flanked by Bill Waterman (navigator) and Lloyd Robinson (bomb aimer). The wireless operator, Flight Sergeant J Butterworth and Sergeant Doug McWha, gunner, are at the front.* Dave Cheetham

many of his RAF counterparts later that night, Schnaufer had great difficulty landing, overshooting the airfield four times until the cloud temporarily dispersed enough for him to get down safely. The radio operator, Fritz Rumpelhardt, commented later that 'the nerves of the crew were stretched to breaking point when, after the fourth attempt, the aerodrome was still not in sight; but then, a miracle, a hole in the cloud and Schnaufer put it down smartly.' It was unsettling enough for Schnaufer to insist later that he had no intention of flying again in such conditions.[12] Meanwhile, the Lancasters flew on, with six more hours left in the air – if they survived that long ...

7 Squadron pilot Pilot Officer Geoff Tyler – yet another Australian – had taken off from Oakington at 4.21 pm. The crew had posed for a picture in the garden of rear gunner Billy Wilson's parents' house in Chesterfield. The photograph stares up at me from the table: Tyler and his men, in uniform, smiling at the future with a slightly preoccupied, apprehensive look, like cricketers waiting to bat. There are leafless trees

*No. 7 Squadron pilot Geoff Tyler at the Wilson family home in Chesterfield; rear gunner Billy Wilson is third from the left and his sister Jean stands in front of Tyler.*
Dave Cheetham

behind them, tall chimneys and the stolid brick of Wilson's home. The rear gunner's sister, sensibly frocked, has Tyler's hands resting on her shoulders: she is smiling as if she likes the tall Australian's attentions. Above them, behind the leaded windows, in shadow, Dave Cheetham told me, is her mother holding the latest arrival in the Wilson family – Jock's brother – young Robert, who would go on to keep goal for Arsenal and Scotland long after the war, and Black Thursday, were over. I recently acquired a second photograph of the same garden with some of the same protagonists: sister Jean in a different frock; the two year old Bob at the front and Tyler alongside his rear gunner into whose parents' house he had been so welcomed. It was Geoff Tyler's twenty-first birthday. In his last letter home Tyler had described his delight at the surprise birthday cake with its twenty-one candles and the lone aircraft in the centre. Billy – like his brother before him – wrote a last letter to his parents, written in anticipation of what might happen. In it he talked of the seven recent raids he had flown in – 'devastating attacks' – and his feelings for his crew and its pilot: '... it has been an honour to fly with my crew, especially my skipper Geoff, whose praises I cannot sing too high ...'[13]

*Celebrating pilot Geoff Tyler's twenty-first birthday in the Wilson garden in Chesterfield. He is on the far left. Future Arsenal and Scotland goalkeeper Bob Wilson is at the front. His brother Billy is next to his pilot.* Bob Wilson

For Tyler and his crew Black Thursday was to be in stark contrast to the tranquillity of this English garden. The Wilson family already knew about tragedy – Billy's elder brother, John – Jock – had been shot down and killed flying a Spitfire in February 1942. He had been nineteen. Billy, for his part, was twenty in December 1943. 'Do not in any way grieve if you should hear I am missing,' he wrote to his parents, signing it off 'I am ever and always your very loving son Billy.'

Far from the peaceful haven of the Wilson garden, the first Tyler knew that the Lancaster had been hit was when the port wing caught fire between the two engines. The damage had been inflicted by cannon fire from a Swiss born, anti-Nazi aristocrat – Prince Heinrich zu Sayn-Wittgenstein – whose own war was not to last much longer.[14] Five minutes investigating such a name on the internet exposes a spider's web of pan-European noble connections: Sayn-Wittgenstein's name sits contentedly alongside the Windsors and the Danish royal family in a flurry of models and princesses, show-jumpers and well heeled diplomats. There is even a photograph of the flying prince out there in cyber-space: he sits, uniformed and medalled, staring into an uncertain future, hair slicked back from an aristocrat's forehead, hands clasped and his cuffs shot to reveal chunky cuff-links and an expensive time-piece. There is white china in front of him: coffee pot and delicate plates, while a roaring fire consumes logs in the bricked grate behind him. The pilot's shadow looms ominously behind his right shoulder.

*Rear gunner Billy Wilson, 7 Squadron.* Bob Wilson

The fighter came round for a second pass at Tyler's Lancaster, unleashing a burst of cannon shells that ripped through the central fuselage. The bomb aimer Sergeant Dennis Woolford had been sitting with the navigator operating the H2S set when suddenly the aircraft shook violently as if it had come shuddering to a halt. This was followed by a battery of noise like kettle drums being pounded. Moments later, the navigator's table disintegrated. Woolford turned to see Tyler – they were close friends – struggling to keep the aircraft flying. There was a flurry of machine gun fire and later Woolford realised he had been hit in the wrist as he scrabbled for his parachute. The flight engineer was blown apart. In the confusion, Woolford heard Tyler giving instructions to bale out and he made for the hatch in the nose of the aircraft. At first he thought he was trapped: the hatch wouldn't open, held in place by the pressure from the aircraft's spinning, wheeling descent. Eventually he kicked his way out, counted to thirty and pulled the rip cord. He had 17,000 feet left to fall.

He never saw the ground until he landed – in a field, while his parachute slowly ballooned and spread itself over a wire fence. It was a hard landing and he hurt one of his ankles. His boots had come off in the escape from the burning aircraft. He saw a barn and made for it, hoping to break in and hide while he gathered his wits. Moments later, he was facing a German farmer, an old man pointing a gun at him. 'All the neighbours came in to have a look and everybody was quite good to me. In the morning the *Luftwaffe* came in a truck to pick me up. There were five coffins in the truck and I knew it was members of my crew. There was a smell like pork and I knew they had been burned.'[15] The farmer had been a survivor of the fighting in the first war. Briefly Woolford had been in the hands of the Gestapo who 'interrogated him and wanted to know about the radar. He told them he was not a Pathfinder but Main Force and that he had been shot down by flak. He was then beaten ... and told he would be shot in the morning.' The *Luftwaffe* came to his rescue and he spent the rest of the war as a POW.[16] The other survivor was the navigator, Flight Sergeant Alex Smillie. 'He told me he hadn't got a 'chute and the pilot handed him his, saying, "Take mine"'. Smillie's parachute had been shredded by gunfire. Not long before Geoff Tyler, the pilot, had volunteered the crew for Pathfinder duties: years later, Woolford would explain that the expectation was that the Stirlings they had been flying were going to be turned over to odd jobs – glider towing, or anti-submarine work. Tyler had been unimpressed: 'I haven't come over from Australia to do odd-jobbing,' he had said, before making his fateful decision.

As the attackers droned across western Germany, the fighter threat temporarily diminished, but not before Flight Lieutenant Petrie had been shot down west of Cloppenburg by Oberleutnant Dietrich Schmidt. This was around 6.45 pm.[17] While the RAF pilots were staring into the darkness, their counterparts were stepping out on to Dutch tarmac, smelling hot oil and metal, cordite, and the damp night fog, and imagining warm coffee, schnapps, and leather chairs circling a blazing log fire. The citizens of Hannover will have heard the thunder of aircraft engines, looked up and wondered, but the convoy steadfastly headed east.

So to Berlin: roofed by cloud, thick with flak, but relatively fighter-free, since the *Luftwaffe* controllers had held off committing their aircraft, worried that the RAF ploy was to swing south towards Leipzig. The losses sustained by the attackers were the result of flak and mid-air collisions, not fighter interventions.

All told twenty-three RAF aircraft came down over Holland and Germany that night. The table below logs them all:

| | Pilot | Squadron | Circumstances | Survivors |
|---|---|---|---|---|
| 1 | Warrant Officer D Baker | 625 | Lost over Diepholz, perhaps 120 miles from the North Sea coast. | 1 |
| 2 | Pilot Officer G B Loney | 619 | Crashed at Eberswalde-Finow 40 miles NE of Berlin, close to the route of the bombers as they headed away from the German capital. | 0 |
| 3 | Flying Officer R S McAra | 576 | Crashed at Lichtenberg, 5 miles ENE of Berlin. Malcolm Western (see text) was this crew's rear gunner.[18] | 0 |
| 4 | Pilot Officer L P Archibald | 426 | Shot down near Verden, north of Hannover by a fighter while flying at 19,000 feet. Only the bomb aimer managed to bale out. | 1 |
| 5 | Flight Lieutenant R J Allen | 207 | Shot down by a night-fighter near Magdeburg, 70 miles west of Berlin. | 5 |
| 6 | Flying Officer P W R Pollett | 166 | Lost over Diepholz, perhaps 120 miles from the North Sea coast. | 0 |
| 7 | Pilot Officer C H Storer | 106 | Crashed near Bramsche, Germany near the Dutch border. | 0 |
| 8 | Flight Sergeant H Campbell | 103 | Crashed near Doberitz. | 0 |
| 9 | Pilot Officer D A Rollin | 44 | Lost over Diepholz, perhaps 120 miles from the North Sea coast. | 1 |
| 10 | Pilot Officer I Black | 9 | Crashed at Salzbergen, near Rheine, fairly close to the Dutch border. | 0 |
| 11 | Pilot Officer R Bayldon | 9 | Crashed at Eberswalde-Finow 40 miles NE of Berlin, close to the route of the bombers as they headed away from the German capital. | 0 |
| 12 | Flight Lieutenant J Petrie | 7 | Crashed 40 km west of Cloppenburg. | 0 |

| | Pilot | Squadron | Circumstances | Survivors |
|---|---|---|---|---|
| 13 | Pilot Officer G Tyler | 7 | Shot down and crashed at Wilsum, close to the Dutch border. | 2 |
| 14 | Warrant Officer W Watson | 7 | Shot down by Schnaufer and crashed on Bangma's farm at Follega. | 0 |
| 15 | Flying Officer F Rush | 7 | Crashed near Alkmaar. | 1 |
| 16 | Pilot Officer G Ratcliffe | 49 | Shot down by Schnaufer over Holland. | 0 |
| 17 | Flying Officer W Fisher | 432 | Shot down by Schnaufer over Holland. This was Fisher's seventeenth operation. | 2 |
| 18 | Flying Officer W Maitland | 408 | Lost without trace. | 0 |
| 19 | Flight Lieutenant C Aubert | 156 | Lost without trace. | 0 |
| 20 | Pilot Officer N Newton | 115 | Crashed in Holland: it exploded in mid-air over Heemskerk. This was a newly assembled crew in a brand new aircraft[19]. | 0 |
| 21 | Flying Officer R MacFarlane | 101 | Shot down by Schnaufer near Lemmer, Holland. | 0 |
| 22 | Flight Sergeant P Head | 101 | Lost without trace. | 0 |
| 23 | Flight Lieutenant D Brill | 97 | Lost without trace. | 0 |

The small number of survivors of these incidents (13) reveals the relative difficulties associated with baling out when an aircraft is on fire and tumbling to destruction. Unlike crashes in England where gunners had the best chance of survival, over enemy territory their chances were slim in the extreme.

Poignantly there was another factor at play in the struggle between German fighters and RAF Lancasters. It was chance that I discovered it, since no survivors had mentioned it to me. For some three years there had been controversy concerning the Identification Friend or Foe (IFF) mechanism on board RAF bombers. The relevant files[20] at the National Archives are titled *The Effect of IFF on German Searchlights* and the origins of the debate stemmed from a report by a Hampden crew, based at Lindholme, but landing at Linton-on-Ouse in October 1940. IFF, as the name suggests, was designed to operate over the United Kingdom and prevent mistaken identity and subsequent mishaps. The Hampden crew under interrogation once they had landed in Yorkshire, according to a memo from HQ 4 Group to Bomber Command HQ, '... mentioned that they had switched on their IFF equipment during a period of

*RAF Waddington, Lincolnshire, early in the war: a Hampden at dispersal. Waddington was the home of 467 Squadron on Black Thursday.* From the Museum of Lincolnshire Life, by courtesy of Lincolnshire County Council

intense searchlight activity . . . and it was observed that the searchlights "doused" . . .' The crew noted that this was not exceptional. It was relatively common practice for IFF to be used over enemy territory to thwart unduly intense searchlight attention – to turn out the lights.

Uncertainty surrounded the issue for years, with no firm conclusions drawn from various experiments to confirm or deny the phenomenon. In the absence of conclusive evidence, Bomber Command HQ took the view that using IFF in this way was worth pursuing '. . . since no evidence has come to light indicating a harmful effect . . . the psychological effect on the crews is sufficient alone to justify its retention . . .'[21] There were those however who thought this unwise: it is unnerving to read a memorandum from R V Jones in the file, since it was his reference to IFF in his book *Most Secret War* that had alerted me to the issue. Jones took the view that, rather than saving crews' lives, the use of IFF over enemy territory was hazardous. His advice dated 12 September 1941 included the phrase 'we should refrain from the use of this treacherous device over enemy territory.' He was ignored.

So it was that on Black Thursday, it seems, some crews turned unerringly to a device that they thought might turn off the lights, confuse the enemy and save their lives . . . 'According to the Germans' own (Enigma) reports 6 out of 26 (sic) (aircraft were lost) on . . . 16/17th December'[22] as a direct result of the Germans homing in on active IFF equipment in the bombers above them. Switched on in a forlorn attempt to increase the chance of survival, it cruelly triggered their own demise.

# CHAPTER SEVENTEEN
# ON THE GROUND

In rural Buckinghamshire, Arthur Harris was still lying awake, staring into the darkness, unwilling or unable to let sleep take over until he knew that his men were back. His insomnia was shared by thousands of others: Wing Commander Holford's young bride alone in a Lincolnshire pub; WAAFs emotionally bound up with frightened airmen high above Germany, privately willing them to make it back, but following orders with a tight-lipped intensity; and ground crew waiting to hear the incoming roar of the engines they knew so well.

Leading Aircraftman Des Evans was the flight mechanic on Lancaster U-Uncle from 97 Squadron that night: he remembers it as '... dark and drizzly with mist when they took off.'[1] Once the aircraft had left Bourn for Berlin, waved away into the night, he and other members of his crew went to the NAAFI for a drink, preparing to kill time

until the crews started to return in the early hours. This still had some novelty about it for Evans who, having enlisted in 1942, was a relative newcomer to the aerodrome: 'I was the baby of the squadron' was how he put it sixty years later. They congregated at dispersal, amidst the clutter of toolboxes and oily rags, huddling around the stove to fend off the damp chill, waiting and waiting, and occasionally taking anxious looks at the fog pressing against the windows. Inevitably, they were wondering what the rest of the night would bring: if U-Uncle was damaged, they might need to work through until morning, with an hour or so of snatched sleep, in order to get the aircraft serviceable for the

*Ground crew: Des Evans and Dennis Mooney at Coningsby in 1944. 'We had been working through the night – that's why we look a little scruffy.'* Des Evans

*The De Wesselow crew (97 Squadron) – the pilot is on the extreme left.* Des Evans

following night's operation if the fog cleared enough to make it fit for flying.

Once the aircraft started to return, Evans heard 'one or two bangs' but thought no more about them once his own crew in U-Uncle came in. 'I heard it and saw the silhouette above me in the fog.' He guided the aircraft across the tarmac with the special torches provided for the purpose. Pete de Wesselow was the last to land at Bourn that night.[2] It was two or three days later before he found out what had happened: that the squadron had sustained significant losses that night was clear enough, but that the principal problem had been so close to home was not. 'Ginger, one of my mates, was taken away to stand by the crashed aircraft ... when aircraft crashed they seized our toolboxes' – even before the grey morning of the 17th had dawned, the emphasis had already turned to investigating the events of that night and finding who to blame. Scrutiny of the mechanic's tool-box might show up the negligence of a tired engine fitter perhaps. If not, there was 'pilot error', that stark judgement so easily reached but which ignores the challenges facing these young men battling with fatigue, fighters, anti-aircraft fire, distance, shortage of fuel, cruel weather and darkness. Evans was clear about the immediate cause: '... it was an absolute cock-up from the briefing onwards ... stacking over the airfield was the problem and they ran out of fuel. The early ones in had some sort of chance ...'

The relationship between ground crew and fliers could be very close: the corporal-fitter in charge of Canadian pilot Jimmy Munro's aircraft resolutely refused to take his leave until he knew the crew had successfully completed its second tour: with one operation remaining there had been a series of postponements. 'This was a considerable sacrifice, for ground crew got very little leave, and worked outside ... in sometimes quite atrocious conditions ...'[3] Des Evans still refers poignantly to 'my' skipper Ted Porter, the wing commander of 97 Squadron, who led raids as a 'Master Bomber': '... He was a fantastic guy ... so courteous, he would take us for a pint and had no regard for rank. He was a pacifist, but his sister had got killed in an air raid on London and afterwards he hated Germans.' Evans came back from leave in mid-August 1944 to find the dispersal eerily empty: Porter had returned from leave early and stood in for another pilot, taking another crew on an operation. He never came back.[4] 'My skipper died in Stettin,' Evans said. Later he told me that he and three other members of his crew had dedicated a tree to Porter's memory in the 97 Squadron Memorial Garden.

\*    \*    \*    \*

### Midnight, somewhere in Lincolnshire

It is a shifting problem of arithmetic: three engines, so many thousand feet, thirty-five Lancasters to land before you, and petrol diminishing at the rate of several hundred gallons an hour. You watch the night, look for holes in the cloud, worry about a chance collision – or an intruder – and stare at the fuel gauges as if intensity of focus will somehow reduce consumption. Your turn comes round, and you hope that the moment coincides with a first fleeting glimpse of land. Your hands flex on the controls and the eyes stare ahead into nothing. Then there is a glow which really only serves to confuse, and at the point when you are only too aware of the fact, the bomb aimer tells you that you are way too high. Well, thank you SO much. But you know he has the better view. He'll be judging the height from the strips of red light across the landing strip and you should really pull out and go round again. But you'd rather take the chance when the ground is as close as this. You may never see it again after all. This is the moment when you never want to fly again. 'I'm buggered if I'm going to overshoot on a night like this!' you tell him. 'Almost at once there's the thump of wheels against tarmac – all seven of you are conclusively down, with every rivet and bolt of the aircraft shaken to its core. Hell, this is too bloody fast, and the runway is disappearing too quickly ... you roar onwards over grass and into the edge of a field of cabbages. Painfully, you ease the aircraft round and back on to the perimeter track and roll to a standstill. Maybe you'll make Christmas after all. There is enough fuel left, it seems, to fill a cigarette lighter.[5]

### Diverted – where?

Too many aircraft trying to get down at Ludford: so we'll head for Leconfield instead. Bugger-all petrol left. We're all there with eyeballs out on stalks looking for lights, the ground, home, anything to get us out of this mess. Yes! The bomb aimer can see circuit lights down there somewhere, a sudden break in the curtain of fog. Too good to miss, so I shall put the aircraft down through the gap, breaking the cloud at around 250 feet. Down and down again. Landfall – somewhere. Stepping out of the aircraft, we ask the embarrassing question: 'Where the hell are we?' 'Grimsby,' someone says. 'This is Grimsby.' Not far away, there are flames, where someone not so lucky as us has bought it.

### And so to bed

Long trip. Too long. Feel exhausted and desperate to get down. Nothing visible but fires – some poor bastards there before us and they must've hit the deck. And then ... there's this debate across the intercom: should we chance it or bale out? OK, if that's the way you want it. 'I'll take her up to five thousand and anyone who wants to bale out has my permission to do so.' Thanks for the vote of confidence lads. Silence – that shut them up. We circle and circle, just waiting. Then: 'A-Able, you may pancake.' How thoughtful. 'Right, everyone,' I say, sounding more bullish than I feel, 'I'll put this cow down if it's the last thing I do.' Bravado – it might just be the last thing after all. Turn, then straighten. Steady, steady ... 'PULL UP!! I can see the deck!' This from the rear gunner who's best placed to see after all. Up she goes, nose in the air. Who the hell is right? The gunner or the altimeter? That was saying 300 feet. Call the tower and get a new QFE. Start all over again ... look for the flare path and hope ... Briefing and bed are waiting ...

\*    \*    \*    \*

Faced with the confusion in the night sky beyond the windows, Flying Control flirted with loss of control. Calm WAAF voices persisted with soothing tones despite the clamour of voices across the air waves. Give out the QFE; your turn to pancake E-Easy; try Ludford or Leconfield, J-Johnny. If anything was clear on this night of chaos, I thought, it was that no airfield other than in Scotland and Cornwall was fog-free – pilots would have to take their chance, get down somehow here or be diverted elsewhere. Many crews found themselves feeling their way down into an unfamiliar landfall: X-X-Ray from 408 at Linton-on-Ouse landed at Rufforth six miles away (it was three days before the weather was clear enough to fly home), and six others of the seventeen who flew that night were diverted – to Dalton, near Darlington, for example. The prevailing sense is of mayhem and confusion at every turn. The experience of Pilot Officer L J Halley (115 Squadron) and his crew was typical: '... there was fog over Witchford ... (so) we were diverted to Foulsham ... we recognised we were over the airfield as we could see an occasional orange light. We got on to the circuit but could only see one light at a time ...'[6] Of the fourteen aircraft from 115 Squadron, 11 were diverted (the remainder were either 'early returns' or lost over the continent). The crews of 625 Squadron at Kelstern were similarly forced into a flurry of diversions. Only two landed at base and the pilots spoke of 'hazardous' and 'tricky' conditions.[7] But then I spoke to another survivor who made me think again ...

Squadron Leader Sandy Sandison flew with 619 Squadron at Woodhall Spa, some twenty miles southeast of Lincoln. Berlin on Black Thursday was his twenty-first trip. He was with his regular crew and a second dickey, along for the experience. I had written to him prior to our telephone conversation setting out some questions to get him talking, and prompt his memory: occasionally a veteran would say to me, 'It was more than sixty years ago you know!' Those that did remember had, until now, spoken or written vividly of a traumatic night. Sandison was different: 'I'm not sure I can help you,' he said. 'It was a straightforward trip. The weather was OK. We flew out from Woodhall and back there again – no diversion. We weren't held up over the airfield at all.'

'What about the fog?' I said.

'The fog had gone,' Sandy said, coughing gently.

There was one 619 Squadron crash on return which I had assumed was down to bad weather: Flight Lieutenant A H Tomlin and his crew had survived the accident which happened near the airfield's outer beacon. He had also crashed on his return from Berlin on 27 November. The weather was not to blame though – there was NO FOG! – instead, Tomlin was struggling with a badly damaged aircraft. 'They were late out and late back,' Sandison said. 'He got badly shot up and flew back with his bomb doors stuck open. He saw the lights as he approached Woodhall and turned into the funnel. Then his starboard inner engine failed and he couldn't turn any more. As he landed he caught a lot of hedgerow in the open bomb doors.' He ended up in a field of beet. I had a sudden image of mud and branches, tearing metal, crewmen braced against the impact and the fuselage filling with brutally and prematurely pruned hedge. The smell of cut wood and damp earth. 'Tomlin's navigator shot a big line about how he dutifully signed his log book before calmly stepping out of the aircraft, cool as you like.' I saw him, in my mind's eye, pausing as he looked out at the night and the damage, breathing in clean night air, running a nonchalant hand through his brylcreemed hair, and stepping down as if he always arrived somewhere in this turbulent, harum-scarum fashion. It was Flight Lieutenant Tomlin's last trip.

Then Sandison made me think: 'I wonder why 1 Group aircraft weren't diverted to Woodhall and elsewhere where there was no fog.' That was the question I was already asking myself. 'I guess there was such confusion everywhere,' I said, 'and so many aircraft arriving at the same time.' I didn't find the response totally convincing. Going through the Squadron ORBs later made me even more uncertain: why was it that 115 Squadron at Witchford (3 Group) could divert eleven aircraft, while 97 Squadron (8 Group) at Bourn – only fifteen miles away – diverted just one, despite the appalling weather? An alternative view might be that Groups operated in splendid isolation, habitually relying on their own resources, rather than thinking beyond the confines of Group territory.

'Well, anyway,' he said, 'there was no fog that night.' I thanked him, hung up and went to find my map of Lincolnshire: Woodhall to Elsham Wolds, for example, was, say thirty-five miles; Grimsby maybe fifty. Ten or fifteen minutes' flying time. Later I had an e-mail[8] suggesting that 44 Squadron at nearby Dunholme Lodge, five miles north of Lincoln was also untroubled by bad weather: 'I had a call from Ted Mercer, a pilot on the Berlin Raid of 16/17 December. He says he cannot recall anything untoward about the raid or the recovery to the UK – it was just another ordinary raid (if there could ever be such an event!) He has checked his records (log book) and there are no comments.' A month later, another e-mail made the same point: 'I have just received a note from E Hedley who flew on the night raid you are interested in. He says, "I checked my log book for the night in question, but nothing out of the ordinary happened, certainly no crash."' 'Nothing out of the ordinary'! Um ... Then ex-619 Squadron bomb-aimer Charles Clarke rang me to convey the same message. 'Nothing to say,' he said. 'It was just another trip.. You land, count your blessings and off to bed. That night the weather cleared.'[9]

So it looked as if in this blanket of thick fog which I had assumed stretched in an unbroken swathe the length of eastern England, there was a window of clarity. It explained those pilots who, in the debrief, talked of a raid that was 'quiet' and 'uneventful'; 'no incidents of interest', reported Flight Lieutenant C J Ginder (106 Squadron, Metheringham).[10] How big was the window, I wondered, and could more have been done to get more crews through it and down to safety? It was unsettling to find that for some aircrew that night Black Thursday was uniformly grey: simply straightforward, even fairly forgettable. Just one more trip on a long tour. It dawned on me that I had concentrated too much on those who had been lost that night, without focusing enough on why so many had survived. I needed to think more about that. It might even clarify who or what was predominantly to blame.

# CHAPTER EIGHTEEN
# FITNESS FOR FLYING

The ORB microfiche[1] is scratchy, the words fogged sometimes, but there is a harsh, unforgiving clarity about the way in which the official records log the fate of Squadron Leader Ernie Deverill and others from 97 Squadron that night. Deverill took off from Bourn at 4.45 pm within the twenty-five minute window which saw twenty-one Lancasters from 97 Squadron airborne. They rolled away at the rate of one a minute. Flying Officer Mooney was the last to ease his aircraft's wheels from the runway at 5.05 pm. His aircraft never touched down again.

The sky was filled with man-made thunder, while the aircraft climbed and circled before heading for the coast. Of the twenty-one aircraft sent aloft at Bourn, four had 'second dickeys' aboard, while several others were on their first operation. Deverill's return at 12.15 am on the 17th is logged, with cruel irony, as 'landing' and the description of it is terse: '*Crashed at GRAVELEY on returning from attack on Berlin, owing to very bad visibility and low cloud.*' The morning after, typewriters clacked slowly, consigning the grim facts to posterity: 97 Squadron lost seven aircraft on return and twenty-nine aircrew died. Senior officers reluctantly turned to best notepaper to break painful news, while outside the windows the sky was obscured. Too late, the weather was undeniably not fit for flying.

It was clear that I needed to know much more about the weather that day. In York I knew it had been grim for a week or more: in the York City Archive, close to the city wall and Minster, I pored over the weather records, small blue notebooks the size of diaries and full of fountain-penned data. The research assistant had lain them before me like an attentive waitress, served up for my delectation. The barometric pressure had been rising for a week or more, so that by the 15th it had reached 1037.6. There was a minimal downturn the following day – more towards evening. The wind scarcely rose above Force 1, swinging gently between north and east. It was cold all week and freezing at night: six degrees below freezing (26 Fahrenheit) on the night of the 15th. It was misty, overcast, or just plain foggy all week. It made me shiver to think about it.

Before the disconcerting telephone calls from Squadron Leader Sandy Sandison and others ('There was no fog that night!'), I had searched through the records at the National Meteorological Archive which

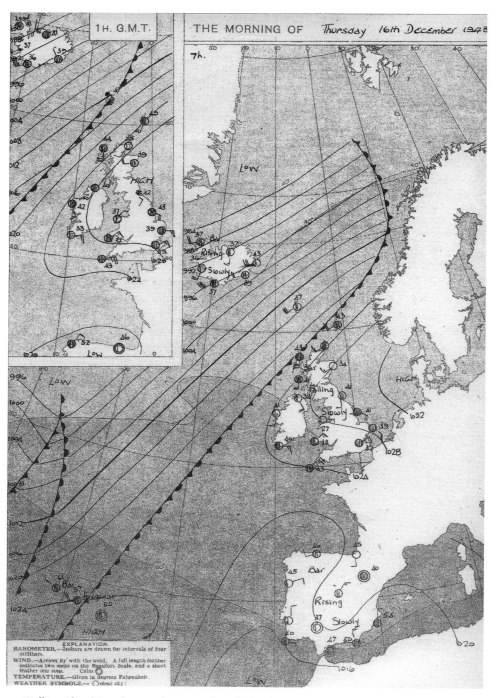

*'Falling Slowly' – the weather map for Black Thursday.* National Meteorological Archive

FORECASTS FOR THE 24 HOURS COMMENCING 12 NOON, G.M.T. Thursday 16th December 1943.

Light or moderate east to southeast winds; cloudy and dull, with general smoke haze and local fog; cold.

16 Orkneys and Shetlands — As 13-15

17 N.W. Ireland / 18 N.E. Ireland / 19 S.E. Ireland / 20 S.W. Ireland — Light southerly winds, cloudy; rather cold.

Light southerly winds, cloudy, visibility poor, with some fog; rather cold.

**GENERAL INFERENCE**

A wedge of high pressure over the British Isles is almost stationary and weakening. Weather will be cloudy in most districts, with local drizzle in the northwest. Visibility will be poor over England, Wales and South Scotland; local fog; cold.

Light or moderate southwest winds, fresh to strong at times in northwest; cloudy; local drizzle in northwest; appreciable bright intervals in northeast; cold.

**FURTHER OUTLOOK**

Rain in extreme western and northwestern districts; dry and dull elsewhere. Gale warning in operation in districts 16 (part of) Time of issue 2330 15 Dec.

Forecasts issued at 1030.

NELSON K. JOHNSON, K.C.B., D.Sc., Director
Meteorological Office, Air Ministry, Kingsway, London, W.C.2

*The weather forecast for Thursday 16 December 1943.* National Meteorological Archive

at that time was located in an unprepossessing building on a Bracknell industrial estate. It has now moved to Exeter. What had I learned on that first visit? Within five minutes of arriving I had the original documents in front of me – the snappily titled *Large Pocket Register of the Eye Observations of Pressure, Temperature, Cloud, Weather and Visibility.*[2] They had the look and feel of sixth formers' A-level notebooks: thick and well-thumbed pages with grey hand-worn covers and the observers' names inked on the front. Where are you now Margaret Rawson and Anne Lawrence from East Moor, Yorkshire? Inside each there are columns of figures and coded letters invariably penned in airforce blue ink. Something about the writing hints at a different age: is it the flourish of a pen dipped into an inkwell? I imagined grumpily conducted

*And for the previous day.* National Meteorological Archive

FORECASTS FOR THE 24 HOURS COMMENCING 12 NOON, G.M.T. Wednesday 15th December, 1943.

Light northeast or east wind; mainly dull; rather cold.

Light variable winds; rather extensive and persistent fog; cold.

Light or moderate east winds mainly cloudy, some local rain later; cold.

Light variable winds; foggy in east, fair elsewhere; cold.

As 13-4.

Moderate southwest winds, fresh to strong on northwest seaboard; mainly cloudy, but some bright periods in east; local rain or drizzle; rather cold.

16 Orkneys and Shetlands — As 13A 7/5.

17 N.W. Ireland / 18 N.E. Ireland / 19 S.E. Ireland / 20 S.W. Ireland — Light or moderate south or southeast wi. cloudy, some local rain in northwest; ra

**GENERAL INFERENCE**

An anticyclone centred off Northeast England is declini moving slowly eastwards. Some local rain will occur o northeast seaboard, and later in southwest England. E it will be dry, but mainly dull with a large area of pe over the Midlands, north England and South Scotland. I cold or rather cold.

**FURTHER OUTLOOK**

Little change.

Forecasts issued at 10.30

NELSON K. JOHNSON, K.C.B., I
Meteorological Office, Air Ministry, Kingswa

checks of the weather data, gloved hands struggling with notebooks, the remains of snow on the ground, feet being stamped on the iron-hard earth, coat collar turned up against a stiff east wind. Pages impregnated with December damp. Then back to the desk and the meticulous collation of data, entered up line by line at the beck and call of more senior officers and the station clock.

I looked at the weather for Bourn: what did Deverill, Mooney, Smith and the rest have to face at take-off – and later? At 4 pm[3] – the closest to the take-off time – there was thick cloud, but visibility was some 2,500 yards (it had been 3,900 yards three hours earlier); there was a gentle south easterly breeze. The cloud base was approximately 1,000 feet. By the early hours, visibility was reduced to eighty yards (4 am), and the normally minimalist entries for cloud base have been dispensed with – inadequate for such harsh conditions. In such circumstances, you need words, not code. The observers have written 'Less than 150 feet' and 'Sky obscured'. At one in the morning, the cloud base was at the surface: sky and earth had met.

Weather data for the other bases I scrutinised then matched that of Bourn: it was raw cold – about 37 degrees at take-off time (East Moor); early morning drizzle and 34 degrees, dropping below freezing towards midnight (Ludford Magna in Lincolnshire); barometric pressure was dropping slowly; winds ranged from 4 mph (Warboys) to 15 (Linton-on-Ouse); the cloud base at Elsham Wolds was as low as 600 feet at 3.45 pm. The pattern was the same: then I noticed a difference between the Bourn notebook and some of the others: the latter had a column headed 'Weather Fitness'. It was, it seemed, a judgement on the suitability of the weather for flying. 'The scale of Fitness numbers is 0–9, figure 0 referring to the worst conditions and figure 9 to the best ...'[4] On that basis, I surmised that a figure of 4 or 5 was acceptable, but below 3 was definitely not. I checked back at the bases where the column had been completed for 'weather fitness' at 1600 hours and for the return:

| Station | Fitness at 1600 | Fitness at midnight |
| --- | --- | --- |
| Elsham Wolds | 5 | 2 |
| Ludford Magna | 4 | 2 |
| East Moor | 6 | 4 |
| Warboys | 4 | 2 |
| Linton-on-Ouse | 5 | 4 |
| Binbrook | 5 | 3 |
| Grimsby | 6 | 3 |
| Wickenby | 6 | 5 |

It seemed to show that the crews left England in conditions that were generally regarded as acceptable for flying, but that they had deteriorated to the point where flying was unsafe; that conditions in Yorkshire afflicting 6 Group in particular were very challenging, but not quite as bad as those further south. In parts of Cambridgeshire they were at their worst. I was reminded that crashes in the north that night were largely the result of crews blundering around the fog-bound skies and coming to grief against high ground; while elsewhere the difficulty was getting the aircraft down in the vicinity of the aerodrome. Landing a Lancaster required about 1,000 yards of runway, while the pilots could see less than 300. The mix of cloud, fog, and smoke from coke fires was lethal. 'It's just down the road from bloody Sheffield!' was how one ex-RAF man[5] put it in a conversation we had about the prevalence of fog in wartime Yorkshire.

All this was very well, but I would have to go back to the records; I had only looked at those RAF stations where the losses had been incurred. What was the weather data for Dunholme Lodge, Fiskerton, and Woodhall Spa? How big was that gaping hole in the fog? What chances were missed that night, and how many airmen could have been saved?

I wrote to the Met Archive:

'Very recently I have been talking to a survivor whose first reaction was 'there was no fog!' It opens up the possibility that there was a window of clear sky around the airfields nearest Lincoln (he was based at Woodhall Spa). My scrutiny of the books when I visited Bracknell concentrated on those stations where there were crashes. Is there any possibility that you could send me the data for Skellingthorpe, Woodhall Spa, Coningsby, Dunholme Lodge, Fiskerton and Metheringham?' A few days later, the documents came. It was true: southern Lincolnshire was blessed with relative clarity.

| Fitness for Flying at 1.0 am on 17 December (out of 9) | |
|---|---|
| Woodhall | 5 |
| Metheringham | 3 |
| Skellingthorpe | 5 |
| Fiskerton | 4 |
| Dunholme Lodge | 5 |
| Coningsby | 6 |

What I had seen as a total blanket of cloud was now revealed as an untruth: 5 Group survived in large measure because it didn't have to cope with the full extent of the appalling conditions to the north and south.

For a long time I had baulked at the idea of reading each squadron's ORB for that night: what was to be gained by a laborious trawl through the records of each of the thirty-two squadrons of Lancasters flying on Black Thursday? Each ORB lists take-off and landing times; pilot and crew names; and a description of the main events. These latter vary in detail and often concentrate on weight and type of bombs, or the efficiency of the markers. They can have the feel of hurried bureaucracy. But I knew now that I needed to be this thorough: how else could I be sure that I had got as close to that night as possible?

The process was revealing. It was possible now to quantify the number of early returns; how many aircraft were diverted; the average time for the trip there and back. But it also showed up some key facts that I had been in danger of glossing over. The key one was the variation between Groups' experiences that night. For example, 5 Group's squadrons – based at Bardney, East Kirkby, Metheringham, Skellingthorpe, Spilsby, Waddington and Woodhall Spa – had a significantly easier time than those of the other groups: there were just five diversions, and five 'early returns'; three aircraft were shot down, and, most tellingly of all, just *two* crashes on return. By contrast, 8 (Pathfinder) Group – with fewer stations operational that night (Bourn, Oakington, Gransden Lodge, Warboys and Wyton) – had eleven diversions and twelve crashed or baled out. 1 Group's experience was even worse. A table at Appendix F summarises the ORBs. This table shows the crashes by group:

| Group | Crashes |
|---|---|
| 1 | 17 |
| 3 | 1 |
| 5 | 2 |
| 6 | 5 |
| 8 | 12 |

It was apparent that, contrary to what I had thought, Black Thursday was blacker for some than others. The weather was not uniform for one thing. Later too I found that 5 Group was held up as an exemplar to the others by the Inspector General: in a report on RAF Waddington early in 1944, he had noted that the group had developed a 'quick and efficient method of landing aircraft at night after operations. It was claimed after a recent operation that they had landed twenty-eight aircraft in forty-seven minutes ...'[6] Not everyone was so efficient or prepared.

# CHAPTER NINETEEN
# FIDO

Tighten the last nut. Check the last fluid level. Get the pilot to sign Form 700 for the kite and leave him to it. If you weren't flying, all the ground crew could do was wait. So too intelligence and met men, staff officers and padres. The seven men in the air were effectively reliant on their own devices for survival, that and creaky technology, and luck. A soft-voiced WAAF would be there on the R/T, as they droned overhead, layer upon layer of Lancasters, burning petrol and losing patience, but she wasn't going to save your life. You were effectively alone. Help on a night of fog was fire on the ground – literally, but only if you were in the right place at the right time. The only meaningful weapon in fighting fog was the system with the whimsical acronym FIDO – Fog Intensive Dispersal Operation. This was not sophisticated technology. The basic principle was that intense petrol-stoked fires on either side of the runway would burn the fog away. It worked well enough, but there were some snags, not least the challenge of putting an aircraft down between parallel lines of fire. Perhaps the biggest snag of all was that the system was not available on most airfields.

Losses of returning aircraft were not a new phenomenon in December 1943: as early as 16/17 October 1940, on a raid on various German targets, thirteen aircraft out of seventy-three were lost – ten of them crashing in fog on return. Churchill was sufficiently concerned to memo his newly appointed Chief of the Air Staff: '... What arrangements have we got for blind landings for aircraft?... It ought to be possible to guide them down quite safely as commercial aircraft were before the war in spite of fog. Let me have full particulars ...'[1] The losses, however, continued: eleven out of eighty-two bombers were lost in a raid on Berlin on 14/15 November, 1940. Churchill found himself calculating the loss percentage (8 per cent) and arguing for a reduction in operating in 'very adverse weather conditions'. The instruction seems to have had minimal effect. Eventually, after a further disastrous series of crashes after raids on Genoa and Frankfurt, Lord Cherwell, Churchill's scientific adviser, undertook some investigations, while at the same time, 'The Chief of the Air Staff undertook to look into the possibility of dispelling fog on aerodromes by heat or other means'. Lord Cherwell reported to the Prime Minister in the following terms: '... For some years, work

*A Lancaster lands in FIDO.* Photograph courtesy of the Imperial War Museum, London. Negative: CH 15272

*FIDO was dependent on huge quantities of fuel. These pumps have an output of 80,000 gallons an hour down the runway.* Photograph courtesy of the Imperial War Museum, London. Negative: CH 15275

*Aircrew from an airfield where FIDO is being installed talk to the Secretary of the Petroleum Warfare Department, Mr Geoffrey Lloyd.* Photograph courtesy of the Imperial War Museum, London. Negative: CH 15276

was done in a leisurely fashion by the Air Ministry ... the experiments were promising (but) they were discontinued ...'[2]

Meanwhile the losses continued: on the night of 7/8 November 1941, a major raid on Berlin by 392 aircraft, mainly Hampdens and Whitleys, saw thirty-seven aircraft fail to return or crash in England. The likelihood is that many plunged into the North Sea, dragged down by chronic icing or running out of fuel.[3] Churchill gave a typically robust response: '... I have several times in Cabinet deprecated forcing the night bombing of Germany without due regard to weather conditions. There is no need to fight the enemy and the weather at the same time!' That mantra again. The immediate result was that on 13 November the Air Ministry issued instructions to reduce the scale of operations against Germany, especially when the weather was bad.

It was many months, however, before significant progress on fog dispersal was made: on 26 September 1942, Churchill fired a minute to Geoffrey Lloyd, the minister responsible for the Petroleum Warfare Department (PWD) requiring immediate action: '... It is of great importance to find a means to dissipate fog at aerodromes so that aircraft can land safely. Let full experiments be put in hand by PWD

*Navigator's map: Cambridgeshire. 'Bourn' has been inked in by the navigator himself.*
Arthur Spencer

with all expedition ...' Five months later, the first FIDO landing took place at Graveley in Cambridgeshire; the pilot was Group Captain Donald Bennett: '... I took a Lancaster myself from Oakington over to Graveley one night and did the first landing with FIDO burning ... The glare was certainly considerable, and there was some turbulence ...' But Bennett was convinced it would work – not least perhaps because his experiment was done in visibility of about 100 yards – and expressed his total confidence in it: '... I made it a rule that whenever I wished to fly I did so regardless of the weather, on the basis that FIDO was always there to save my miserable neck should the need arise ...'[4]

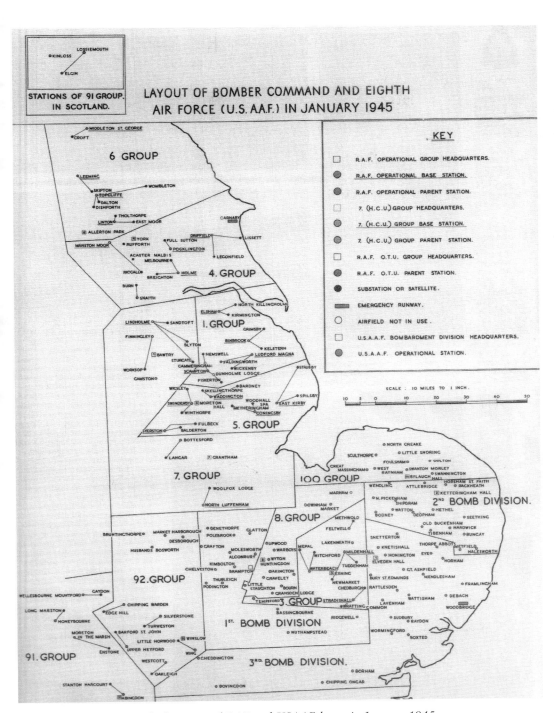

*A map showing the location of RAF and USAAF bases in January 1945.*

FIDO was introduced at Graveley in January 1943, followed by Downham Market in Norfolk shortly afterwards. Bennett's successful trial – on 18 February 1943 – encouraged the deployment of FIDO to a further six stations, including in the north and eastern counties, Ludford Magna on the Lincolnshire Wolds; Melbourne in east Yorkshire; and Fiskerton near Lincoln. These installations were in place by November 1943, but only Graveley was operational by the middle of the following month,[5] and the system was very much in its infancy. Experiments were conducted at Graveley on the 10, 19 and 22 November: 'on the night of the 19th the FIDO was burned successfully for the four aircraft returning from an operational sortie. There was thick fog to a depth of fifty feet (visibility 200 yards) and very satisfactory landings were carried out.'[6] This was the first occasion on which a FIDO installation had been used in actual operations. Churchill was delighted: 'Congratulations to all concerned,' he wrote, and his approval was conveyed down the line by a series of internal memoranda. However, as we shall see, circumstances dictated that Graveley with its Halifax aircraft was not operational that night and the system was not lit until relatively late. The basic principle of FIDO was that lines of burning petrol along the runway caused the temperature to rise and, with it, the fog. It was startling for observers and aircrew alike: one observer commented that '... the ignition of the petrol in the starting up period caused a terrific black pall of smoke over its whole length, just like a tanker on fire at sea...',[7] while pilot Hamish Mahaddie described landing under – or through – it thus: '... we are getting lower and I am watching that altimeter until we seem to be almost on the ground – 60 feet or something like that. Then we burst through and there are these flames burning away as far as the eye can see ...' It was, as one navigator put it, '... a navigator's salvation – we saw it 150 miles away!' For all that, while it cast a fiery light into the night on Black Thursday, its impact on the saving of lives that night was minimal. It was a case of too little, too late.

\*    \*    \*    \*

The road from St Neots back to the aerodrome ran parallel to the main runway. It was cold – close to freezing – and heavy clouds obscured the moon. Cycling in the winter darkness was something that Mike Hedgeland[8] had got used to in the past twelve months. On the night of 16 December 1943 he had pedalled over to his girlfriend's house; 35 Squadron based at Graveley flew Halifaxes and that night's operation targeted at Berlin was an all Lancaster affair. No flying then for them that night, but Hedgeland preferred his girlfriend's company to the

*The view across Graveley airfield: fields now, not runways.*

hastily arranged dance back at base. It was between eleven and midnight. The fog was down and he could see not much more than a quarter of a mile ahead. At about that distance he could see flames licking up at the sky, and turning north towards the village of Graveley,

*A tangible reminder of the past: the monument to the squadrons flying from Graveley set amidst farmland.*

and cycling past the eastern end of the runway, he realised that FIDO had been lit. Only later did he recognise that some of the fires were caused by burning aircraft. He cycled back to his hut, registering for the first time how low the cloud base was – a fact signalled by the orange reflection of FIDO's burning petrol across the entire sky. 'I could … hear the sound of aircraft invisible above. A few minutes later I heard a tremendous thud and to my horror saw that an aircraft had crashed about 200 yards away. On reflection, I think it must have run out of fuel for it did not burst into flames …'

The aircraft had been heading for the runway but, to Hedgeland's mind, 'at almost right angles to it …' He knew that the aircraft had been doomed on that angle of approach. He was joined by other air-men from his hut as he ran towards the stricken Lancaster. There were bodies thrown clear by the impact, clearly dead. Soon after an ambulance arrived and the bodies were stretchered away. Hedgeland never knew the identity of the aircraft or its occupants.

The fog at Graveley that night was exacerbated by smoke drifting slowly across the airfield:[9] it was 500 feet deep and compounded by stratus cloud packed thickly above it for 3,000 feet. Lighting FIDO took some twenty minutes and the fact that the station was stood down for the night meant there was a critical delay in getting the system to begin to disperse the fog. This it duly did: '… the fog on the runway was cleared so that horizontal visibility improved to 1,600 yards. Unfortunately there was no way the apparatus could shift three thousand feet of stratus, nor could the glow from the burners penetrate the blanket, so that pilots attempting an approach had only a vague idea of where the runway lay …'[10]

*   *   *   *

The confusion in the sky over Graveley was matched by that in the control tower, and in the various accounts of the night's events. With the aircraft barely into the return flight, it was already evident that the night's problems had only just begun …[11]

At 21.10 Graveley is told to stand by for diversions – the DREM lighting is switched on at 23.57 and the first diverted aircraft lands moments later. Three minutes later – around midnight[12] – four aircraft are heard over the airfield. Moments later one crashes to the north east. This would appear to be the aircraft of 97 Squadron's Flight Sergeant Scott (RAAF) 97 Squadron. Chorley times this crash at 1.01.[13] The aircraft comes down near the village of Papworth St Agnes. There are no survivors.

By 00.16 four aircraft – squadrons unknown – are overhead. They are given permission to land, but moments later, communication with them suddenly dries up. At 00.39 FIDO is finally lit (some three and a half hours after the first indication of potential diversions). As the lights begin to take effect, aircraft H-Henry lands safely.

More aircraft are given permission to land – but in the event are diverted to Wyton and Warboys, not far away to the north east. At 00.51 P-Peter and J-Jig are ordered to divert there, while C-Charlie reports that he has only fifteen minutes of petrol left. He is told to divert to Warboys. S-Sugar piloted by Pilot Officer Leo Mooney (97 Squadron) is told the same. Time has run out, however, and Mooney and his crew bale out 'owing to weather conditions making landing too dangerous'.[14] They all survive and one lucky soul lands in the middle of the WAAF quarters.[15]

P-Peter radios in with a desperate message: 'There's no future at Wyton, can I have a crack at your FIDO?' His approach to the runway is at right angles to it.[16] At the very moment when landing seems inevitable, he suddenly chooses to race the engines. Cruelly they simply cut out and the aircraft thunders into the bomb dump, bursting into flames. The pilot was Squadron Leader Ernie Deverill, vastly experienced and on his third tour of operations. Only one crew member survives: Warrant Officer James Benbow, the mid-upper gunner. He has second degree burns on his face and hands, and fractured tibia and fibula. He is taken to the RAF Hospital at Ely. At 00.50 Flight Lieutenant Allan (RCAF) from 405 Squadron crashes two miles south-east of Graveley. He survives briefly, dying in hospital in Oxford on 28 December. Three men survive.

No amount of stark officialese can disguise what must have been an atmosphere of mounting panic: darkness punctuated eventually by the controlled fire of FIDO, and then burning aircraft; strangled voices on the intercom; thunder of engines and aircraft hitting the ground; the muddle of rescue – water, hosepipes, ambulance crews, telephones ringing; and the reek of burning petrol. Isabelle Burton, a WAAF driver, speaks for all who were there: 'I shall never forget that night ... There was a nasty eerie reddish glow all around ... It was said that they were dazzled by FIDO.' To the pilots who got down thanks to FIDO that night – and they were few in number – the experience was like landing in hell.[17] It was, however, better than the alternative: a different sort of fire on the ground.

# CHAPTER TWENTY

# 'WHAT'S IT TO BE – BOMBS OR FUEL?'

The sky above Berlin – around 8 pm. Pilot Officer Russell Ewens (49 Squadron) is at the controls of J-JIG – its lettering acquired when the previous J-JIG crashed two weeks previously. He felt the kick of the aircraft as their largest bomb was released. He contemplated home and safety, although he knew that their incendiaries had still to be dropped. Suddenly there was a burst of lethal cannon fire from a night-fighter and things began to fall apart: Ewens systematically checked the damage. Not least of his problems was that the bomb doors remained open; that, and a piece of jagged metal standing away from the mainframe, was significantly slowing the aircraft down. It would be a slow, tense return to England. Then Flight Engineer Doug Tritton drew his attention to the fuel gauges: fuel was leaking away from one of the larger tanks. It would be necessary to switch things so that for a while all four engines ran from the leaking tank. He began to make calculations about whether the fuel would last.

\* \* \* \*

Aircraft needed two precious commodities: trained aircrew and aviation fuel. In both cases circumstance conspired to erode that provision: trainee pilots persistently crashed into hills, runways, barns, trees and each other, while fuel could as easily end up staining the Atlantic black when torpedoed oil tankers spilled their cargoes. A fully laden Lancaster was a thirsty beast: 1 Group Headquarters calculated[1] that flying to the target it used 210 gallons per hour. For an eight hour plus operation to Berlin, this meant a Lancaster taking off with some 1,800 gallons aboard. The sheer quantity of fuel used on a raid of this kind beggars belief: 482 fuel loads of 1,800 gallons each is a startling 867,600 gallons at a time when every barrel of oil had to be ferried in by oil tankers ever threatened by German submarines.[2]

\* \* \* \*

Tritton juggled figures in his head: he thought they would have enough fuel to get them back. He scarcely took his eyes off the gauges as they crossed the North Sea, lower and slower than usual. Over Lincolnshire, there were no landing lights visible. Later he wrote: 'Lincolnshire was a carpet of blackness.'[3] Phil Griffiths, the wireless operator, requested a bearing for their home base of Fiskerton, near Lincoln, and Tritton's anxiety was increased when the navigator reported that they had unknowingly flown over it. Griffiths was on the point of seeking another fix when anxiety turned to acute concern: the fuel situation had suddenly become critical and Tritton stepped in: 'We must land immediately!'

\*    \*    \*    \*

By early December 1943,[4] Bomber Command Headquarters was expressing concern about the variation in the methods by which fuel allocations were being made: 'There appears to be considerable lack of agreement between Groups as to the methods of calculating the operational performance of various types and marks of aircraft, and of assessing the allowances which should be made for fuel reserve, inexperienced crews etc ...' There were, without doubt, marked differences in fuel consumption depending on the way pilots flew their aircraft – intense evasive tactics for example were heavy on fuel – and it is markedly evident in looking at the experience of some of the crews on Black Thursday. For example, take two of 97 Squadron's pilots: Flying Officer Mooney ran out of fuel after seven hours forty minutes in the air while Squadron Leader Deverill was flying for nearly an hour longer. The Groups' responses to HQ's memorandum about fuel allocation were distinctly uneasy: 6 Group (based in north Yorkshire) defended its allocation by pointing out its relative isolation – 'our aircraft have fewer nearby stations to which they may be diverted' – while 5 Group noted that 7 per cent of their aircraft landed with less than 100 gallons remaining in the tanks. Later, in March 1944, it was noted by Air Vice-Marshal Cochrane of 5 Group that 'the variation in consumption between the pilot who handles the aircraft carefully and in accordance with the detailed instructions to obtain maximum fuel economy, and that obtained by a pilot who is careless or inexperienced in these matters, is such that this is probably the biggest factor in deciding the amount of fuel to carry ...' He might have pointed out that fuel loss caused by enemy action over Europe was also a major factor. It certainly was for Lancaster J-Jig running out of petrol over Lincolnshire that night.

\*    \*    \*    \*

Ewens put out a distress call and, shortly afterwards, saw below them the lights of RAF Ingham in Lincolnshire. 'We can't afford an overshoot, skip,' Tritton said. 'No circuit procedure. Approach as high as you can, and be prepared to lose all power at any moment.' Ewens gulped and began the manoeuvre ...

\*   \*   \*   \*

The calculations to be made were not just concerned with fuel, how much should be set aside for contingency, and what was the extent of latitude that could be made for a fuel-extravagant pilot, or a crisis caused by damage. Air staff knew that the aircraft's weight was a key factor in survival: the heavier the aircraft, the slower and less manoeuvrable it was. There were in effect only two variables when considering the overall weight of the aircraft: fuel and the bombs that the aircraft could carry. And bombs were the very *raison d'etre* of the bomber after all. The ratio of bombs to fuel was the kind of problem that provoked head-scratching and urgent, tetchy correspondence amongst bureaucrats, and resentment amongst those whose aircraft were burning the fuel and dropping the bombs. Len Whitehead's view was typical of the latter. 'It was the policy to reduce the amount of fuel to an amount required to fly the distance plus a small allowance in case of trouble. This was to allow the maximum amount of bombs to be loaded. Unfortunately the amount of reserve was sometimes insufficient and I suspect that was the case on 16 December.'[5] I asked Sandy Sandison whether he thought fuel was sacrificed to increase bomb loads. 'Not with us,' he said, 'but we'd heard that it was true of 1 Group.' Air staff would fiercely resist such an accusation, but there was a widespread and heartfelt perception amongst air crew that the tonnage of bombs carried and dropped mattered more than the need to provide enough fuel on board to cope with exceptional contingencies – like impenetrably thick fog blanketing dozens of airfields from the north of Yorkshire to Cambridgeshire on a bitter December night.

\*   \*   \*   \*

Ingham's runway was grass[6] and J-Jig came down without the use of brakes. Ewens cut the engines straight away and the aircraft rolled to a halt. Minutes later, he and his crew inspected the damage with shaking torches. The damage was extensive: the incendiary canisters were full of holes; the fuselage and tailplane were extensively damaged, close to the perches of wireless operator and rear gunner. It had been a close call, but it was two more days before they realised how close to death they had come. The flight sergeant in charge of A Flight ground crew had travelled to Ingham to empty the fuel tanks on J-Jig. He assumed when he found them dry that the Ingham ground staff had done the job for him. Later Tritton put him right: 'We had agreed on the spot that our own crew would handle the aircraft. "But the tanks were dry," protested the flight sergeant, "not merely empty with a drop swilling about in the bottom, not even damp!"'

## CHAPTER TWENTY-ONE
# DEVERILL AT DOCKING

Ernest Deverill was the pilot of P-Peter whose anguished plea in the darkness – 'Can I have a crack at your FIDO?' before his aircraft careered into the Graveley bomb dump – echoes across the years. The trauma of that night makes him sound like some greenhorn when he was anything but.

I am looking at a picture[1] of him, right leg crossed over left, a slight, hunched figure, older (at twenty-seven) than the others around him, fingers of his left hand resting calmly on his right, cap set rakishly, casting a shadow over his left eye. He looks the sort of man you could have trusted: firm chin, fatherly smile, leaning towards you as if he cared what you thought of him. With him as your pilot you would have thought, 'If anyone can get me home, Ernie can.' The photograph records the decoration he received after his heroics in a raid on Augsburg (17 April 1942): steadfastly completing a bombing run with the aircraft on fire, flames continuing to engulf one engine. Somehow he and his crew managed to douse the flames and get home to Woodhall Spa, despite a three metre rip along the Lancaster's fuselage caused by the wing of another aircraft from his squadron. The operation had been experimental: in daylight, with a small force of twelve aircraft operating at low level. The target was a factory making diesel engines. The leader of the raid, Squadron Leader John Nettleton of 44 Squadron, was awarded the Victoria Cross and Deverill gained the first of his two DFCs.[2] Only five aircraft got back.

Deverill was born in Gillingham, Kent in the middle of the first war; he died in the middle of the second, buried in the churchyard of the Norfolk community into which he had married: the wedding to Joyce Burgis of North Farm, Docking brightened the village's summer in 1940, while further south, blue skies were full of skirmishing fighter pilots and plummeting German bombers. Unusually for a squadron leader, he had worked his way up the system – from ground crew, rather than ground floor, having been an apprentice at the School of Technical Training at RAF Halton. Such experience of life at the bottom of the pile earned you the unflattering soubriquet 'Halton Brat'. In truth, it was a label that made a man proud. The man whom circumstances had reduced to asking for a last ditch attempt at landing at Graveley was a pilot of the highest quality, having survived more than one hundred operations, initially with Coastal Command. Black Thursday was the first raid of his third tour: he had been posted back only eleven days before from 1660 HCU at Swinderby. He had patiently waited to return to the fray until the weather improved enough to fly – and fight – again ...

Docking is tucked away in the corn fields and gently rolling hills of north Norfolk between King's Lynn and the coast. There are not many reasons for going there, though I had one. On a summer day in 2004 – on 24 July it was just one day shy of the sixty-fourth anniversary of Ernest and Joyce Deverill's wedding – the light had that tell-tale glint of nearby coast, and the dark green hedgerows neatly divided up dusty yellow fields. The church at Docking is a peaceful island in a busy village: the churchyard shadowed near the church by dark yew trees. There was one other person there, a widow tending her husband's grave I guessed. I patrolled up and down the lines of gravestones – so unlike the clean regimentation of the Canadian tombs at Stonefall – but could not find Deverill's which I had read was on the north-western side. Many of the stones were so weathered by wind and sea air that the names had long since gone, air-brushed by time, and one corner – to the north-west – had been allowed to run wild, so the nettles were waist high and the gravestones barely visible in the green tumult. Foiled, I looked for Joyce Deverill's gravestone – she died in 1975 without remarrying – but she seemed not to be there either.

Later, driving away, I reasoned that the only graves I had seen were either very old, or relatively new: it was the graves of the 1930s and 1940s that had been allowed to revert to nature. Nevertheless, I was glad I had gone there: somehow being there – graveyard, crash site, runway – brings those lost days closer.

## CHAPTER TWENTY-TWO

# JUMPING SHIP

The women who packed parachutes held both precious parachute silk – there was an acute shortage in 1943 – and men's lives in their nimble fingers. It had to be done just so, since only one man had ever survived baling out parachute-less. That lucky man was rear gunner Flight Sergeant Nicholas Alkemade who baled out from a Lancaster near Berlin on 24 March 1944 at 18,000 feet and landed in a snowdrift deep enough to break his fall.[1] Acquiring a parachute that opened in the right way and at the right time was quite literally a matter of life and death. You wouldn't want one that had been prepared by a packer with her mind on something else. Leading Aircraftwoman Olive Snow worked as a parachute packer at Ringway aerodrome: 'You'd only pack about 20 parachutes each day. Even when you'd been there a while and you might have thought you could do it with your eyes closed, you didn't; a man's life depended on each and every parachute ... There were only a few deaths when I was there, but only one was a packer's fault. She hadn't packed the rigging right, so the parachute didn't open – it was a Roman candle. Of course they moved her from the camp straightaway, but it was a terrible thing for all of us; it could have been any of us who made that mistake.'[2]

Then there was getting out of the aircraft itself. It wasn't designed for ease of egress. 'Hatch in floor of nose should be used by all members of the crew if time is available; it is released by handle in centre, lifted inwards and jettisoned.'[3] Put like that – in cold functional English without a whiff of fear – makes it seem as if escaping from a doomed aircraft might be relatively straightforward, but the reality was much starker. So much so that stepping out into the dark was a reluctant and despairing option for many aircrew, and one which remained unspoken of and largely unpractised. This is why....

Your petrol is fast fading away, caught as you are in a droning stack of aircraft over a fogbound airfield. You can see no lights and there is an ominous silence – you are past the point of crisp exchanges with Flying Control, since everyone else is running short of fuel too. You need height to bale out – time and space for the 'chute to open – so a decision has to be taken to climb, an action which further increases the use of fuel. If the emergency were to be over enemy territory, the dilemma is worse since you will probably be on fire with the aircraft yawing

*Parachute packers in 1944. Note the warning on the wall.* Photograph courtesy of the Imperial War Museum, London. Negative: CH 13267

and rocking in the darkness: smoke, screams and anguished confusion. As pilot it is your decision, though you might be tempted to rely on democracy and canvass opinion from the crew. That takes more time of course. The escape hatch is just twenty-two inches wide and far to the front of the aircraft: your pencil-thin bomb aimer is best placed to escape, while things are significantly less sanguine for your chubby wireless operator. You should be OK but, as skipper, there is an obligation to leave the aircraft last. The rear gunner, cooped in his perspex straitjacket, is least well-placed since he cannot wear his parachute while you are flying. It is stowed in the fuselage. The alternative escape route – via the opened doors of the turret and falling backwards into the fiery night – is singularly unattractive in such circumstances. You cannot imagine there is time for him to line the turret up, open the doors, clamber half out of the turret to reach the parachute (what's that so far? thirty seconds?), clip the chute on, climb back into the turret (nearly a minute?), disentangle himself from the belts of ammunition and other gunner's paraphernalia; swing the turret through ninety degrees and then fall out backwards (too late, too late!). It makes you flinch to think of his legs being caught and pinning him in while the rest of the crew tumble groundwards. You give the instruction to abandon the aircraft and head for the hatch, fumbling with your own 'chute . . .

There is so much that can go wrong: the parachute might not be correctly clipped on on both sides; you might pull the ripcord too soon (the discipline of counting to ten!); or the straps of your 'chute might get caught on the bombsight.[4] The potential for the silk or cords of the parachute catching on parts of the aircraft are high. Navigator Johnnie Clark found the escape hatch jammed and, as he did so, inadvertently opened his 'chute in the aircraft. Controlling his mounting panic, he eventually freed the hatch and gathered the silk folds of the parachute around himself, and then jumped into the void.[5]

Then you are clear of the Lancaster, watching it drift east towards the North Sea with the automatic pilot maintaining a predetermined course. You are falling through the darkness in biting cold, and instinctively pull the ripcord. (Did I count? Was it slow enough?). There is a sudden jolt that takes your breath away and you feel the globe of silk catch the wind and your tumbling trajectory is checked. You wait for the ground to come up to meet you and hope that the landing is soft and level. Having made the decision to jump you do not want to end up straddling telegraph wires, or impaled on a church spire or worse. The wind rushes past you and then suddenly you hit the ground with a thump, roll over and start to gather the saviour silk around you. There is silence – no voices now, and the roar of the Lancaster's engines has faded away in the distance.

426 Squadron pilot, Roger Coulombe, contemplated ordering his crew to bale out on Black Thursday but in the end preferred to trust his navigator and his flying instruments: 'I took the gambling chance of flying totally blind',[6] he said, rather than jump ship. Baling out was the final throw of the dice. Two weeks before he had returned from Berlin in desperate circumstances. Flying over the North Sea on one and a half engines, and losing height constantly, he had instructed the crew to stand by to jump. He sent out a distress call and flashed an SOS on the light on the belly of his aircraft. Immediately, an airfield – it was an American B-17 base at Snetterton Heath, Norfolk – turned on its runway lights and Coulombe brought the aircraft down with the crew braced for a crash landing since there was only one undercarriage wheel functioning. He got the Lancaster down – and the crew's parachutes remained resolutely packed away for another time.

\*     \*     \*     \*

So how do you know when to jump? Mid-upper gunner Len Whitehead, 61 Squadron, commented: 'I cannot remember hearing it at briefing, but it was understood that if unable to land we were to fly over the base on a given heading which would take the aircraft out to the North Sea, engage George, the automatic pilot, and bale out over base.' Coulombe took the same broad view: 'It was totally left to the decision of the pilot when realising he couldn't possible land his aircraft in such foggy conditions.'

The Form 1180 for Flight Sergeant Miller's crash (166 Squadron) notes '... crews to consider baling out of non-essential members before attempting landing ...' But there seemed to be no criteria for making such a critical decision: a fact underlined by the variations in the timings of crews baling that night. One pilot and his crew parted company with their aircraft after less than seven hours in the air. Sergeant Miller's crew didn't bale although they had been airborne for seven and a quarter hours. 97 Squadron's Leo Mooney jumped into the night sky above Ely after seven and a half hours. Why did some of 97 Squadron's pilots and crews, for example, *not* jump before it was too late? Both Squadron Leader Mackenzie and Flying Officer Thackway were in the air for substantially longer than the average flight time of 450 minutes (thirty and thirty-five minutes respectively). The answer probably lies in a combination of acute anxiety about the process; profound determination to get the aircraft down; and going past the point where the aircraft had enough height to make baling out a realistic survival option. Petrol almost gone, you can hardly climb to 7,000 feet from a point just above the hedgerows.

## CHAPTER TWENTY-THREE

# SMITHY AT IKEN

97 Squadron's Lancaster Y-York came down less than three miles from the North Sea in Suffolk near the village of Sudbourne. The coast here has an air of whimsy about it: the River Alde seems bent on an uncomplicated rendezvous with the sea, only to turn due south at the last minute to form the long spit of Orford Ness, a wriggling worm of land that must look even odder from the air than it does on the map. Above the river there are gently undulating hills, high enough to interrupt the downward flight of an aircraft on its final descent, petrol and hope long since gone. I cycled into Sudbourne along the B road from Orford to Snape, a road edged by dense woodland and bracken. There seemed few people around to ask about the crash: a window cleaner up a ladder, and a man cutting a hedge. The village has no pub or shop and not much sign of life. The hedge-cutter scratched his head: he knew nothing about a crash – 'I'm racking my brains to think of someone who would know ... the window cleaner? No, he's from out of the village.' Not for the first time I faced the absurdity of asking people to remember things sixty years and more ago. Then he said, 'Mind you, I've got the compass from a Lancaster at home!' It was, he said, given to him years ago by a friend in Orford who had since died. Did it belong, I wondered, to Lancaster Y-York?

\*     \*     \*     \*

It was Pilot Officer F Smith's first operation. He took off from Bourn, the home of 97 Squadron, at ten to five in the late afternoon. The outward journey was not without incident: only violent evasive action – the aircraft dropping like a stone for some seconds – ended the interest of a prowling German fighter. The remainder of the trip was routine, though nobody on board recognised it as such, until they got close to home. If finding Berlin had been a challenge, then identifying the location of Bourn in the fog was to be infinitely worse. It wasn't helped by problems with SBA – Pilot Officer John Arthurson, the aircraft's navigator, remembers that 'the system was not working well.' Flying Control told Smith to circle the airfield at several thousand feet. The crew knew this meant a long delay while they waited their turn. Arthurson later estimated that there were eighteen Lancasters stacked above the Cambridgeshire fields waiting to land. Sergeant Maurice

Durn, the flight engineer, calculated the fuel would run out well before the time-consuming SBA process could be completed.

Thwarted, Smith headed north west for Graveley. He was reliant on dead reckoning and hoping to see a promised flare fired from the ground at Graveley. Nothing could be seen however – flare, ground, lights – nothing. Smith let the aircraft's wheels and flaps down, peering through the fog and slowly descending, praying for a sight of the ground. Training didn't prepare you for this – playing this game of life and death after eight hours in the air and your eyes blindfolded. Bomb aimer, Flight Sergeant J A Wilson, was in the nose straining his eyes to see something – anything – and he gave an anxious commentary to the pilot – 'Up a bit!' 'No, down a bit...' – with occasional sharp intakes of breath as a looming hazard passed beneath them. Suddenly there was the unmistakeable light of Graveley's FIDO: a glimpse of a runway, a narrow strip between all-consuming rows of fire. Such relief! There were rousing cheers and Smith, confidence boosted, eased the aircraft round to align it with the runway. One last turn ... Here we go! But – in turning he lost sight of it. FIDO had disappeared in the fog. That wasn't meant to happen ... Frantically they searched, turning and turning, but saw nothing but fog. FOG! The remaining fuel would now keep them aloft for maybe fifteen minutes – no more.

Arthurson suggested climbing and then baling out. Two others immediately agreed: Sergeant Cliff Bradshaw, the rear gunner, and Sergeant Gordon Townend, the wireless operator. Smith was reluctant. They continued the search. Then Smith asked what height he would need to get to and was told that seven thousand feet should be enough to guarantee that, if the parachute didn't open, the owner would be none the wiser. Smith climbed and headed the aircraft towards the North Sea; then he clarified which exit each crew member should use, and then, finally, gave the last dramatic instruction to jump. The pilot was the last to leave, switching on his automatic replacement, checking that he was indeed alone, and then stepping out into the night via the front hatch. At seven thousand feet they were in bright moonlight above the banks of fog. There was a bright moon. Y-York disappeared 'like a ghost ship in the night';[1] the roar of her engines faded as the giant bomber throbbed eastwards towards the distant sea, sixty miles away. Towards Sudbourne and rural Suffolk.

*     *     *     *

Both Sudbourne and the neighbouring village of Iken were seized by the Ministry of Defence in July 1942: the populations of both, some 300 people, were evacuated – given two weeks' notice – and the land given over to tank training. It became the Orford Battle School. The land, all 3,500 acres of it, was literally fenced off by barbed wire. Four major farms were swallowed by it, together with a number of smallholdings. It remained like this for several years after the war ended. The *Suffolk Chronicle* of 11 April 1947 leads with a story headed 'ORFORD BATTLE SCHOOL CREEPS BACK TO LIFE' describing in great detail the damage done to good agricultural land: churned mud, shell holes, rusting field guns. 'This part of Suffolk might be any continental battlefield.'[2] The formal ceremony by which Sudbourne was returned to its people took place on 4 March 1948. Iken followed soon afterwards.

The barbed wire fence separating the unpopulated acres of the Orford Battle School and the rest of rural Suffolk extended along the narrow lane to Iken whose parish church sits precariously on a promontory overlooking the Long Reach, a tidal lake in the midst of swaying reed beds. I talked to a Sudbourne resident who had been on holiday in nearby Leiston when war broke out that far-off September and stayed there with an aunt and never went home. Her father was the groom to an Italian count who was interned once the war began. She had a story to tell – of her school choir entertaining American airmen; jumping from the truck wearing white ankle socks and landing in a puddle, and later, provoking the headmaster's wrath, when over-full of lemonade and cake, the choir seriously underperformed. But she knew nothing of the Lancaster crash on Black Thursday ...

*    *    *    *

The parachutes opened with a jolt. Each of them hung there suspended, apparently unmoving, until they careered through the cloud bank, and, moments later, hit the ground. Arthurson, the navigator, landed in a muddy ploughed field. He was alone in the darkness, shivering with cold and shock, and disorientated by the thick fog. He shrugged off his parachute and harness, and dutifully folded them under his arm. He blundered through the darkness and eventually came to a hedge. Having intended a scrupulous following of the rules in returning his 'chute, he changed his mind, leaving the parachute in a hedge and blundered on. He walked for a while and then came to some huts at the edge of Graveley airfield. He was reunited with Maurice Durn, and the MO insisted on both sleeping for twenty-four hours – standard practice in cases of baling out.

They all got down safely, although rear gunner Bradshaw's experience was singular: his exit from the aircraft was messy – he caught his right foot between the door step and the fuselage and this swung him under the aircraft. He hit his head on the tail wheel and the impact

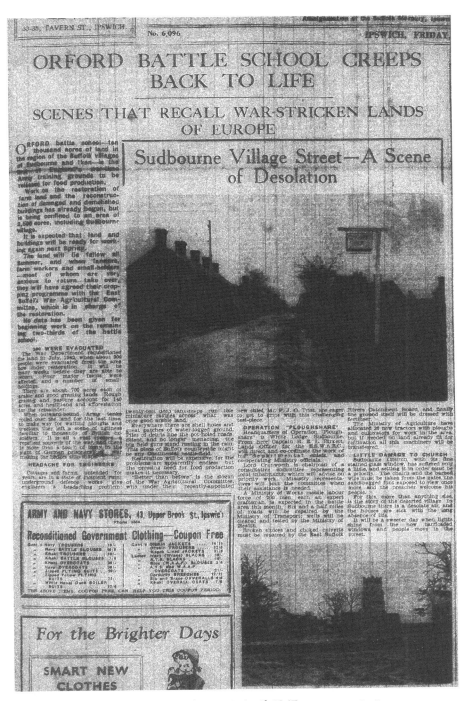

# ORFORD BATTLE SCHOOL CREEPS BACK TO LIFE

## SCENES THAT RECALL WAR-STRICKEN LANDS OF EUROPE

### Sudbourne Village Street—A Scene of Desolation

*Front page of the* Suffolk Chronicle *on 11 April 1947.* Suffolk Record Office

knocked him out. Somehow he landed – albeit roughly, bumping his head again in the process. When he came round he could see flames in the fog – presumably a fiery blend of FIDO and crashed Lancasters – but in his confusion he assumed he had baled out over Germany and what he could see were the fires consuming Berlin. He snapped into action, knowing that the Germans would be on the scene soon to search for survivors. He removed his badges and anything which would reveal his rank, buried his 'chute, flying suit etc in a ditch, and set off in the darkness. He avoided houses and walked for a long time. He was thirsty. Finally he decided to give himself up. What followed was a bizarre scene where the farmer's wife assumed he was a German spy and Bradshaw grappled with the conundrum as to why this country *hausfrau* spoke such impeccable English. It took some time to get the roles sorted out. Bradshaw was finally collected by the local police who took him back to Bourn. Once there, still concussed and obsessed with avoiding what he still believed to be German captors, he escaped, only to be picked up again near a railway siding in Cambridge.

The following day they were required to go out in the van to pick up equipment and soon after, in a moment of official sympathy, given an

*Just a few miles from the North Sea: the site at Iken Common, Suffolk where the Lancaster of 97 Squadron's P/O Smith crashed. He and his crew had baled out to safety.*
Brian Boulton

PHOTOGRAPH OF
SCENE TAKEN
FROM HERE ON
SANDY LANE.

TAKEN FROM THE ORDNANCE SURVEY MAP OF THE IPSWICH AREA.
SECOND WAR REVISION 1940 - SHEET 87.

LOCATION OF LANCASTER BOMBER CRASH SITE AS INDICATED IN THE EAST SUFFOLK POLICE REPORT
DATED FRIDAY, 17 DECEMBER 1943.

*Map showing the location of the crash at Iken, Suffolk.* Brian Boulton

opportunity to go home for Christmas on a forty-eight hour leave. They
were flying operations again by 29 December. Five of the crew survived
the war. Maurice Durn never flew with Smith again. He was killed in a
mid-air accident on 23 June 1944. Sergeant Harry Stewart had died two
months before when flying as a replacement with another crew.

Y-York came down finally on flat grazing land very close to the River
Alde: there are sheep there now and the flat land is overlooked by
an unbroken curtain of trees. It was an empty landscape into which
this empty aircraft fell – flat and depopulated, guns and wire, tank-
traps and oil-streaked puddles – within a few miles of the North Sea to
which Pilot Officer Smith had dutifully consigned the aircraft in his last
moments in the cockpit. The police report, signed by PC 61 Robert
Howard, notes that 'about 0200 hours today Friday 17th December
1943 a "Lancaster" aircraft with markings ... Y JB 531 crashed in the
parish of Iken. Map reference M 864736. The aircraft was extensively
damaged. The area where the plane crashed is in the Orford Battle
Area ...' An indication of the confusion that grey morning is the

Form No. 18.                                    Headquarter Reference No.

# EAST SUFFOLK POLICE.

TUNSTALL. _Station,_

17th. _day of_ December., 19 43.

**Subject of Correspondence**

Crashed Lancaster

Air craft at Iken

0200 hours 17/12/43.

Superintendent Boreham. M.B.E./

    I beg to report that about 0200 hours today Friday 17th. December., 1943 a 'Lancaster' aircraft with markings O.F. -Y. J.B. 531 crashed in the parish of Iken. Map reference M. 864736. The aircraft was extensively damaged. The area where the plane crashed is in the Orford Battle Area.

    No members of the crew were in the aircraft. All members of the crew with the exception of one named Cameron have been accounted for in another area. War duties room information is to the effect that the base of the aircraft is Dunsfold, Horsham, Sussex.

    A guard has been supplied by the Air Ministry.

_Robert A. Howard._

P.c. No. 61.

_PC 61's report the day after the crash at Iken._ Suffolk Record Office

assertion by PC Howard that only one crew member is unaccounted for – he names a Sergeant Cameron who had in fact baled out elsewhere the previous night.[3] Finally, Howard reports that the Air Ministry has posted a guard to watch over the wreck in this desolate lonely landscape. A cold posting he had of it.

# CHAPTER TWENTY-FOUR

# FLYING A DESK AT CASTLE DISMAL

It would be hard to find a starker contrast than that between an English country house in high summer 2004 and the Nissen huts scattered across windswept airfields in the bleak midwinter of 1943. Allerton Park, the headquarters of the Canadian 6 Group, may have been called Castle Dismal by the aircrews, but its seventy-five rooms offered a degree of comfort not to be found in the lives of the men who flew.[1] It lies at the centre of a two thousand acre estate, on a slight hill that allows it to brood over the main road north. It has improbable turrets and weathered stone. The view south is across the Vale of York – flat agricultural land, with, on a clear day, a hint of the high moors west of Harrogate. To the north is an ancient cedar tree, a crumbling wall held in place it seems by creepers, and meadows with grazing sheep. Little has changed since the day the Canadians took over the house from its owner, Lord Mowbray, who resented the temporary loss of his property.

June 2004: it is 25 degrees with high clouds and blue sky – twenty miles of visibility. Allerton is open to the public and an elderly retainer takes my money. The house has a recusant feel to it: high windows and oak-panelled rooms; flamboyant dark wood furniture and a soaring hallway whose ceiling is the height of the highest turret in the building. The library was 6 Group's Operations Room, and the billiard room was the officers' mess. The walls were protected during the war by high plywood panelling, the top brass keen to minimise the damage from mess room high jinks and capers. In the basement, there are candle holders in the wall. In wartime, as twilight fell, routine required each candle would be lit to dispel the darkness in that electricity-free corridor. Five years ago, it seems, the very men whose job it was to light them each night returned to the house, elderly Canadians chasing memories.

There is a small museum dedicated to the Canadian airmen in some outbuildings off the cobbled courtyard to the east side of the house. It is dusty and half forgotten, its notices peeling and faded from the sun, with camouflage netting draped over framed photographs. There is the order of battle for the raid on Peenemunde on a large wooden framed notice-board. Pinned to the corridor wall are several extracts from the

*'Castle Dismal' hidden behind a wintry tree: Allerton Park, HQ of 6 Group and the temporary home of Air Vice-Marshal George Brookes.*

war diary of Air Vice-Marshal George Brookes. Brookes was English – indeed a Yorkshireman, born in Ingleton. He was forty-nine years old and a veteran of the First World War when he had been shot down and seriously wounded in 1917. Later, I discover that Sir Arthur Harris had little time for Brookes; while others found him 'amiable (and) talkative', Harris noted that he was known as Babbling Brook. 'I am frankly alarmed at the prospects of that Group'.[2] The diary is written in black fountain pen ink and, frustratingly for me, the extract stops a few months short of 16 December ...

\*    \*    \*    \*

Allerton is now owned by an American, Dr Gerald Arthur Rolph, who for more than twenty years has deployed much of the wealth he has accrued from the computer industry in a battle to keep this most English of houses alive. His first intervention saved the roof just as it seemed destined to leak irreparably. It isn't just money that he brings to the exercise: I saw him painstakingly applying imitation gilt to a mirror, in a room whose shelves were full of paint and glue, turpentine and wood.

I wrote to him, explaining the background and asking where he had acquired the diary. His reply came on notepaper whose heading was an intricate pen and ink sketch of the house – 'Castle' now – and ornate lettering. There was no source in his files he wrote, and he passed me on to Vern White, a former RCAF bomb aimer with 427 Squadron.

White's responding e-mail was prompt: but he had missed the Battle of Berlin by a matter of months, having been shot down on a raid on the Ruhr earlier in 1943. I looked him up: his Halifax had taken off from Leeming at 23.07 on 24 June 1943 (the light lingers late into the evening on a Yorkshire night in June). The aircraft came down over Holland, burying itself in a Dutch polder, near Rotterdam. Two of its crew were only disinterred from the heavy mud in 1967. One body has never been recovered, and only Vern and one of the gunners survived. By the time the Battle of Berlin was fought, Vern was a POW. He had no idea where Brookes's diary was: 'I have heard,' he wrote, 'that it contains personal and anecdotal notations and nothing of an operational nature.' That only made it the more interesting to me: I like the 'personal and anecdotal'. I kept wondering what it was like to be so close to the unrelenting tragedy of the air war, stationed in baronial splendour, while a few miles away heavy bombers rumbled down runways heading for fire and retribution, with young men staring into the darkness, not expecting to live much longer. So, without much expectation or hope, I wrote to the National Defence Headquarters in Ottawa. Two weeks later, I sat in the garden holding a photocopy of the diary entries Brookes had written throughout that dark December so long ago. I held myself back from going straight for Black Thursday, and read the document chronologically ...

*  *  *  *

George Brookes sat upright in bed surrounded by the Gothic splendour of Allerton Park and, a stickler for routine, wrote his diary. It was 2 December 1943 and he tersely noted the attendance at the 'usual conferences'. He had felt unwell, blaming, as men do, 'the flu'. He stayed in bed throughout the next day, reading, pleased at the timely arrival of 'the illustrated papers.' He tried to ignore the grim weather, fretting instead at the ongoing problem of crews' early returns. On the Saturday (the 3rd), he was back at his desk before finding time to drive to Harrogate where he sent flowers to his wife, Dorothy, and bought coffee beans.

It was a life of conferences, church on Sundays, haircuts and cycling; food and quiet reading; social engagements and cancelled operations – the consequence of 'tricky weather.' On the 6th he cycled to Boroughbridge to take tea with friends, not forgetting to put a tin of nut and date loaf into his saddlebag. On the 10th, less than a week before Black Thursday, he spent the evening reading in the comfort of the great house. His diary carefully notes the 'comfort food' of his supper: bully beef and bread and pickles and a large cup of chocolate malted milk. He was in bed by 10.30, taking a last look out of the window on to a clear night, with a fine moon, and the beginnings of a frost.

As the week of Black Thursday begins, Brookes continues to note the round of meetings, chores, and cancelled operations. The weather is a constant theme: full moon and no cloud on Sunday; 'rather poor conditions' on Monday; fog on Tuesday and Wednesday, continuing throughout the day. The fog is bad enough on the Tuesday (14th) to make driving difficult: he had arranged interviews with three NCOs ('doubtful commissioning cases') – who were they? I wondered – and the journey into Allerton proves problematic. You have a sense that blundering through thick mist with hooded headlights along the A59 Harrogate Road is quite as challenging as flying by night in deep cloud, starved of sleep and watching the petrol gauge dwindle. Later that evening he can be found reading by an open log fire while outside the fog rolls in, thicker by the hour. It presses against the mansion's windows while he sleeps soundly in four-poster comfort. The fog lingers throughout the following day (Wednesday) and it is relatively early in the day when the decision is taken that flying is out of the question.

So I had reached the 16th – Black Thursday. I expected a change in tone, some sense of events being both unusual and deeply tragic. And yes, the entry for the day is longer than some others, and there is a detailed note about the weather at take-off time in the top right-hand corner. But there is little sign of anxiety or regret. No pain or guilt, or there by the grace of God ... Brookes attends his conferences, absorbs reports with half-furrowed brow. He notes that the day was 'routine' and declares himself pleased with the operational planning and weather forecast. So that's OK then.

While briefings are delivered and preparations are made, he reads, deals with Church affairs, discusses issues to do with funerals in Harrogate and goes to church to help plan Christmas arrangements. In his own phrase, he 'takes it easy' after dinner, and then sets out to visit local bases with a view to being on hand for the interrogation of returning crews. In the Ops room by 11.15 pm, it is apparent that the cloud base is falling and the airwaves are humming with suggestions about aircraft diversions. There was a discussion about where best to greet the returning crews and they elect to make for Leeming, rather than head for Linton. His diary entry is laconic, noting only that most aircraft got down in their own aerodromes – and failing to comment on the fact that none landed at Leeming. It all reads like just another day.

Nonplussed, I turned to the entry for the following day, sure that at some point the night's events would touch a nerve, some flicker of emotion. But it is stoically ordinary, a quick note of the 'usual conferences'; then a passing reference to four aircraft being missing and four having crashed. The weather, he writes, proved a problem, and 1 Group had a worse time of it than they did. He had a lunchtime drink and ate in the mess; cleared up some files in the early afternoon, and then, keen to make up for the previous night's lack of sleep, rested from 1500 hours to 1730. The evening was similarly banal: evening meal in the mess; 9 o'clock news and an early night with the 'illustrated papers'.

Three days later the crews took off for Frankfurt. Brookes had what he engagingly called 'a jolly good sleep', while the night saw ten more aircraft lost from 6 Group.

Towards the end of 1943, he was awarded an OBE and presented with the insignia of the Commander of the Bath at Buckingham Palace on 1 February 1944.[3] The citation could not have focused on bravery under fire, but there is something admirable in his determined, stolid pursuit of normality amidst that fire and brimstone. How else do you manage loss?

# CHAPTER TWENTY-FIVE
# A BOMBER CREW'S EDUCATION

It is the first day of Spring in Yorkshire: mid-March and daffodils cautiously opening their faces to the sun. From a washed blue sky beyond my window there is that evocative drone of aircraft engines that has never seemed far away during the time I have been writing this book. Whether or not they are trainers taking advantage of good flying weather I don't know, but it is the training of wartime Lancaster crews for a chaotic night of fog that has been preoccupying me this balmy spring morning. Was the training fit for purpose? Were they taught enough to stand a chance?

Sergeant Len Whitehead survived Black Thursday, despite the fact that it was his first operation. A mid-upper gunner with 61 Squadron, he had only arrived at RAF Skellingthorpe on Monday 13 December. 'I ... reported to the Gunnery Leader who was shocked to find that I had never been up at night, had never been in a Lancaster, and had never been in a mid-upper turret.'[1] He was sent off at twilight that night and got forty minutes in on the Wainfleet bombing range. 'The next time I flew,' Whitehead wrote, 'was on the 16th. Black Thursday.' He doesn't record what his more experienced crew members felt about the novice in the turret: led by Flying Officer Bernard Fitch, they had already flown ten operations[2]. Sixty-one years later, he notes that the man he replaced that night, regular gunner Flight Sergeant H W Pronger, died after baling out over the sea on return from Nuremburg on 30 March 1944. His body was never found. 'During my tour I flew with six pilots. Three were lost.'

Whitehead's training consisted of preliminary square bashing; air gunnery school on the Isle of Man; a broken ankle from a nasty tackle during PE and hence delay; and then a direct posting to HCU (Heavy Conversion Unit) on 22 November. 'They were uncertain what to do with us so we were sent to 1485 Gunnery Flight for three days to learn evasive action where we flew for three hours in Wellingtons to learn the corkscrew and shoot off some cine film from the rear turret.' Reading it now, it seems, as a training programme, to have an unduly strong element of happenstance about it. Certainly it has that sense of the individual being at the mercy of the RAF's arcane logistics that characterises many descriptions of aircrew training. Arthur Spencer's[3] route to operations, for example, wove its circuitous way from Toronto, through Florida, Bournemouth, Bobington (Staffordshire), Upper Heyford in Oxfordshire, and Swinderby (Lincolnshire) to Woodhall Spa. It was as if the RAF planners were keen to disorientate their navigators – 'They don't even know their arse from their elbow' – as much as instil the finer points of air navigation.

Imagine the enormity of the task though: in the early days of the war, furrow-browed air staff at the ministry burning midnight oil while far below Londoners scurry through the blacked-out streets and wonder if the Phoney War will ever end. So much to do, and so little time: airfields to survey and build; new aircraft; fuel to obtain and store; bombs and bomb sights; maps and bullets; food and blankets and parachutes and uniforms; and, of course, men to recruit, deploy and render fit for service. They would have sat round air ministry tables and, in a fug of cigarette smoke, drinking ersatz coffee, defined the things they wanted the training to do: make individuals into tight-knit teams; find and hit the target; take evasive action; identify enemy aircraft in the dark; escape from an aircraft if it hit the sea; jump clear and trust to a parachute; and become dab hands at the things that made survival more likely. After all, all this training had a hefty price tag. 'The education of a bomber crew was the most expensive in the world; it cost some £10,000 for each man, enough to send ten men to Oxford or Cambridge for three years.'[4] Logic, as well as morality, required that training should give them every chance of getting home on a dark, foggy night in December. So they'll need to rely on their ability to use GEE and SBA, not just in easy flying conditions, but when the cloud-base begins on the ground, and the ice is accumulating on the wings.

Training was a dangerous occupation: at 11 Operational Training Unit (OTU) in October 1943 there was an accident every 274 flying hours.[5] Accidents often meant death: a grim consequence of the ill-starred juxtaposition of inexperience, bad weather, unfortunately located hills, decrepit aircraft, and tired training staff still suffering from the after effects of a tour of operations over enemy territory. The collective wisdom of beleaguered air staff might have agonised over the content and style of training, but survivors' memories are less than fulsome when describing the experience. It was a world of sleeping thirty to a chilly wooden hut in a windswept corner of a lonely RAF station, surrounded by mud and watery pot-holes. You killed time by dozing on the iron bedstead, listening to dance music and the news on the hut wireless or playing endless games of cards. You wrote chin-up letters home and reassured them about your safety ('You need have no fear about this re-mustering, mother. A WOP/AG is not the rear gunner and he is safe as the pilot'[6]). You were on a constant lookout for fags, or scrounging for coke in the early hours to fend off the cold in that miserable hut. Glimmers of light relief came from a George Formby concert or a film. Or a damn good binge. There were flurries of written examinations and scores ('passed above average 81.8 per cent with 91 per cent on compasses' for one navigator,[7] or ever higher morse words per minute if you were a wireless operator). Tests too – of night vision for example.

WOP/Air-gunner Edwin Thomas enjoyed the bayonet practice, sticking the end of the bayonet into an uncomplaining sack and not questioning when the skill might come in useful while operating guns at 20,000 feet. There was PT – white vests and shorts, just like school. There were hut inspections (sheets and blankets folded just so, with the correct angle of turn) and kit inspections (mirrored shine on boots). You were 'treated like the lowest form of animal life'[8] and when it came to earning a commission, the key questions were often to do with what school you went to ('Never heard of it!'). The critical job of 'crewing up', when decisions were made about who flew with whom, was left to a process akin to the school dance, when the wallflowers got left to the end ('Do you chaps need a navigator?'). Time in the air was a relentless cycle of flying on dual controls or solo, practising landings, flying on fewer engines, cross countries, bombing practice, firing the guns, practising beam approach, and, sometimes, when the devil took you, hairy descents over the local pub where the buxom barmaid held sway, hoping that the thunder of the engines would bring her rushing to the door, bar cloth in hand, and later, a special smile as she pulled a pint and caught your eye – you are *naughty*!

Even so, despite the treadmill and the remorseless moves from RAF station to RAF station – Scotland perhaps to Cornwall, or Kent to north Yorkshire – on overcrowded, blacked-out trains criss-crossing the countryside, crews were arriving at operational bases with gaps in their knowledge that caused concern. The minutes of a Bomber Command conference in November 1943 noted that 'crews were arriving with insufficient knowledge of the DR (Dead Reckoning) compass... navigators on their first few sorties got very poor GEE range due to their inability to cope with enemy jamming, (and) ... in view of navigators arriving from OTUs with practically no GEE experience, it was necessary to give them the maximum GEE training possible'.[9]

Pilots too were a cause of concern: how much night flying practice prepared you for nights of flak, fog and fighters? Roger Coulombe (426

Squadron) had 'just about 100 hours of night flying time (dual and solo flying) when I flew on my first op.'[10] Arthur Spencer's crew got in nearly thirty-six hours at OTU[11] ( '... possibly Jimmy (pilot) did more when the pilots went off to a satellite field for a fortnight to convert to Wellingtons.')[12] In addition, they completed two long cross countries at night; eight hours at HCU; twelve hours and twenty-five minutes on the squadron before they operated. Spencer calculates the figure was five minutes over fifty-six hours. 'Then, of course, we did a 6 hr. 35 min. mining trip to the Gironde (very cushy) before we were trusted with a 97 Lanc over Germany.' Rookie crews frequently got given the oldest aircraft in which to fly. Despite the hours of practice, there were profound concerns about pilot readiness: in the weeks preceding Black Thursday one inspector commented in an official report[13] that 'the number of accidents which still occur through aircraft being flown into the ground, or through getting out of control in clouds or in bad visibility, surely indicates something wrong with our method of training our pilots in flying safely under these conditions ...' In September 1943, the Inspectorate General noted:[14] 'Amongst the papers sent to me in connection with this inquiry is one in which it is stated that aircraft accidents are at present costing us a loss of air crew at the rate of 6,000 lives a year. Including overseas air forces that loss is estimated as of the order of 10,000 trained and semi-trained flying men each year. Here then is a foe within our gates who is slaying our airmen at a rate which is probably higher than that achieved by all Germany's allied nations put together (excluding Germany herself). In fact, our incidence of aircraft accidents is the enemy's best friend and ally in the promotion of his air war against us; and possibly accounts for almost as many of our aircraft as the *Luftwaffe* itself.' The report goes on to equate this level of loss with the destruction of one hundred service squadrons a year; notes the 'contingent loss of some £90 million,' but holds that such a financial loss is minimal when compared to the loss of trained air crew. The Inspector General later refers to these claims as 'facts'. He is critical too of 'cloud breaking techniques' and deficiencies in SBA protocols in some bases. Three months later, it wasn't just the *Luftwaffe* which littered eastern England with burning aircraft.

CHAPTER TWENTY-SIX

# POP WALKER

The weather forecast was wrong: the Lincolnshire wolds had been predicted heavy rain, but the sky was blue, clouds high and the light golden on this autumn day in October 2004. I looked across a line of fields, ploughed furrows with neat hedgerows, towards the point where Flight Sergeant Arthur Brown's aircraft had crashed.[1] The farm's brick outbuildings straggled away from the road on a slight rise above the village of Barrow upon Humber. The incline is the first slope away from the broad expanse of the river and leaves the farm about 100 feet above sea level. High enough to be a threat. On a day like this – bright autumn sunshine, trees turning in a gentle breeze – thick fog on a bitter winter's night seems very distant. Flight Sergeant Brown had been flying for seven and a quarter hours and was intent on returning to base at Kirmington – now Humberside Airport – when he came to grief. He was 'attempting to find the airfield through low cloud base over high ground.'[2] According to the ORB, he was '. . . below very low cloud when descending to locate aerodrome . . .'[3] The aircraft narrowly missed the farmhouse roof with an accompanying terminal roar that the farmer's son, Norman Rolinson, would never forget. It took the top off a hayrick instead of the house and ended its brutal onrush about 250 yards in front of the building. The crew all died.[4]

Nineteen aircraft from 166 Squadron left Kirmington for Berlin as daylight faded: three returned early and one, piloted by Flying Officer P W R Pollett, a law graduate in another life before the war, came down over Germany. Pollett had survived an eight minute joust with a Me 110 on his previous flight. It didn't help this time out. Poignantly he had been promoted to acting Flight Lieutenant on 27 November. The remainder of the squadron struggled to land back at Kirmington in 10/10 cloud and with a cloud base at around 500 feet. The ORB blithely notes '. . . the weather conditions were as forecast, low cloud and fog enveloped the target . . .' It covered swathes of England too of course. Arthur Brown was not the only pilot defeated by the conditions. Two others were diverted: one to Docking, in Norfolk, one to Binbrook. Two miles south of the airfield, after he had been given permission to approach, Flight Sergeant Stanley Miller's aircraft plunged into the hills near Caistor. It was one minute to midnight. These hills stand about 250 feet above sea level and form a rim to the aerodrome's southern perimeter. I parked on a strip of airforce concrete, just off the Caistor road, thought of Miller's last moments, and looked across the deep panorama of woodland, low hills and smooth green valleys.[5] The road swept away in a series of curves and a sign heralded 'ICE'. The only sound was a single prop aircraft drifting in to land, its pilot, like me, savouring the clarity of the light.

Market Stainton is quintessential England: soft green hills, church spires, sea gulls patrolling and pecking at ploughed furrows, flecks of chalk in the soil, and trees touched with autumn, green to gold. Behind the village is a ridge whose slopes are wooded and devoid of habitation. Half a mile outside the village is a small church on a grassy knoll, tree-shaded and with no sign of life. Who is there to attend church here? There is no sound but that ever-present hum of an aircraft high above. This corner of England is where Australian pilot Flying Officer F A Randall and his crew came down. Francis Randall had been awarded the DFC three weeks before. He had already had an eventful war: he had been shot down during a raid on Berlin on 3/4 September 1943 and had been interned in Sweden for three weeks. On Black Thursday, he had been given permission to land back at Binbrook as early as 23.04. Eight minutes later, he called Control to say that he could not see the aerodrome. He would not have given a sign of the panic he must have felt in his heart. He had been circling for more than three quarters of an hour. The crew began firing Very cartridges as the aircraft's sweeps took them further south away from Binbrook. At one point, he clipped a tree[6] but he managed temporarily to right the aircraft. Finally around midnight, he ploughed into a wood close to Market Stainton. He hit – of all things in this rural paradise – a bomb dump. Fact of war: trees hide bombs. The crew's ill-starred fortune sits oddly beside the comments of Pilot Officer Howell, another Australian with 460 Squadron, who, on landing back at base close to the time Randall and his crew died, commented on interrogation that the operation had seen '... no trouble, a good route and ... quite a good attack ...'[7] It was difficult to pin down the precise location of Randall's crash:[8] Market Stainton lies on upland surrounded by woods. The aircraft stalled before crashing into the wood; the likely cause was petrol running out.[9] One thing was clear – this was not the sort of place a young Australian would have expected to lose his life, fighting for freedom.

I went to Binbrook; drove around the perimeter where Flight Sergeant Godwin (460 Squadron) put JB704 into a field in an attempt to land, but survived. He too hit the ground just before midnight: part of the chaos of thunder and flame as the 16th turned to the 17th. Godwin's crew had been particularly challenged from the moment when an engine had been feathered over the Dutch coast. The pilot had opted to fly on and eventually bombed the target from 17,000 feet. The return flight was uneventful, although the aircraft's petrol consumption was worryingly high. Fog-bound Lincolnshire was even more of a problem: 'GEE brought them over base at 23.45 hours but no lights seen at 1,000 feet ...' Godwin was increasingly concerned about running out of petrol and called up Control to explain his predicament: '... and as airfield could not be seen he intended to climb and bale out. Control told him to come down to 500 feet. Expecting to break cloud the aircraft hit the deck a few fields short of the runway. All crew are reported safe.'[10] Newly promoted, he went missing over Leipzig in February 1944. Sixty years later, Binbrook was bleak: vast green hangars standing empty; potholed remnants of runway, youths doing wheelies near a dump of discarded microwaves and tyres. The days of sacrifice seemed far off.

*   *   *   *

Then I went to Hainton. In some ways I knew least about the circumstances surrounding this crash other than that the pilot was another Australian, Flight Sergeant H Ross, from 12 Squadron based at nearby Wickenby. But this one was different in that I knew the son of the navigator – he had been until recently the landlord of our local pub. The village of Hainton is at an elbowed bend of the main road from Lincoln to Louth, its proximity signalled by a grey brick inn whose empty car park and dust-streaked windows suggest that trade is slow, or gone for ever. A cluster of houses follows the lane as it meanders gently down through the village and there are fleeting glimpses of the land below this ridged hillside. I am on the very edge of the wolds.

Time might have stood still here, but there is no indication of what happened here six decades ago. The man in the village post office looked uncertain: 'During the war? I'm not old enough to remember and people here now are mostly incomers.' But then he took me to the east-facing window and pointed to an isolated house about half a mile away, its roof gone, standing foursquare looking west and open to the elements. 'The aircraft took the roof off', he said. 'My mother lived there once, but not during the war. She's gone now, so I can't ask her about it.' He told me the house was on private land, but I drove around the lanes looking for a turning – I imagined an overgrown lane, pot-holes, mud and brambles – but found no such thing. Once I had taken my eyes off the broken building to follow the road towards Sixhills, I lost it entirely and didn't see it again until I had completed a full circuit, rolling to a standstill on Hainton's main street.

Flight Lieutenant Arthur Walker was the navigator on Lancaster JB715 which crashed near Hainton. His son Ian was eighteen months old when his father died: he doesn't remember him, but he has a photograph of himself sat on his father's knee. Arthur Walker's log book is a much inked document: he was thirty-one years old – and known therefore with the soubriquet destined for anyone over the age of twenty-six as 'Pop'. He had been flying since February 1940. Berlin, however, was his first operation. Until then the war for him had been relatively safe: flying out of bases in Scotland on missions as diverse as anti-submarine searches and reconnaissance, ironically, so it seems now, looking on one occasion for the 'buoy of a crashed a/c'. There are photographs of him as an instructor at Navigation School surrounded by trainees looking much younger than him. Looking at all those earnest faces, eyes averted from the future, you cannot help wondering how many survived. He responded to teasing about the 'cushy' nature of a life of instruction by volunteering for ops. How I wondered did he explain that to his wife?

Hugh Ross, Pop Walker's pilot, was a sergeant from Victoria. He was twenty-three years old; four of the crew were even younger, while Fred Clark, the flight engineer, was just nineteen. They must have welcomed the experience Pop brought to the art of navigation and his paternal air. The crew were posted to 12 Squadron at Wickenby from 1667 Heavy Conversion Unit on 16 November 1943 and the following day were aloft training. For the next month opportunities for flying were limited by the appalling weather: Ross flew just seven training flights, only two of which were at night. The ORB would suggest that Ross flew to Leipzig on 3 December, but Arthur Walker's log book makes no mention of it. At 16.14 on Thursday 16 December, this greenhorn crew set out for the German capital. They had never flown in U-Uncle before; indeed,

*Arthur 'Pop' Walker, 12 Squadron navigator.*
Ian Walker

*Arthur Walker prior to his operational career – a staff member at Navigation School (front row, third from the right).* Ian Walker

it was a new aircraft which had only been delivered to 12 Squadron two weeks before (30 November). It made it back, surviving the baptism of fire in the night skies, but attempting to locate Wickenby in the rapidly deteriorating weather was a challenge of a different order. Suddenly, at 23.43 Wickenby control made contact and its assessment of the cloud base was acknowledged. There was no further contact. An anguished silence. The aircraft crashed two minutes later at a point on the hillside closer to Ludford Magna than Wickenby some six miles away to the west. The exact location is left blank on the ORB. The Lancaster '... broke cloud over high ground at a highish rate of descent, flew into trees, hit the ground and disintegrated.'[11] The wreck burned, a fierce glow in the foggy darkness. There was one survivor, the rear gunner, Sergeant Ron Whitley, but by the afternoon of the following day, he too was dead.

Arthur Walker's log book, on the desk beside me, has enough pages to record his flying hours clocked up for decades beyond the 1940s. It is a thick tome looking much less than its sixty-four years old: Ian Walker has evidently looked after his father's legacy. An anonymous clerk in

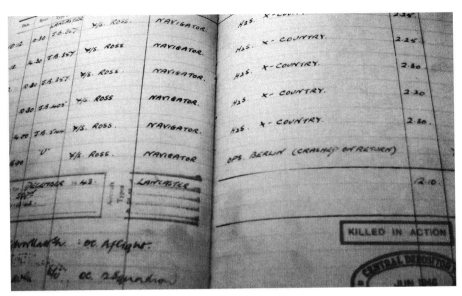

*The final page of F/L Arthur 'Pop' Walker's log book, stamped with 'Killed in Action'.*
Ian Walker

the Wickenby orderly office has inked in the final details: the fatal operation is inscribed in red: 'OPS BERLIN (CRASHED ON RETURN)' and the page is stamped 'KILLED IN ACTION' again in evocatively blood red ink. Senior officers have dutifully signed it; Pop's total hours in the air (an unnervingly neat 444 hours and 45 minutes) are logged and the volume is then consigned to the RAF's Central Depository. A further stamp for June 1946 ends the routine of official procedure. There is no more time in the air to carry forward.

The crew, trained to live cheek by jowl in the Lancaster's confines, were separated in death. The two Australians were deemed too far from home and were buried in the Commonwealth Cemetery in Cambridge. The rest were scattered across England: Norfolk, Sunningdale, Bishop's Castle in Shropshire, Bournemouth. 'Pop' Walker is buried in Whitehaven. Handing over his father's log book to my temporary care, Ian Walker frowned momentarily: 'I've often wondered,' he said, 'whether it was somehow his fault, you know, the crash. He was the navigator, after all.' I demurred, mumbled something about faulty altimeters, the weather, and the numbers of other crews who found the conditions that night beyond them. One former navigator to whom I repeated the story – and who knew what the combination of darkness, fog, and exhaustion could wreak – was more forthright than me: 'If anyone was to blame, it was Butch Harris.'

The story of Arthur 'Pop' Walker has a strange sequel: years later, the Sunday Times published an account by the comedian, and star of *The Goon Show*, Michael Bentine of his 'paranormal experiences'. Bentine was a briefing officer at Wickenby at the time of Black Thursday and knew Arthur Walker well. He described Arthur[12] as 'a large affable northerner with a sound serious streak' – his son is tall, affable and serious too – and remembers a brief discussion with him shortly before he went on a forty-eight-hour leave and Walker flew to Berlin. Leave over, Bentine returned to an airfield covered in midwinter snow that crunched underfoot as he walked towards his hut in the minutes before midnight. The night, according to Bentine, was lit by a bright moon, occasionally obscured by drifting clouds. As he reached his Nissen hut in the woods, he saw 'Pop' Walker walking towards him on the path: characteristically tall and sturdy. Bentine waved as the airman headed off towards his own hut. There was no returning wave – it was as if the Yorkshireman hadn't seen him. He was swallowed up by the trees. The following morning, in the fine tradition of good ghost stories, Bentine's batman told him that he was clearly mistaken since Walker was already dead, having crashed into the woods, the victim of the low cloud. The Intelligence Officer looked askance, believing in his heart that it was Walker's ghost he saw that frosty night amongst the pine trees.

Ian Walker and his mother – who never remarried, like Joyce Deverill – waited patiently after a talk given by Bentine in Yorkshire in 1989 to present themselves to the man who had known their long dead husband and father. Ian still possesses a battered copy of Bentine's book which the comedian signed for them both. The dedication is poignant: 'To "Ma" Walker with great love to you and "Pop" '.

# CHAPTER TWENTY-SEVEN
# JUST JANE AND EARLY RETURNS

I walked across the tarmac towards the hangar. The windsock was flapping angrily in a fierce east wind that still held a hint of the North Sea to its back: East Kirkby, Lincolnshire on an early summer's day in 2005. The lines of trees planted to mark lost airmen leaned away from the cold wind, young leaves hanging on for dear life against the gusts. The hangar doors were half pulled back but only enough to reveal shadow until I got to the entrance itself, and there, brooding in the half-light was the Lancaster, black and big enough to make me stop and take her in, the size and threat of her. *Just Jane*, complete with cartoon pin-up, long-legged and scantily clad, painted on the aircraft's nose. A Mark VII Lancaster, she is now reduced to flightless journeys the length of the East Kirkby runway: she taxies; she broods – nothing more. Engines stilled, she seemed to fill the hangar, wing tips reaching towards the shadowy walls in the darkness, guns and perspex tilted skywards; wheels as high as me. But **seven** men? In that narrow, shapely fuselage? This was a weapon not built for comfort, but for power: four engines the size of concrete mixers; a cricket pitch of wing width; a cavernous bomb bay – but for the crew, enforced intimacy and potential claustrophobia. The rear gunner's eyrie even looked in the opposite direction from the rest of the crew, an afterthought, a blister of perspex like an insect's head, focused on where the aircraft had come from, and where the danger in turn might come. I stood looking at the small ladder where the crew stepped in, or down, and, for a moment, it was me destined for the next raid in the dark. I shivered and turned away. Wondering how I would have measured up.

\* \* \* \*

Aircrew were left in no doubt about the need to reach the target: briefings invariably ended with homilies about the need to 'press on regardless'[1] and to avoid early returns. The latter were regarded as a test of a squadron or group's morale: there were doubts, for example, about the Canadian 6 Group in mid-1943. It 'kept recording the highest percentages of aircraft abandoning their sorties before reaching their targets. Reasons varied from mechanical troubles to gastric problems

*Just Jane*, a Lancaster at rest in the hangar at East Kirkby, Lincolnshire.

among the crews.'[2] A pilot who turned back was only too aware that an aborted operation would not count towards the completion of a tour of duty, and that he would in all probability face an investigation once he was back at base. 'The result was what the chiefs of Bomber Command wanted – men who were reluctant to turn back'.[3] Men often preferred to 'carry on regardless' in such circumstances: Lancaster navigator Arthur White flew the nine hundred mile trip to Munich with 'one engine out of action virtually the whole way, navigation instruments not working and the oxygen supply defective.' The pilot even made a highly risky second run into the mayhem over the target to ensure the attack was pressed home as Harris would have wanted.[4]

Inevitably there were early returns on 16 December: 427 of the 482 aircraft bombed Berlin that night, ten bombed alternative targets, while thirty-five turned back.[5] Three of these, for example, were from 166 Squadron, including Warrant Officer Woodcock-Stevens who was forced to abandon because he was unable to get his Lancaster above 16,000 feet. Elsewhere there were problems with oxygen (Pilot Officer J H Hewitt from 156 Squadron; Pilot Officer B N Dickenson, 101 Squadron), or there were problems with engines: loss of oil pressure, or coolant leakage, for example. Squadron Leader J A Whittet (103 Squadron) had problems with lights stubbornly remaining on; he bombed the Dutch island of Texel instead and turned for home. The crew were debriefed, suppered and in bed by 10 pm. Others had turrets that wouldn't swivel; or were drenched in oil; intercoms that wouldn't work; engines overheated ... 'Mission abandoned ... 1827 hrs. 16,000 feet unable to gain height ... jettisoned at 52.50N 00.39E' is a typical entry in the ORB.[6] Those returning faced searching questions about the cause of the aborted operation: hours before they might well have been sent off with the station commander's cheery 'Good luck! Good bombing! *And no early returns!*' ringing in their ears. For ignoring that last exhortation a pilot and his crew would be subjected to probing and insistent interrogation. The purpose was clear: to encourage a mentality which would accept nothing less than dogged and total commitment to each operation's plan: a steadfast arrow to the enemy's black heart; unwavering acceptance of flak, fighters and engine failure; and then enough persistence to go round twice at least to get the bombs to fall where the fires would burn most fiercely and effectively. Anything less and the job wouldn't get done.

## CHAPTER TWENTY-EIGHT

# THE UNLUCKY
# SQUADRON

As the weather deteriorated, the 143 airmen[1] of 97 Squadron were in a race against time: whether they or the cloud base would reach the ground first. Towards quarter past eleven, the first of the returning aircraft could be heard, if not seen: Pilot Officer C R Snell was the first back after a round trip of six and three quarter hours. Plummeting through the cloud and darkness, and trusting to instinct, providence and his navigator's calculations, he touched down safely at 23.25. It was more than two hours before the last survivor did the same. The chalked names on the operations board listed both survivors and the lost – Snell, Wilson, Owen, Pelletier, Kirkwood, Deverill, Roberts, Riches, Nicholls, Billing, Flack, Cawdery, Mooney, Smith, Scott, Brill, McKenzie, de Wesselow, Mansbridge, Thackway and Coates. Of these, six names, once erased, were never written up again. 97 Squadron lost eight aircraft that night: two crews baled out (Smith and Mooney), but the remaining six pilots died, together with most of their comrades on board. Twelve were bombing Frankfurt just four days later – and three of them did not survive beyond the end of January 1944. One of the survivors, Flying Officer Leo Mooney, who had seemed to have a charmed life – baled out on Black Thursday and survived, was posted as 'Missing' on 20 December (when in fact he did not take off) – but disappeared over Berlin on New Year's Day 1944.

\*     \*     \*     \*

In the twilight of Black Thursday – mist already gathering to end this day of raw December – 97 Squadron's twenty-one Lancasters took off in typically random order ... Riches, De Wesselow, Pelletier, Nicholls, Wilson, Billing, Flack, Brill, McKenzie, Cawdery, Roberts, Owen, Snell, Mansbridge, Smith, Scott, Deverill, Kirkwood, Mooney, Thackway and Coates ... all bound for Germany. The process took some twenty-five minutes, one aircraft heaving itself from the runway to be replaced by the next in line. A minute or so to goad the engines into the frenzy required for lift-off, and then vacate the oil-streaked concrete for the next man in line. All told, there were 151 crew on board: four of the Lancasters had second pilots flying to learn the ropes: Pelletier, Flack, and Owen each had a wide-eyed novice beside them, oblivious to the lurking fog, but soon to be astonished by the intensity of the night's blackness, and then the fire and light over Berlin. Flight Lieutenant David Brill was accompanied by Flight Lieutenant Ernest Handley who had considerable experience, but in a different sphere of war: with 37 Squadron flying Wellingtons in the Middle East. Take your choice then: who would you bank on to get you home? Would you gamble on experience, or decide that survival was more likely if you had taken off early? Were the pilots with least operational experience at the greatest risk that night? Go on – there's a seat, even a spare parachute waiting for you. But there is a 25 per cent chance that you won't survive the night.[2]

The first to run into trouble was Pilot Officer Smith – 'Smithy of Iken'. It was his first operation and, if you're on board his aircraft, you are in for an eventful night. Over enemy territory, the rear gunner, Cliff Bradshaw, saw an enemy fighter, prompting Smithy to throw the aircraft into a desperate dive. It worked, although the manoeuvre cost them time and briefly a sense of where they were.

Flight Lieutenant David Brill and his crew were not so lucky and were the first members of 97 Squadron to die that night, shot down over enemy territory. Two of the men on board were flying their first operation with 97 Squadron: Handley had only joined the squadron from 12 OTU on 1 December, while Flying Officer Norman McIntyre, an Australian navigator married to an Englishwoman, was even more recently arrived, coming in from 35 Squadron just eleven days before. Luck was fickle to RAF aircrew: the regular navigator, Arthur Weston, was spared – illness taking him off operations during early December. The unfortunate McIntyre replaced him. Weston's fortuitous reprieve was short-lived, however: he would die on operations five months later.

*Flying Officer Norman McIntyre pictured during aircrew training. An Australian, he was with 97 Squadron on Black Thursday when he flew with Flight Lieutenant DJ Brill.* Des Evans

Brill and his crew were the only 97 Squadron losses over enemy territory that night. Flight Lieutenant J Pelletier had come unscathed through a skirmish with a JU 88 at 18.53. Otherwise all seemed well enough. The remaining twenty Lancasters were able to bomb – albeit blind[3] – and turn resolutely for home. All the signs were that this would be an unexceptional night. One pilot, Charles Owen, later noted in his diary that 'the trip was quieter than usual.'[4] Pilot Officer Snell's return in fifteen minutes short of seven hours was the shortest of the trips that night: with the longest being eight and a half hours.[5] Flight Lieutenant C Wilson was next in at ten to midnight ...

On the ground, in the foggy darkness, they heard the bomber long before it burst out below the ceiling of cloud. The aircraft's wheels touched, then bounced along the ground, but too far down the runway and Wilson, able to see in front of him at last, knew a few moments of panic as the aircraft's momentum took it thundering prematurely towards what seemed an inevitable collision. As the space for landing rapidly disappeared, he succeeded in swinging the heavy aircraft to one side as the engines roared, tyres squealed, crew cursed and watching ground crew held their breath. The manoeuvre gave them a momentary respite, but almost immediately they struck a transformer, the point of principal contact being the aircraft's tail wheel. The starboard fin and the rudder were damaged and the rear gunner, Sergeant Playdell, felt sufficiently threatened by the rending sound of metal and the fear of fire that as soon as the aircraft came to a chaotic standstill, he hacked his way out of the rear turret with his axe. Wilson and his crew had survived – but only for a month. He was posted missing over Berlin in January 1944.

AUS/414154  F/O. N.G. McINTYRE
R.A.A.F.
17 DEC 43

Fifteen more minutes and a third aircraft roared in: this was the Lancaster of twenty year old Flight Lieutenant Charles Owen who had survived losing

*Flying Officer Norman McIntyre's final resting place: Berlin War Cemetery.* Des Evans

his wireless and GEE on the way home and had relied on navigator Bill Shires' instincts and skill to locate Bourn in the fog. Owen's diary entry[6] for the night reads: 'Homed on to base on SBA beam, breaking cloud at 250 feet to find fog, rain and visibility about 300 yards and deteriorating. R/T then packed up, so after circling for ten minutes at 200 feet, landed without permission in appalling conditions.' Owen pulled no punches in his debrief and the ORB notes that he reported 'dangerous landing conditions at base due to fog.' Interestingly, one aircraft piloted by Flying Officer WBB Cloutier of 405 Squadron was diverted *to* Bourn from Gransden Lodge and had landed safely at 23.36. Flight Lieutenant Pelletier whose aircraft landed similarly at 00.05 was more laconic: 'No results. Cloud.' Does that terseness disguise anger or resignation, or just plain exhaustion? At all events, Owen and Pelletier – and his second dickey, Henson – all survived to fly again. Like most of 97 Squadron's survivors they were on ops to Frankfurt just four days later.

While Owen and Pelletier were successfully piercing the Bourn cloud base, another 97 Squadron aircraft was in acute difficulty a few miles

to the south west. Pilot Officer J Kirkwood had elected to land at Gransden Lodge but the attempt proved fatal: the ORB without a trace of irony has his 'landing time' as 00.10,[7] but in fact Kirkwood's Lancaster missed the runway and instead ploughed into Hayley Wood close to a railway cutting on the Sandy to Cambridge branch line. 'Crashed ... owing to bad visibility and low cloud.'[8] Not for the only time that night, the combination of dense trees and gentle hills was enough to bring the aircraft to a premature and catastrophic end. Nor were Kirkwood's crew alone in being recently posted and then lost on Black Thursday:[9] in their case, the crew had arrived at Bourn on 27 November from 207 Squadron. It wasn't until daylight the following morning that the aircraft was found; there were no survivors.

*Pilot Officer Jim Kirkwood who crashed into woods close to Gransden Lodge in the early hours of 17 December.* Des Evans

The conditions were probably at their worst in the hour after mid-night – while the lucky ones smoked, answered the round of debriefing questions and ultimately slept like dead men, the chances of survival fell away as the clock slipped towards one in the morning. At 12.05, there were still sixteen Lancasters from 97 Squadron in the air; of them, only ten landed safely. Flight Sergeant Scott has no landing – or crashing – time in the ORB: there is no entry in that column. The same mix of 'fog and low cloud' is blamed. Like Kirkwood's aircraft, the ashy remains and burned, twisted metal of the Lancaster and its dead crew were not discovered until the early morning. The Australian Scott, on only his second operation – he was twenty years old – came down a mile or so north east of Graveley. The crash site is not far from the bomb dump where Ernest Deverill came to grief.

This was an hour of madness and desperate confusion: several 97 Squadron Lancasters landed safely at Wyton and Graveley – Roberts,

*Debrief: Flight Sergeant G Atkins, a navigator with 432 Squadron, had just completed his seventh operation, the Black Thursday raid on Berlin. The questions are being asked by Group Captain HM Carscallen, station commander at East Moor, Yorkshire. Atkins went on to complete his tour and was posted to OTU on 31 March 1944.* Memorial Room at RAF Linton-on-Ouse

Riches, Nicholls, Billing, Flack, Cawdery, de Wesselow made it back somehow. But the toll was considerable: Deverill's flight came to a brutal end at 00.15; Mooney and his crew, having weighed their chances of survival, and shivered at the shortage of petrol, baled out at 00.35,[10] McKenzie and his crew bulldozed into the ground at 00.45 (the ORB notes: 'Crashed on landing at base. Captain, flight engineer and air bomber killed.') Smith and his crew jumped into the night and watched their aircraft disappear to its rendezvous with the Suffolk coast. Flight Lieutenant P Mansbridge landed without mishap at 00.50, later reporting 'low cloud at 400 feet ... made landing very dangerous.'[11] The last aircraft to land at Bourn that night was that of Flight Lieutenant Pete de Wesselow. By 12.55 am there were only two aircraft unaccounted for: the Lancasters of Flying Officer Ted Thackway and Sergeant Bill Coates. They were still out there somewhere, two pilots with red-rimmed eyes staring ahead into the night, crews silently calculating how realistic a hope it was that they would live to see

*Victims of Black Thursday: the coffins of Squadron Leader D F MacKenzie and six other aircrew at Cambridge City Cemetery.* Des Evans

another day. Part of the calculation would have taken account of the fact that both pilots were on their first trip.

*   *   *   *

High above Bourn, Flying Officer Ted Thackway '... brought the Lancaster down below cloud level. They were now only 100, then fifty feet off the deck. Visibility was 150 yards or less, and as the huge Lancaster shot across the countryside at around 110 mph, the swirling mists rushed up to part before the windscreen. Ted must have been acutely aware of the appalling gravity of their situation, but he was calm and level-headed by nature and the paramount responsibility which fell upon him, the skipper, kept his natural fear in check. As K-King made her final descent, the white vapours parted and the anxiously watching crew saw a hedge looming obliquely in front of them. A semi-wild hedge of thorn trees and a few other native species,

174527
**F/O  J.M. BALDWIN**
R.C.A.F.
161794
**P/O  W.D. COATES**
1504558
**F/SJT. S. NUTTALL**
1149773
**SJT.  W. CHAPMAN**
1298586
**SJT. B.M. NICHOLAS**
1594296
**SJT.   W.L. YORK**
1590427
**SJT. F. THOMPSON**
R.A.F.

25.3.44     25.3.44     25.3.44

*The crosses marking the loss of the Coates crew. While they lived to fight another day after Black Thursday, they did not survive the war.* Des Evans

it was neither a particularly high nor a solid obstacle. The plane took a chunk out of it with one of her wheels and carried on regardless. Moments later, she landed perfectly, beginning a 300 yard run up the muddy field. Then the undercarriage collapsed. The body of the aircraft hit the ground ... Once down, K-King slid forward with huge velocity, breaking up and catching fire as she went.'[12] There were only two survivors.

Bill Coates and the crew of N-Nan were not to reach Bourn that night. Over Berlin, they had been hit by incendiaries whistling down from another Lancaster. The bombs crashed down on their port wing and amidships, damaging one of the turrets, and within minutes the aircraft caught fire. Coates reacted promptly by ordering the crew to put on their parachutes

*Sergeant W Chapman, the wireless operator with 97 Squadron's Sergeant W D Coates, whose heroics got them home on Black Thursday. They were lost over Berlin, however, on 24 March 1944.* Des Evans

and, at the same time, he flung the bomber into a dive in an attempt to dislodge the incendiaries. The onrush of cold air doused the fires, but also disabled the DR compass gyro and other connected instruments. Coates steadily regained height however and eventually reached the relative safety of 21,000 feet. Their night, however, was far from over. The Lancaster was soon badly hit by flak with consequent damage to the starboard inner engine, sections of which sheered off, severing hydraulic pipes and damaging the tail plane. To make matters worse, the starboard outer engine was also hit and both engines were necessarily shut down. The aircraft was badly crippled: powered by just its two port engines, it slowly drifted lower. Somehow Coates managed to head for Denmark and then towards home, but with little realistic hope of making it across the bleak North Sea. At one point, some twenty miles out from the Danish coast, the aircraft plummeted towards the waves, apparently conclusively, and Coates issued instructions for the crew to take up their positions for ditching into the sea. This was the last grim resort – black December, freezing water, fog, many hours until a wintry daylight – all conspired to fill the crew's hearts with something close to despair. He simultaneously broadcast an SOS. The ocean looked more likely a resting place than an English airfield.

Unwilling to ditch the aircraft and trust to a lifeboat and forlorn flares fired into the gloom, Coates battled to claw back some height and the aircraft coughed its way back to the mainland. Reaching Bourn, however, was out of the question. Instead, after a misdirected flirtation with RAF Marham, Bill Coates headed for Downham Market in Norfolk, a base with a working FIDO installation. The cloud base was at 400 feet and at one point, there were as many as thirty-six aircraft circling, impatiently waiting their turn to land. Coates and his crew were now faced with arguably their biggest challenge of the night: most of the aircraft's instruments were useless, while the absence of hydraulics meant the undercarriage had to be lowered using the emergency mechanism. Landing was fraught with risk. Coates tentatively dipped the aircraft down through the cloud, wondering if there was one last irreversible catastrophe waiting for them all. Then, like the pink beginnings of a foggy dawn, the darkness was broken by the strengthening glow of FIDO: Coates could see again and he plunged the Lancaster into the fiery turbulence and straight between the two lines of flame. Fire, which had threatened to consume them hours before, was now the means by which the nightmare ended. Minutes later, the crew emerged from the charred and blistered aircraft, only half aware of the punctured holes in the fuselage, and carrying their pilot on their tired shoulders as if the Yorkshire-born pilot had scored a faultless hundred at Headingley. He was glad of the lift since the eight and a half hours at the controls had taken its toll: in particular, his feet had been locked against the rudder bar for so long that walking was, for the moment, beyond him.

# CHAPTER TWENTY-NINE

# CAMBRIDGESHIRE GHOSTS AND PROPERTY DEVELOPERS

The view from Graveley airfield is mostly sky. I am on a broad plateau stretching away northwards to a low line of hills, a far horizon defined by trees. What colour there is – the clouds scudding in from the west are unremittingly gunmetal grey – comes from fields of oil seed rape, with that unhealthy paint-box yellow which seems to seep into everything nearby, a canary haze. The geography of the place doesn't lie: this is demonstrably airfield territory. After this long I can recognise the signs within moments of turning a corner. It is high enough at 170 feet above sea level and the land falls away on each side, making it that much easier to drag a heavily loaded bomber into the air. It is a lonely spot, with a gusting wind that sweeps across the early wheat. The telegraph wires whistle in the westerly breeze. It is crops that dominate the site: the runways are covered in green and all the buildings bar an isolated farmhouse have been demolished. Unless you know, this looks like a bleak farm untouched by history. There is, however, a dark grey monument fronted by yellow tulips at the farm's entrance. I drive around the perimeter and, on the southern edge, follow the route that Mike Hedgeland took as he cycled back from St Neots that December evening many years ago.[1] I feel he is with me. It is a long, gentle incline that would have made him push hard at the pedals, the effort warming cold hands. I stop at the point where he would have done, imagining the glow of fire he would have seen reflected against the shroud of fog to the north. He saw FIDO and Deverill's burning Lancaster, and in my mind's eye I see them too.

Deverill almost made it, but 97 Squadron's Australian Flight Sergeant Scott crashed a little further away near Papworth St Agnes, more than a mile from the airfield. The village is at the end of a winding narrow lane which peters out in a cluster of neat cottages. The fields hereabouts are unequivocally Tory, partisan signboards emphatically pounded into soft pre-Election earth. You can sense the neighbourhood watch. To the north is an unspectacular scarp overlooking the road – it seems high enough to be the likely point where Scott came down, oblivious to the shift in contours in the foggy darkness. I drive on towards Gransden Lodge where Pilot Officer Kirkwood crashed three quarters of an hour after Scott. Hayley Wood where the aircraft came down is a lengthy sweep of mixed trees still not fully green although April is nearly done. A disused railway, its bridge over the Gransden–Longstowe road long since de-spanned, goes straight through the wood. It is quiet here, except for a man on a motor mower cutting the grass outside the farm opposite the entrance to the airfield, and the drone of a single-engined aircraft.

The airfield is now home to the Cambridge Gliding Club and also hosts clay pigeon shooting.[2] I drive uneasily up the approach road, expecting to be stopped, past the green and rusty paraphernalia that launches the clay targets. To my surprise I find myself slowly rumbling along what must have been original airfield concrete paving, if not runway, then perimeter track. My tyres are thumping rhythmically against crumbling ruts and I am thinking of bomb-heavy aeroplanes lumbering here before me. All I can see is waist-high rape, this old road with green veins of weed, and then an expanse of eastern sky. Later I eat a sandwich looking out over the airfield and note how close poor Kirkwood's copse was; the radio mast high above Sandy; tatterdemalion hedgerows hiding scrubby ditches; an unmoving red tractor; a church spire; two white arms of the Gransden windmill, its base just below the ridge; and an orange wind-sock facing west and flicking its tail in the sharp wind. Like Graveley, Gransden Lodge is suitably isolated: it takes no great effort to reinvent the past.

The same is not true of Bourn, from where 97 Squadron's crews flew. It is too close to Cambridge to have survived the onslaught of property developers. I came here twenty years ago with my father-in-law and we found the overgrown remains of old Nissen huts and it was possible to imagine it as it once was. It felt like untouched countryside. Now it is a confusion of new roads; estates with road names like Cavendish Mews and Cambridge Meadows protected by squads of sleeping policemen; Bryant Homes' show houses spruce and soulless beneath flapping gold-topped flagpoles; and sprawling business parks specialising in obscure technologies, or warehousing and logistics, fenced in by leylandii and barbed wire. I drive around the airfield, looking for The Hay where Ted Thackway came down, and Two Pots farmhouse, the site of McKenzie's crash. The main A428 Bedford to Cambridge blasts straight past the farm: it is busy suburban England now, with no time to stop and think. Go less than sixty and you are seriously at odds with the world. Finally, I can make out where Thackway hit the ground – a sequence of small fields hedged with scrubby trees in the hinterland south of Highfield Farm. Away from the main road there are ancient cars and farm vehicles gathering rust and moss, half hidden by trees. Bourn was sad – little hope of ghosts here since the emphasis was on easy commuting to well-paid jobs in town and using the airfield for the next massive Car Boot Sale.

I set off back towards Graveley, hoping to find Ingle's Farm where Flying Officer McLennan had died. It was just outside the village of Yelling – a neat building with well-tended garden, but its flaunted security discouraged scrutiny. Once again, rural England taking exception to prying eyes: I found myself flinching at the sign I had already seen in Hunsingore, Yorkshire months before: 'I can reach the fence in 5 seconds – can you?' and a picture of a dog whose hunger and vengeful nature was all too evident. They don't take prisoners here, I thought, and headed for home.

## CHAPTER THIRTY

# THE RUST ON REBECCA

The air museum at Flixton. Just inside the hut door there is the only fragment I had seen of an aircraft that crashed on Black Thursday. Tucked away on a low shelf it would have been easy to miss. It looks unexceptional: a curl of black cable and some intersecting pieces of dull black metal encrusted with rust, the result of spending nearly forty years in the River Deben. This is 'Rebecca'. She allowed aircrew to talk to agents on the ground in Special Operations Executive (SOE) clandestine operations over France and elsewhere. It is all that remains of a Halifax from 161 Squadron which crashed into the water near Felixstowe in the early hours of 17 December on its return from mid-France.[1]

\* \* \* \*

*The rusting Rebecca receiving aerial belonging to Flying Officer Harborow's crashed Halifax. It was recovered from the river Deben nearly forty years after Black Thursday and is now at the Norfolk and Suffolk Aviation Museum at Flixton.*

*Squadron Leader James 'Waggy' Wagland's sharp eyes and some Michelin maps were enough to get him and his pilot's Lysander back from France.* Graham Pitchfork

It was not just bombs that got dropped on enemy territory – on Black Thursday, four B17s from the USAAF[2] dropped nearly two million leaflets over Germany, France and Belgium. They found visibility over the target 'hazy' but 'all aircraft returned safely.' In addition, there were supplies and personnel intended to support resistance on the ground in France. Aircraft from 138 and 161 Squadrons, flying that night from Tangmere in Sussex and Tempsford in Bedfordshire – were involved, detailed to provide transport support for Special Operations Executive. SOE had been set up to cause maximum disruption on mainland Europe: the blowing of bridges; attacks on railway infrastructure; factory sabotage; the gathering of information, and the spread of disinformation; the nurturing of committed resistance and its co-ordination. Churchill wanted them to 'set Europe ablaze.' That entailed the steady supply of agents, stores and ammunition on bright moonlit nights from low-flying aircraft. On 16 December, as well as the Lancasters and Mosquitoes bombing Berlin from 20,000 feet, there were Halifaxes and Lysanders sweeping into France below the level of radar, at around 600 feet, on secret missions for SOE and the Special Intelligence Service (SIS).

\*   \*   \*   \*

Tangmere was close to the English Channel: just a brief trip from the French mainland even for a single-engined Lysander. At 8 pm on 16 December, buoyed by an optimistic weather forecast, Squadron Leader Lewis 'Bob' Hodges gunned the tiny monoplane down the runway and was soon being buffeted by the flak over the French coast. He was conscious of having tried and failed to make the same pick-up the night before and was worried too about the fog forecast for later that night. He was in a hurry to get there and back in good time. Navigation on a Lysander was normally an additional duty for the pilot, but Hodges had help with him this time in the shape of Squadron Leader James 'Waggy' Wagland.[3] No sophisticated navigational aids on this trip, just Wagland, some Michelin road maps and observant eyes picking out landmarks in the darkness: the flurry of surf where sea met land; moonlight reflected from sweeping curves in large rivers, or canals; the glint of metal from railway tracks; a road straight as a die, chalky white against the surrounding forest darkness. Hodges crossed the river Loire, near Saumur, its chateau standing high above the river in the pale light of the moon, and headed south towards Poitiers. He was looking for a lonely field between Poitiers and Angouleme.

The rules governing where airstrips could be located were precise and spelled out to SOE operatives in training:[4] open space about 700 yards square; *not* agricultural land or swamp, but rather grassy parkland with some cover; not too many trees however, for fear of tangled parachutes; no high-tension cables or telegraph poles; narrow valleys should be avoided; so should the proximity of aerodromes. There should be a long enough strip of straight, unhindered land for ease of take-off. A 'safe house' should be located within one mile of the chosen site. As Hodges's Lysander droned south, the chosen field lay in darkness still, but the moonlight was giving excellent visibility. He recognised the small town he had identified as a 'marker' and, using his compass, altered course, timing his run to the target. Below, in the French night, a solitary Citroen hurried to the rendezvous, headlights picking out ominous shadows in the narrow lanes. The Lysander circled briefly; then Hodges saw the car headlights sweeping into a field below him and, moments later, figures running, distributing landing lights in the familiar pattern. He eased the monoplane down and on to the firm, smooth stubble, turning the aircraft into the wind in case he had to make an unexpectedly rapid departure. This was not a time for niceties: agents on the ground were under strict orders: 'You are in charge of a military operation. Whatever the rank or importance of your passengers they must be under your orders. There must be no family parties on the field. If the pilot sees a crowd he may not land. Ensure that at the moment of landing you and your passengers and NOBODY ELSE are on the left of Light A, and your assistant on the left of Light B. Anybody anywhere else, especially anybody approaching the aircraft from the right, is liable to be shot by the pilot.'[5]

Two men scrambled on board, one of them was agent Jean (Joseph Dubar); the other was Flight Lieutenant Robin Hooper who had been stranded in France for weeks when his Lysander had got inextricably bogged down in a field near Chatellerault: it had even resisted the combined pulling weight of a team of bullocks and had to be burned before Hooper made his escape. Hodges was not so unlucky: within minutes he had taken off and was heading north towards England. France was still bathed in moonlight; the Channel too was clear. Only when he approached the English coast did he see a bank of low cloud. Then Tangmere Control came on the air warning of falling visibility and a cloud base at 500 feet. Strangely, above the cloud, there was still a steely bright moon. Hodges was instructed to make a landing on instruments alone: Lysanders though had no SBA, just VHF radio/telephone equipment. He ploughed into the cloud, watched it billow and fill around the perspex dome from which he viewed the world. He emerged below the cloud with 300 feet between the aircraft and the ground: he could see the runway lights now, and moments later he was down, his second landfall of the night. It was 'mere minutes before the fog closed in completely'[6] and there were other aircraft still aloft.

Flying Officer James McBride was flying a Lysander too and heading for Tangmere returning from Operation *Diablo*. He too had passengers – for whom there were no parachutes, making baling out for McBride an unacceptable option, despite the gathering fog and diminishing fuel.[7] He would have to chance a blind approach as the weather rapidly declined. Tangmere Control talked him toward the runway and he made a convincing approach through the murk. Suddenly he saw a red light directly ahead and it made him abort the landing – 'You're flying me into the hangars!' – and come around for another try. Then the R/T went dead. The silence was palpable and the fog got even worse, bad enough to make searching for the missing aircraft difficult. Eventually, after working backwards from the runway along the approach, across fields and ditches, they found the Lysander, its nose buried in the ground and consumed by fire. McBride was trapped in the cockpit and died there, but the two agents scrambled clear, 'crawling out of the blazing wreck.'[8] Stunned, they were driven off to the agents' base – the Cottage – at Tangmere. Escaping death through foul English weather must have seemed much less likely than at the hands of the Gestapo.

There was more to come: Flight Lieutenant Stephen Hankey tried to land at Ford, a naval airbase not far from Tangmere. He hit a hill, lost control and crashed. He and his two passengers (a male White Russian and a female agent) all died. Four men were killed when a Halifax from 138 Squadron crashed into the sea off Harwich; five more died when Flight Sergeant Watson failed to find the FIDO-lit runway at Woodbridge and hit the ground at Capel Green. At nearby Capel St Andrew another FIDO-seeking Halifax came down, with the loss of its pilot Flight Lieutenant Gray and two others. Another crew baled out near Spilsby in Lincolnshire, leaving the aircraft to dive into the North Sea off Skegness.

Flying Officer Harborow had taken off from Tempsford at 20.34 pm. It was to be a long and eventful night. On return, his Halifax hit a high wooden receiver mast west of Bawdsey close to the Suffolk coastline. At 05.25 in the morning of the 17th, he crashed into mudflats on the river Deben, upstream from the Felixstowe ferry crossing. Flying Officer Wilson McMaster was flung clear and lost consciousness, landing face down in the cloying mud. He suffocated. The aircraft slowly slid deeper into the mud: fuselage, then wings and propellers sucked further down. The Rebecca aerial sank with the rest as the early hours of the

*161 Squadron's Flying Officer D R Harborow clipped the wooden radio mast overlooking the North Sea at Bawdsey, Suffolk and crashed into the nearby River Deben. This is the mast's successor.*

17 December dawned, in a spectral half-light. The river flowed, the tide turned, and later, grim-faced rescuers stared at the mud-choked wreckage as the fog swirled across the wintry estuary.

\*    \*    \*    \*

Suffolk in the rain, deep puddles and storm-blown trees. Roads thick with mud. Heading out towards the Deben estuary, looking for the location of the crashed Halifax, it feels like edging out on a limb of England. I have had the same feeling on the way to Spurn Point, that arthritic finger of land curling into the river Humber, separating it from the sea. Between the road and the sea, on a slight wooded rise is a high mast and I take it to be the spot where Harborow's Halifax sliced through its wooden predecessor. To the east is the sea, while to the west is marshland, the Deben floodplain with a few scrubby bushes and little else. The road ends at Bawdsey Quay where the ferry plies across what today is a choppy stretch of water. Where the river meets the sea there are white breakers, and beyond a container ship marks the horizon heading out of Felixstowe docks. The mudflats where the Halifax crashed are hidden today by the highest of tides.

I headed north towards the sites of the other crashes. The rain intensifies and the puddles deepen. Capel St Andrew is little more than a sprawling farm, while Capel Green is even smaller – three houses, including another farm. The farmhouse is on a sharp bend: tractor parked under a tree and a neat garden. Beyond the hamlet is a wood of oak trees, green and dripping on a low hill, while the narrow lane climbs towards the plateau that holds RAF Woodbridge. This is Rendlesham Forest and I stop briefly at the end of the Woodbridge runway, a long expanse of concrete rising gently to a curved summit in the west. In this foul summer weather, it takes no great imagination to see returning heavy bombers in bleak midwinter darkness.

# CHAPTER THIRTY-ONE
# FRIDAY THE SEVENTEENTH

The morning of the 17th dawned grey and cold: there was snow on the northern wolds and elsewhere the fog lingered. The crews were soon stood down, with the weathermen predicting little change. Armed guards were placed on crashed aircraft: lone RAF policemen with beads of damp dripping from caps, and eyes straining to see through the mist stood watch over broken – often burned – Lancasters. Morose senior officers mooched around crash sites: Wing Commander Swetman and the Squadron Engineering Officer from 426 Squadron among them.[1] Others, with resigned sighs, started composing letters of regret. It was a task that required stamina and a hardened heart, rather than imagination and literary skills. The search continued for aircraft still not accounted for, and airmen woke to find unoccupied and undisturbed beds providing stark reminders of colleagues who had not returned. Ground crew circled damaged Lancasters and scratched their heads at the work to be done. At Bourn, Linton, Elsham Wolds, Waltham and the rest of the stations where crews had failed to complete the return from Germany the previous night, the atmosphere was heavy with loss. The persistent, rolling fog meant no resumption of flying and so there were unfilled hours to brood over what had happened. In north Yorkshire, it was three days before the fog had cleared enough for 408 Squadron's diverted aircraft to return to Linton-on-Ouse.[2] I e-mailed Roger Coulombe to tap his memories of the aftermath. 'To hear,' Roger replied, 'that so many corpses from the crashes had been (recovered) from the crashed Lancasters just a few miles from our base were guys that we knew and liked and that those guys were with us just a few hours ago taking off for Berlin made it more difficult to accept. In addition, the word spread around that a great number of coffins were taken away to Harrogate for burial to Stonefall Cemetery ... from one of the hangars where they had been kept for a few hours ... In war, it seems that losing friends through enemy action is easier to take than losing them because of defective equipment or because of human error ... the Friday (the 17th) was a dismal day both because of the continuing foggy weather and because of the feeling of loss of many buddies that we liked and whose comradeship and friendship we used to enjoy every day at work around the flight.'[3]

The bright morning in November 2004 was a sharp contrast: a Lincolnshire sky empty of cloud, a washed blue backdrop with a low winter sun. There was a crisp frost. The Red Arrows were practising over Scampton, scrawling vapour trails above the A15. The road to Lincoln runs north to south, Roman fashion and pencil-straight, its signposts a constant reminder of airfields long since closed: Fiskerton and Faldingworth, Binbrook and Kelstern. Their time seemed long gone. Later, though, I found myself much closer, thinking – not for the first time – of the morning after Black Thursday: the smell of burning, the exhausted crews and the sense of things never being the same again. I had gone to the Lincolnshire County Archive to read the Chief Constable's Daily Situation Report written on 17 December 1943: an earlier inquiry had indicated that it contained a reference to the crash of 'Pop' Walker's Lancaster near Hainton. The file[4] contained a tissue-thin carbon copy of the letter sent to the police duty officer in the Police War Duty Room at the Home Office in Whitehall. The file itself was interesting in that the police seemed concerned about just three things: bombing incursions by the enemy; crashes of RAF aircraft, and strikes by workers: dockers, for example, or the refusal to work by the bus drivers and conductresses of the Lincolnshire Red Car Company in September 1942. There was also the promised reference to the crash at Hainton:

'*I write to inform you that there was no enemy activity during the night of the 16/17th December 1943, but...*' – standard format clearly ... then a lengthy account of the collision at Ulceby[5] before the writer turned to another of the night's crashes: '*Another Lancaster bomber crashed near Hainton (40/642037) resulting in damage to some army lorries. A minor road from Torrington to Hainton was blocked until midday today...*' The bracketed number looked like an Ordnance Survey grid reference and I left the Archive building thinking I had pinpointed exactly where the 12 Squadron Lancaster had come down. I hadn't quite yet, but I was close, thanks to the internet: an on-line calculation turning the Cassini grid[6] into conventional longitude (almost exactly zero) and latitude (53 degrees or so); it even printed a map with the familiar fiddler's elbow of a bend on the main Lincoln to Louth road and a star marking the crash site. X marks the spot – but it wasn't where I expected it from the conversation I'd had with the man in the village post office four months before. Then we had looked east towards an isolated house with tall chimneys and a ramshackle roof; now, the site seemed to be closer to the village, past the church, on the road leading west, back towards Wickenby from where Ross and his crew had taken off.

*    *    *    *

Several months later, in mid-February I went to the Record Office in Lincoln again, for once not searching for wartime documents: I had spent the day reading the school Log Book from West Deeping Primary School where my aunt had been headmistress in the years between the wars ('May 24th, 1927 – The timetable was not followed today. The children sang patriotic songs. The Head Teacher told the story of the Empire.') A day that had been cold and cloudless enough in the morning for the Red Arrows to do their usual blue-sky routine for me driving south down the A15 had, by late afternoon, turned more February-like. The light was beginning to fade, while a thin, mean rain fell, casting a grey pall over countryside that looked as if spring would never come. The cloud was suitably low, giving me a reminder of what wintry Lincolnshire can look like at this, the take-off hour.

I drove towards Hainton from the Torringtons, West and East, through the driving rain, as the light began to fade. The road was narrow and awash with mud. It turned back on itself, gaining height in a leisurely fashion, turning slowly from flat farmland to a line of low hills, in a fold of which sat the village of Hainton, brick cottages and tall trees. The Cassini map had a road coming in from the left before I got to the point where the aircraft is thought to have hit the ground. Passing it, I glanced across, looking north along the incoming lane. It fell away across rolling farmland. Yes! Here's where it must be: a straggling copse the length of a football pitch to the south side of the Torrington road. The ground was white with snowdrops. Looking beyond the trees, the boundary marked by a tumbledown fence, I caught a glimpse of a mansion set back amongst the trees – Hainton Hall – so placed that any glimpse of it from the road would be fleeting. I drove slowly, sensing I was close, but dissatisfied too, I suppose because there was no definitive proof, nothing to mark the spot out from just another country lane in the middle of nowhere. The rain was getting harder and twilight closer. I almost turned for home.

No harm though, in a second pass, so I drove back along the length of the lane. Then back again. In the gloom ahead of me there was a man walking his dogs. He stood willingly in the rain while I asked the familiar questions: No, he didn't know where. Yes, he had heard of such a thing; Mel at the Post Office might know; oh, you've spoken to him already; well ...

'I suppose Mr Heneage might know something about it.'

'Who's he?'

'He owns the village – and the next one – Sixhills. He's the landlord, good one too. Approachable, but you couldn't just turn up on his doorstep. He keeps records of the village.' We agreed a telephone call or letter might be best and I drove away into what had become a fierce rainstorm, thinking how coincidental it was that, earlier in the Lincoln Record Office, I had noticed in passing a file marked 'Heneage of Hainton'. I wondered too if the reason the aircraft had hit army lorries was because the Hall had been requisitioned by the Army during the war. I wrote and, while the reply confirmed the requisitioning, James Heneage was apologetic: 'I have looked into the matter of the crashed Lancaster but have not been successful in coming up with anything.'

*　　*　　*　　*

I returned to Hunsingore at the turn of the year: to another crash site whose precise location I had struggled with initially.[7] Two o'clock December sun and lengthening shadows already after a day of winter blue. Visiting the Memorial Room at RAF Linton-on-Ouse I had come across a more accurate description of the crash location of 426 Squadron's DS779 piloted by Canadian Flight Sergeant R D Stewart. The place was even closer to the A1 than I had thought, more than a mile from the village whose church spire I could see above a line of winter trees.

I turned off the A59 Harrogate to York road, close to the entrance to Allerton Park. This is territory where Air Vice-Marshal Brookes bicycled when the demands of high office permitted. The road to Northlands Farm Hopperton was a car's width wide and slick with mud. A railway branch line bisected the road and the gates were shut. The Network Rail man repeated the warning of the makeshift sign I had just passed to the effect that there was no way through to the motorway. I told him why I wanted to go further down the lane. 'I'm more of a *Luftwaffe* man myself!' he said, giving every impression of a man who liked to sit in his hut and read military history books while he drank railwayman's tea, enjoyed the fug, and every hour or so saluted a passing train. While I waited and we talked, he waved a Harrogate-bound train through with a proprietorial air. 'Just blow the horn when you want to come back!' he said to me, pulling at the white-barred gates.

Northlands farm faces due west, presiding over fields of heavy clay, its neat grey bricks lit by the late sun. The light shows this stalwart building off at its best, giving the brickwork a hint of colour and illuminating the cream paint of a dovecote over a barn. To the north is a slight rise where the village of Wixley separates this landscape from the serpentine loops of the river Ouse. There is, of course, no sign of the crash: no deep crater, no evidence of remembrance. Indeed there is no sign of life in these fields, just standing water in puddles, a line of bare trees at what passes for the low point in this gently undulating farm-land. There is green moss marking the middle of the country lane. It is easy to imagine this isolated spot being much the same decades ago on such a winter afternoon. Again I am struck by the similarity of these crash sites: trees, a hint of hillside, and a farm at the centre of a clutch of barns and sheds. Often too it is quiet, but here I can hear the swish of the motorway, and for once no aircraft prowling overhead.

## CHAPTER THIRTY-TWO

# PILOT ERROR?

Air investigators were well versed in the rituals of picking over aircraft debris and asking the right questions of tired airmen who had survived: while RAF police guarded the sites, they picked through charred metal fragments, shattered perspex, scattered ammunition, maps and lucky mascots, and human remains, and made their observations and notes. They stamped their feet against the cold, looked at the lie of the land – that hill, those trees – and stood in sombre groups pointing out lines of approach and apportioning blame while their breath turned to mist in the December cold.

Within a fortnight, one of the Groups at least – 1 Group based at Bawtry Hall in south Yorkshire – had reflected enough to determine its conclusions. Two weeks was a long time when there was a war to be won. In its Group Summary sent out to all squadrons in the Group at the end of December it noted: '... on December 16/17, a widespread and unpredicted deterioration in the weather at our home bases occurred. No diversion areas were available and many deplorable accidents resulted while our aircraft were endeavouring to break cloud and land ...' So sorry boys – blame the weather for not doing what we expected, and you surely can't expect us to guarantee an alternative airfield. That's not what we're here for! No, if anyone's to blame I'm afraid, it's down to you lot ...

The report continued: 'An investigation has now been completed which shows the accidents cannot be attributed to a common factor. Some aircraft broke cloud too quickly (how could you pilots **DO** that!), some broke cloud too slowly and continued to sink, whilst others 'slipped in' on a turn while endeavouring to keep the airfield lights in view. Conditions were vile and unexpected yet 136 aircraft landed safely. We must continue to strive for better airmanship and more effective ground control.'[1] Such well-intentioned exhortation did not seem to me enough to stop it happening again.

* * * *

For each crashed aircraft that night, there is an accident card – Form 1180. I have all of them beside me, with 12 Squadron's Ross on the top of the pile. It is coldly bureaucratic: two pages of columns and boxes, abbreviations and inked data. Around the outside there are holes to be punched where the shorthand code fits the circumstances: so 'Fatal' is punched under CAS, for 'Casualties', and 'Ground' under FIRE. The date, time and location of the crash, numbers of the engines, rank and nationality of the pilot are all painstakingly ledgered, together with other information of the kind that organisations collect when things go wrong – plenty of numbers, cross-referenced files and cryptic initials. In each case, there is a commentary in connected, often terse prose providing a gloss on what happened. This is usually written by a senior officer, with additional, even more terse, points made by the next one up in the hierarchy – station commander, and AOC. The comment on Ross's crash is brief, if graphic: 'A/C broke cloud over high ground and as the descent was unnecessarily fast pilot was unable to check before hitting ground – a/c disintegrated and caught fire.' Writing it down now I am conscious that it seems so few words to consign a seven man crew to history and the out-tray; why, the scribe spurns eloquence for business-like brevity, dispensing with commas and emotion in equal measure! As for blame, I think back to Ian Walker's anxiety that it was his navigator father's error that had consigned this crew to a fiery death. The finger of blame in the 1180 however points straight at pilot Hugh Ross himself, descending too fast to stop his aircraft's precipitate fall to earth. Indeed, that is the way of the men behind the desks in the days after Black Thursday: shift the blame to the men in the cockpit.

Most dismissive of all are the comments on the pilots from 97 Squadron: the same form of words suffices for five of them. In each case, the judgement is unforgiving, so much so that the phrase pilot 'error of judgement' is restricted to a perfunctory 'E of J'. Let Acting Squadron Leader Mackenzie stand for all of them. His 1180 reads: 'A/C attempting to locate a/field in low cloud and bad vis. (CO) Pilot should have practised SBA. (Stn. CO) E of J in bad vis. (AOC:AOC i/c) One of 12 accidents which are subject of special report.' So Scott, Thackway, Kirkwood, Deverill, Mooney and Mackenzie (97 Squadron) are all held accountable over their collective failure to use SBA; Holford (100) was lost and dazzled by lights; Proudfoot (100) 'probably thought he was still in cloud'; Allan (405) was inexperienced; Clark (408) lacked skill in cloud-breaking techniques; Scott and Richter (576 and 103) 'both disobeyed briefing'; Cooper (101) was 'lost and apparently panicked', and so on. Pilots! The finger of blame is pointing at YOU.

*    *    *    *

Military bureaucracy does not welcome uncertainty or fence-sitting. So it was that if you didn't use SBA to land then you were culpable and duly attracted the 'E of J' judgement. And yet, SBA was an on-going issue of debate ...

Autumn in wartime Buckinghamshire: at Bomber Command HQ in High Wycombe; the Commander-in-Chief's deputy, Robert Saundby is composing a letter intended for each of Bomber Command's Groups. The date is 4 November 1943: six weeks before Black Thursday. The letter is a sensitive one and requires delicate phrasing since he knows there will be sharply held views, and Group commanders can be all too readily stirred to disagreement.

'You are aware,' he writes, 'that the Air Ministry are giving serious consideration to the possibility of giving up SBA ... The main arguments for this step are: ... that SBA has not proved a practical means of landing in fog conditions with average operational crews, and its use as a homing aid has now been largely replaced by GEE ...'[2] He proposes a conference to be held on 15 November to discuss the issue.

The response to this was predictably mixed: Don Bennett at 8 Group (Pathfinder Force) in Huntingdon pulled no punches. Writing by return, on 6 November, he urged that SBA should be retained: 'It is not agreed that SBA has not proved a practical means of landing in bad conditions of visibility or where a ground fog has just formed ... SBA is almost compulsory for use with fog dispersal apparatus.' He went on to insist that SBA was far more reliable than any other item of equipment aboard a heavy bomber. Bennett was the most vociferous opponent, but 1 Group also had doubts: the view there was that while it was true that 'SBA is not a practical means of landing large numbers of bombers in fog conditions,' it was realistic that between 100 and 150 Lancasters could be sent out in poor weather and return safely with 'properly sited SBAs.' In the main though the responses tended to accept the proposed abolition of SBA: on the 8th, the officer commanding 92 Group indicated that 'the advantages of abolishing SBA in this Group would outweigh the disadvantages, provided that all OTU aircraft were equipped with GEE.' Air Vice-Marshal Brookes at Allerton Park, North Yorkshire – HQ of 6 Group – wrote a wordy response accepting that SBA is 'not used, except in isolated circumstances for blind landings'. Nonetheless he set a special case for the Group's pilots: 'The stations in this Group lie in a valley between two ranges of hills, namely the Clevelands on the east rising to a height between 1,000 and 1,200 feet, and the Pennines on the west rising to a height of between 2,500 and 3,000 feet. In many cases cloud conditions for return from operations has been such as to obscure, or lie very close to, the top of these hills.' He concludes that SBA is critical when aircraft are 'breaking cloud' – an issue with which

Brookes was preoccupied in the aftermath of Black Thursday, as the Form 1180s he completed clearly indicate.

A decision was taken at the mid-November conference that SBA should be retained for the foreseeable future: the equipment was still readily available until the following September. It was agreed to review the situation in July 1944. A month later, despite the reservations about it expressed through the autumn, the failure to prepare for, and deploy SBA in such grim circumstances provoked accusations by senior officers of neglect by pilots.[3] 'Error of Judgement' might more appropriately have been levelled at those senior men charged with ensuring that their pilots and crews were given every opportunity to survive the worst the Germans, or the weather, could throw at them.

# CHAPTER THIRTY-THREE
# REPEATING HISTORY

December again. Raised eyebrows from the met officer at briefing. Heavy rain filling puddles and a bitter wind making wires and cable sing. Take-off was at 20.05. The aircraft rocked in the blustering squalls as it rolled along the runway. White horses streaked the North Sea and the rain slanted horizontally across the cockpit window. Familiar landmarks: Dogger, Flamborough; the flak battery at Grimsby. Crossing the coast, the pilot changed course for York. Below he could see wet rooftops slick with rain. Flurries of hail battered the windscreen and occasionally the aircraft nosed into thick cloud that muffled like a blanket and stole what visibility there was. 'On the road that led straight to York, a lonely driver put his headlights on every few minutes.' Solid Yorkshire bloody-mindedness: bugger the blackout! Over York, they opened the bomb doors. 'We climbed higher and made out the gas works first. The bombs fell.'

This is no Lancaster but a Dornier with a German pilot and crew. Wheeling away from the city, they saw a tongue of flame stab into the sky, as high as a church tower. 'We must have hit the gasworks.' For miles on their homeward journey, the clouds hung red and heavy over the city.[1] They made it back across the North Sea, the wind and fires behind them.

Browsing idly through the archives at the York City Archive I had suddenly come across a file about a crashed bomber on the North York Moors, near Crow's Nest, Hawnby. Another Dornier, piloted by *Oberleutnant* Rolf Hausner, had careered into a dry stone wall at high speed and broken into pieces which scattered across the farmland near High Banniscue farm. The date was unsettling: 17 December 1942 – a year before Black Thursday. It was perhaps three miles from where Flying Officer Russell Clark was to die a year later: a steep descent down into the valley of the river Rye, wooded and lonely, and then a breathless hike up the other side and across bleak, treeless moor to the isolated Silver Hill farmhouse. Here there was another stone wall to act as an aircraft's last resting place.

The file was less to do with the crash, and more its aftermath: it comprised a letter to the Chief Constable of police seeking information about the crash on behalf of the dead crew's family. The daughter of one of the crew had been taken up to this bleak spot in the 1950s and

174

been distraught by the remaining evidence of the aircraft's grim ending: 'parts of it are still there on the open, lonely hillside.' Unsurprisingly, faced with the rusting metal and the bleak presence of Easterside Hill, all bracken and sheep tracks, she had cried. Her father had been lost on a 'reprisal raid' on York, the aircraft burning fiercely and consuming the bodies. It had been a night of grim weather where the crews had not expected to fly and then were sent on their way by those determined to fight the weather as well as the British. Black Thursday '43 was just another such occasion in a long line of sacrifice, both RAF and *Luftwaffe*.

*  *  *  *

Move forward to 21 December 1944: 5 Group – including 97 Squadron,[2] the squadron for whom Black Thursday had most resonance – is flying on operations to the oil refinery at Politz, near Stettin. The weather had been bad for days: snow and frost; and thick fog. The take-off was bedevilled by thick mist and pilots could only see half the length of the runway. Amongst 97 Squadron's pilots, with Coningsby shrouded in fog, the expectation was that the operation would be cancelled. Had any of the survivors of Black Thursday been flying, they would have been more pessimistic, shrugging resigned shoulders that common sense would not prevail. They were to be in the air for ten and a half hours. And, on return, the fog had worsened.

The result was predictable: Flying Officer Read (9 Squadron) collided with a tree in poor visibility at Bardney: two men died. It was 2.35 in the morning. Eleven minutes later, 83 Squadron's Squadron Leader Hatcher crashed, having diverted to Metheringham whose FIDO proved unable to save him or his crew (seven crew members died). A Lancaster flown by Flying Officer Croker (227 Squadron) was diverted to Wick in Scotland and crashed at 3.07. The aircraft was written off but the crew survived. Flying Officer Joplin (617 Squadron) was diverted to Ludford Magna, its FIDO burning brightly in the thick fog. The Lancaster's port wing grazed the ground on approach and crashed near Market Rasen, with two fatalities. Flying Officer Stockill (630 Squadron) crashed too, with six crew members dying. In all, twenty-three deaths on a wintry night, with the war's end rapidly approaching.

To the bitter end bombers set off for operations in poor weather, and returned to find England cloaked in mist. Take the night of 8 and 9 April 1945, with the end of the war in Europe just weeks away. Raids were launched on Lutzkendorf and Hamburg. Let the experience of Flying Officer Watson (RAAF, 466 squadron) stand for those defeated by the weather, if not the Germans:

'T/O 1946 Driffield. Encountered fog on return and while trying to locate the airfield, the Halifax flew into trees and crashed 0115 at Kirkburn Grange farm, some two miles W of the aerodrome. All rest in various UK cemeteries.'[3]

## CHAPTER THIRTY-FOUR

# LESSONS TO BE LEARNED?

The Prime Minister was prone to terse and tetchy single sentence questions fired at the soft underbelly of his Chief of the Air Staff (CAS), Air Chief Marshal Sir Charles Portal. One of the files at the National Archives[1] includes several such examples before the tide of war turned and Churchill grew content to receive monthly reports written to an unremarkable template: tonnage of bombs; operations flown; estimates of damage. On 10 September 1942, for example, he peremptorily demanded that Portal should 'make me a list of the German towns bombed since August 1, with the weight of bombs dropped on each and the number of aircraft used. I thought of sending it to Premier Stalin.' Optimistically I turned to December 1943: nothing! But I knew the Prime Minister had other things on his mind; on his lungs too. He had been taken ill in Tunis on 10 December and his doctor was alarmed enough to say in retrospect that he expected Churchill to die on the 14th. On the 15th, his heart began to fibrillate. He was out of the country again late on the 16th. He had no occasion to fire a truculent query about losses in the fog over England. I already knew that while the Cabinet were informed in general and brief terms about the raid[2] – tonnage of bombs dropped; numbers of aircraft doing the bombing – there was no report of the losses on the way home. Cabinet's agenda around this time was preoccupied with Indian finance; Ireland; Civil Service leave; and the renewal of the BBC Charter.

I wasn't the first to comb the archives to find a definitive report in the aftermath of Black Thursday. Jennie Gray had concluded that 'there was apparently no detailed inquiry into the night's events.'[3] The Accident Cards made clear however that some of the crashes that night were the 'subject of a special report'. I had already learned that there was an inquiry into the accidents in 1 Group and the idea that those behind desks did not feel duty-bound to probe and blame ran counter to what I knew about how the civil service functions. From a scrutiny of each squadron's ORB I learned too that there were four more crashes that night than had been thought, making a total of forty-three in all.[4]

Eventually I found[5] a key letter written on 14 February 1944 by the Director of Air Safety to Harris at Bomber Command. It made me gasp out loud in the accusing silence of the Reading Room at the National Archives. What I read made clear that 'the Inspector General has recently reported on a number of losses which occurred to the operational aircraft of your Command on return from bombing operations on the night of the 16 December 1943.' The thinking in that report is evident from the letter and the guidance is firmly framed ('I am to request that you will ...' etc). However the report itself remains 'out there' somewhere – destroyed or lost. It matters little since, were the question to be asked of me by a Prime Minister determined to know the truth, I could get as close as anyone now: 'Let me have by the weekend a report on the events of the 16th with recommendations that no such a thing ever occurs again – WSC.'

So this is what I would have written to the impatient man in the siren suit, knowing that he wanted the unvarnished truth and some kind of solution ...

## A REPORT ON THE LOSSES INCURRED ON 16 DECEMBER 1943

*1. Introduction*
This paper describes the circumstances surrounding the operation on Berlin on the night of 16 December 1943. Its purpose is to clarify the reasons why losses were incurred and to suggest the means by which such losses can be avoided or minimised in the future. The basic facts are these: 482 Lancasters and a small number of Mosquitoes took part in the operation. Crews took off in the late afternoon from aerodromes in Yorkshire, Lincolnshire and Cambridgeshire. In addition, crews from 138 and 161 Squadrons at Tempsford and Tangmere were involved in secret operations over France and suffered significant losses on return to this country. Zero hour over Berlin was 20.00 hours and the raid itself was broadly successful, although heavy cloud over the target made accurate assessment of the damage inflicted difficult to confirm. In all a minimum of sixty-five aircraft were lost overall, forty-three of them over England. The following sections consider a number of different factors which contributed to this grim night for Bomber Command.

*2. The Weather*
The weather was cold, windless and misty. In that regard it was little different from the preceding weeks (it had prevented operations since 2 December). There is a view that the absence of activity against the enemy for two weeks increased the pressure on Bomber Command HQ to proceed with this raid on the German capital. Forecasts were for

cloud to increase as the night wore on; it is also true to say that many aircrew were expecting the operation to be cancelled. It would not have been the first time.

By the time the aircraft were returning the fog had descended. The cloud base was very low, on occasions at 300 feet or less. A significant number of pilots encountered major problems in locating their home airfield, or indeed any aerodrome at all. It is also true to say, however, that a high proportion of returning pilots spoke of acceptable conditions and indeed accurate weather forecasts. There is no doubt that conditions at some airfields – Linton, Bourn, Kelstern, Waltham for example – were appalling, with visibility effectively nil, and with conditions worsening by the hour. At Bourn, for example, the 'fitness for flying' quotient was judged as zero by midnight. Overall, the difficulties of the night were such that many pilots – some seventy in all – diverted to alternative airfields.

A key feature, however, is that there appears to have been a window of clearer sky around Lincoln: weather data for Woodhall Spa, Metheringham, Dunholme Lodge, Fiskerton and a number of other 5 Group aerodromes indicated that the fog did not worsen in the hours around midnight and losses amongst the squadrons in 5 Group were minimal. This raises a key question: was it possible for more use to be made of the easier conditions to the east of Lincoln?

There is no doubt overall that the weather conditions were exceptionally problematic, and with the benefit of hindsight the operation should have been aborted. Weighing the damage inflicted on the enemy against the loss of so many aircraft and crew – expensive resources both – it is doubtful whether Bomber Command's determination to 'press on regardless' is fully justified, commendable though the determination to take the fight to the enemy is. The Commander-in-Chief has expressed serious reservations about the distinct independence of the Meteorological Service, believing that it belongs more appropriately within the RAF and he may well take the view that losses of this kind are inevitable when there is not a close enough relation between those who fly; those who judge fitness for flying; and those who provide weather forecasts. At all events, it is an unavoidable fact that a decision was taken at the highest level to send men aloft and abroad on a night when conditions worsened to the point where catastrophe was unavoidable for some. Despite the often expressed view of the Prime Minister – that Bomber Command should confine itself to fighting Nazis, not the weather – a bitter battle with the elements is precisely what happened on the night in question.

### 3. Navigational Problems

Faced with low cloud, fog and poor visibility, the pilot necessarily relies on instruments. There are two which are most relevant here: GEE and Standard Beam Approach (SBA). The former essentially allows a navigator to pinpoint exact location, while the latter is a mechanism whereby a pilot can 'home in' on the approach runway. Both are problematic in the sense that it appears that the practice of both is inconsistent: pilots emerge from training units with only the most rudimentary grasp of GEE, while there is uncertainty about the continuing use of SBA. As recently as a month ago the Air Ministry was proposing its abolition: a move which prompted both support for the notion, and determined opposition (from the Pathfinders who, it might be thought, know best on issues of navigation). The views of the Inspector General[6] are clear: 'The SBA situation is getting very slack again ... many aircraft went off already knowing their diversion area but not being fitted for the SBA requirements for those particular aerodromes.' The use of SBA varies markedly from Group to Group:

*Table 1   Use of Standard Beam Approach (December 1943)*

| GROUP | 1 | 3 | 4 | 5 | 6 | 8 | TOTAL |
|---|---|---|---|---|---|---|---|
| Total number of operations | 832 | 348 | 468 | 912 | 437 | 960 | 3,957 |
| Operations where SBA was used in poor weather | 106 | 30 | 74 | 9 | 8 | 79 | 306 |
| *% use SBA* | *12.7* | *8.6* | *15.8* | *0.99* | *1.8* | *8.2* | *7.7* |

It is evident too from these figures that while the AOC 8 Group might stress the value of SBA – and indeed his senior officers have strenuously exhorted their pilots to make greater use of it in the light of 'Black Thursday' – in fact, it is a minority occupation. This is in part because for some 'average' pilots, the use of SBA in conditions of appalling weather is beyond their capability. The Inspector-General takes the view that heavy losses were 'partly caused due to the lack of any pre-planning and practice of a scheme for homing in bad weather and neglect of SBA ... The night was ideal for SBA, but many stations ordered aircraft to break cloud over the sea and to try and come in under the low cloud, which resulted in accidents due to aircraft flying into high ground and congestion over airfields at low altitude.'[7] If a repetition of this night's debacle is to be avoided it is necessary to

(a) render the SBA method easier to use in hazardous conditions;
(b) improve training and ensure that pilots are not required to undertake missions of this kind before they have had the opportunity to become very familiar with SBA methodology and practice.

## 4. Fuel Shortages

Aircraft bound for Berlin are usually filled with some 1,860 gallons. The rule of thumb is that there is enough fuel for the trip, plus a contingency amount which tends to vary from Group to Group. This is in itself unsatisfactory, and recognised as such by Bomber Command HQ which drew attention to the variation just five days before this operation. Moreover, the problem is exacerbated by the fact that different pilots use different amounts of fuel, depending how they fly. The greater the amount of evasion, the more fuel is used. An inexperienced pilot uses more petrol too – although 1 Group, for example, makes no concession for this fact. Thus a 'heavy fuel using' novice pilot, who has, say, two encounters with Nazi night-fighters, 'corkscrews' violently, and heads for home on three engines, will be much closer to running out of fuel than his more fortunate and conservative counterpart. Short of fuel, pilots would not want to return to thick fog, and skies full of circling bombers desperate to land.

A further factor is that there is a perception that fuel is reduced to cram the maximum tonnage of bombs aboard. There is no evidence to support this, but the very fact that so many aircraft were left short of fuel on the 16 December would indicate that the line between bombs and fuel should be realigned, thereby providing a greater amount of fuel for contingencies. Assuming that lives and/or aircraft would have been saved by another fifteen minutes' worth of petrol in each Lancaster, then an additional fifty gallons would have meant minimal reduction in the tonnage of bombs on board.

## 5. Faulty Altimeters

The Inspector General[8] has suggested that a number of unexplained crashes caused by inexperienced pilots flying into the ground may be due to a lag in altimeters, particularly in those which have been exposed to winter weather at dispersals. This is a major issue since a high proportion of the crashes on the 16th were caused by pilots flying into higher ground. It is proposed to initiate a systematic check by flight engineers on return from operational activities. It is suggested that the flight engineer should, as a matter of routine, take and record the reading of the altimeter at the moment when the wheels touch the ground on return from operations and the QFE set on the altimeter. It is the opinion of the Inspector General that the majority of the lives lost would have been saved if the aircraft had been fitted with the radio altimeter.

### 6. Other Factors

It is troubling to consider that some of the pilots were not ready for this kind of operation: some had spent too few hours flying Lancasters at night prior to an eight hour operation to Berlin. Inexperience was a key issue. In addition, there was insufficient scope for diversions; the weather was worse than forecast; there was uncertainty about the circumstances under which crews could bale out; aircraft stalled; there were radio/telephone and other technical failures; inappropriate use of searchlights and Sandra[9] lights so that pilots were temporarily blinded or confused. Training did not fully prepare these men for their ordeal. Planning and preparation for such situations has not been good enough. Pilots broke cloud too fast, descending too precipitately and the orderly process of 'stacking' was abused by some pilots, and mismanaged by some ground controls.

To bring home the reality of what these men faced, it is worth considering the experience of one crew. Sergeant Walter Evans was one pilot who survived. Attempting to return to Ludford Magna in Lincolnshire, he was in the event diverted to Driffield in east Yorkshire. He could hear R/T messages from three different stations, but could see no lights at all. Then one of the airfields, Catfoss, offered to put up a light for them. Len Brooks, who was the rear gunner in that Lancaster described the situation thus: 'They realised we were very low and put the beam almost parallel to the ground right on us. I remember feeling the power go on, the nose lift and suddenly I saw under the turret chicken huts, a garden shed and finally chimney pots flashing by. That light saved us.'[10] Too many others that night were less fortunate.

### 7. Recommendations

- Criteria defining the minimum acceptable weather conditions under which operations can be conducted should be agreed and disseminated.
- Arrangements for diverting aircraft away from their home station should be improved. This includes greater emphasis being placed on pilots being fully aware of such arrangements –

including for example knowing the SBA frequencies for potential diversionary aerodromes; and for greater cooperation between bases so that information about possible better weather conditions is made available rapidly to others.

- Navigators should emerge from training confident in their ability to make use of GEE to locate runways in poor weather conditions.
- The use of SBA should be continued until a viable alternative is available and accepted. There should be greater consistency of use across the various Groups. Training in the use of SBA should be regular and on-going.
- Pilots who have not reached an acceptable level of performance in the use of SBA should not fly in poor weather.
- Research should be conducted on variations in the use of fuel and allocations revised in the light of that. The amount of contingency fuel should be increased to allow for a further thirty minutes of flying time over base.
- The 'lag' between what altimeters indicate as being height above sea level, and the *actual* height on landing should be researched, and average 'lag' factored into pilot calculations.
- The use of radio altimeters should be expedited as a matter of the highest urgency.
- There should be greater clarity for pilots on the conditions under which baling out of the aircraft over base is judged acceptable and appropriate.
- The use of FIDO should be urgently extended, so that all squadrons have access to a functioning FIDO runway on return to England in fog.
- Pre-planning for bad weather conditions is not of a consistent quality across Bomber Command. The Inspector General[11] also found that the method of return employed in 5 Group and laid down in their Air Staff Instruction TRG/14 dated 29 December 1943 was effective in the conditions encountered on the night of the 16th December. This system of bad weather planning should be adopted by others, or, where this is not practicable, an alternative plan should be made to suit local conditions.

## 8. Conclusions

The sacrifices made by the crews of Bomber Command are unequalled in the course of this air war. It is self evident however that the nation can ill afford the losses incurred on the Berlin operation of 16 December

1943. This report and the recommendations outlined in the previous paragraph clearly indicate that there are steps which can – and must – be taken to ensure that lessons have been learned and such losses arising from the kind of bad weather which characterises the typical English winter never occur again.

# CHAPTER THIRTY-FIVE

# LOST AIRMEN

Almost the last piece of research I did was to look forward in time from Black Thursday: I had my definitive list of pilots flying that night, and I had Chorley's weighty tome listing the losses for 1944. I had come to feel an affinity with these men – my survivors and it was with trepidation that I looked into their future. It was a chilling glimpse into their destinies. Of the 417 pilots that my research had identified as survivors from Black Thursday, 156 had crashed by the end of March 1944, most of them to their deaths; 37 per cent. 7 Squadron had lost nine; 156 – eleven. Some had been shot down within seventy-two hours of Black Thursday: attacking Frankfurt on 20 December, Pilot Officer R W G Evans (44 Squadron) and one other crew member survived to be POWs; Pilot Officer A Blackmore (49 Squadron) was less fortunate on the same raid.

Some old friends suffered too: the pilot of the first aircraft to take off on 16 December – Pilot Officer C Grannum (12 Squadron) came down over Berlin on 27/28 January 1944. He successfully evaded capture. Others weren't so lucky this time round. Flight Sergeant Hurley, who had survived the ditching in the North Sea, lost his life on a raid to Wesseling on 22 June 1944. Flying Officer A L Lazenby (101 Squadron), who had baled out on the 16th, was shot down two weeks later over Berlin. He and three of his crew – the same crew – died. 97 Squadron's Leo Mooney, another pilot who had jumped ship, lost his life the night before Lazenby – again over Berlin (1/2 January). Pilot Officer McLean (83 Squadron) who had tangled with another aircraft above the misty hills of Lincolnshire and survived, was killed in August 1944 in a daylight raid over Brest. Flying Officer Bob West – one of whose gunners was the diarist Bernard Clark who had written of their first raid and returning to the ground crew's cheers – died over Berlin a month later. Sergeant Coates (97 Squadron) who had performed miracles on returning from Berlin on two engines and landing at 1.30 on the morning of Black Thursday Plus One, came down over the Big City in late March 1944. He, like so many others did not survive. Fleetingly I remembered the list of names from 97 Squadron's order of battle on the 16th – twenty-one of them. By the Spring of 1944, only ten survived. Such was the price of the onslaught Harris unleashed on Germany.

\* \* \* \*

Just as the location of bomber aerodromes have certain common characteristics – broad expanses of upland; no steep valley sides; high blue hills only in the distance – so the crash sites on Black Thursday seemed to me to have a singular uniformity. Invariably, there were unpopulated areas: not one crash caused a civilian casualty. Damage was confined to stone walls, farm buildings and outhouses, chicken sheds – the back to backs of industrial Britain were far away. Mostly there were hills, often rolling wolds, and trees leaning into the prevailing westerly winds. In Lincolnshire, in particular, the scarp overlooking middle England constituted a hazard to all lost airmen: flat fens, then suddenly this sharp ridge buried in cloud. Off the beaten track, much of it, narrow lanes and hedgerow, and thatched cottages draped in honeysuckle. So much that is inescapably English, and where young volunteers from Australia and Canada – as well as Wiltshire and Wales, Durham and Derby – died all too soon. Decades later, you can be sure if you are driving through this half of England – where hazard is a speed camera or a lorry driver on his mobile phone – that somewhere within the nearby fields and hillsides there are the lingering remains of rusting aircraft and young men's lives brought low by war and bad weather, lost over the land for which they were fighting, rather than in the fire and tumult over blazing Berlin.

# MAPS OF THE CRASH SITES

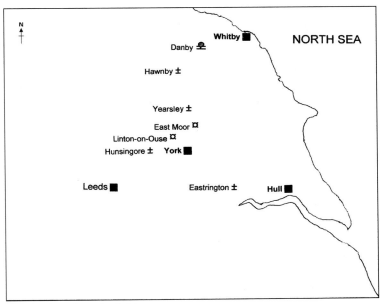

*Black Thursday: Yorkshire*

*Black Thursday: Lincolnshire*

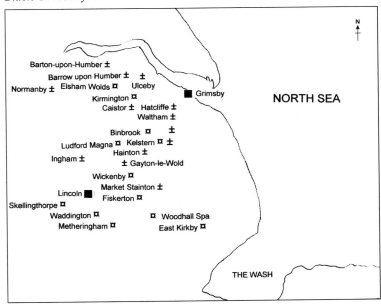

| | |
|---|---|
| ± | : crash site |
| ⚉ | : crew baled out |

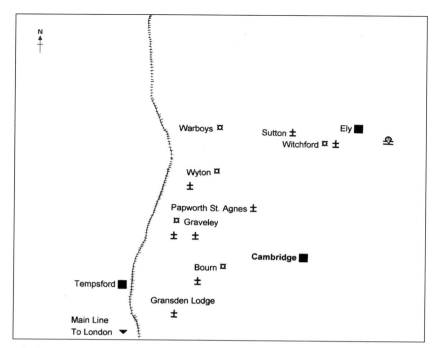

*Black Thursday: Cambridgeshire*

# CRASH LOCATIONS AND DETAILS

| | Location | Pilot | Squadron | Comments |
|---|---|---|---|---|
| 1 | *Murton Common near Hawnby* on the North York Moors. | Flying Officer Russell S Clark | 408 | Clark, a Canadian, hit a wall and outbuildings at Silver Hill Farm on high ground in north Yorkshire. He survived until 21 December. Four other crew members died, but two of the gunners survived. The farm is now ruined. |
| 2 | *Hunsingore, Yorkshire.* Four miles NE of Wetherby and six miles from Linton-on-Ouse. | Flight Sergeant R D Stewart | 426 | Stewart, the Canadian pilot, was killed. Relatively inexperienced, he had done two 'dickey' trips to Berlin, and his first operation had been in October: he had returned early with technical problems. Four other crew members died, but two of the gunners survived, including Sergeant D S Jamieson, from Winnipeg, Manitoba. He was not to survive the war, being shot by the Gestapo in 1944. |
| 3 | *Yearsley, Yorkshire.* Fifteen miles N of York; ten miles NE of Linton. | Squadron Leader Thomas M Kneale | 426 | Squadron Leader Kneale was another Canadian. Aged twenty-nine, he was from Woodstock, Ontario. He had completed sixteen sorties and was commander of B Flight: he had therefore commanded Roger Coulombe (see text). It appears that the aircraft flew into the hill top where the village cross roads are and crashed across the road narrowly missing houses and other buildings. |
| 4 | *Danby Beacon, Yorkshire.* | Flying Officer H B Hatfield | 432 | Hatfield and his crew baled out over Castleton; they were out of fuel and had been diverted to Leeming. They all survived, landing on high moorland on the slopes of Danby Beacon, not far from the North Sea. The aircraft came to rest in boggy land near Danby. |

| | Location | Pilot | Squadron | Comments |
|---|---|---|---|---|
| 5 | *Eastrington* near Howden in East Yorkshire. | Sergeant N M Cooper | 101 | Six of the crew died when Cooper crashed trying to land at Holme-upon-Spalding Moor. Six crew members, including a second pilot, died. The two gunners survived. |
| 6 | *Hainton, Lincolnshire* – between Louth and Lincoln, some six miles from the base at Wickenby. | Flight Sergeant H Ross | 12 | The crew all died, though the rear gunner survived for several days. The crew was a novice one, and the navigator was 'Pop' Walker (see text) who had been a navigator instructor but who, at the age of thirty-one, had volunteered for operations. The Lancaster hit army lorries parked in the grounds of Hainton Hall which had been requisitioned for the war. |
| 7 | *North Sea.* | Sergeant J Hinde | 57 | Ditched in the North Sea on return; only wireless operator Flight Sergeant Hurley survived, having been drifting at sea for thirty-six hours. (See 'Ditched' in main text.) |
| 8 | *Wyton, Cambridgeshire.* | Pilot Officer F F McLean | 83 | With one exception, the crew escaped despite crashing – and nearly colliding with Wing Commander Joe Northrop on approaching Wyton. The bomb aimer Greg Tankard died. McLean died over Brest eight months later. |
| 9 | *Papworth St Agnes, Cambridgeshire.* | Flight Sergeant I M Scott | 97 | Crashed close to Graveley airfield. All seven crew members died. |
| 10 | *Bourn, Cambridgeshire.* | Squadron Leader D F MacKenzie | 97 | Four survivors from this crash which occurred at Two Pots farmhouse, opposite the entrance to RAF Bourn, on the main Bedford to Cambridge road. |
| 11 | *Bourn, Cambridgeshire.* | Flying Officer E Thackway | 97 | Crashed near Highfield Farm to the east of Bourn airfield. There were two survivors. |

| | Location | Pilot | Squadron | Comments |
|---|---|---|---|---|
| 12 | *Hayley Wood, close to Gransden Lodge airfield, Cambridgeshire.* | Pilot Officer J Kirkwood | 97 | All seven crew members died when the Lancaster came down in woodland close to the Sandy to Cambridge railway line. |
| 13 | *Graveley, Cambridgeshire.* | Squadron Leader E A Deverill | 97 | Crashed at Graveley with the loss of six crew; one of the gunners survived. The search for Deverill's grave in a Norfolk churchyard is described in the main text. Rear gunner Donald Penfold figures in this book's introduction. |
| 14 | *North Sea.* | Flying Officer R L Mooney | 97 | The crew baled out over Ely, and the aircraft came down in the North Sea. Mooney went missing over Berlin two weeks later. |
| 15 | *Iken Common, near Sudbourne, Suffolk.* | Pilot Officer F Smith | 97 | Smith was on his first operation. He and his crew baled out – short of fuel – and the aircraft came down close to the North Sea in land that had been requisitioned by the MOD for tank training. |
| 16 | *Kelstern, Lincolnshire.* | Wing Commander D Holford | 100 | Holford was squadron commander and highly experienced. His wife was waiting for him in a nearby hotel. Dazzled by lights, he crashed close to the base at Kelstern and was found the following morning in a snowdrift at the side of the road. Two crew members survived. |
| 17 | *Hatcliffe Top, Lincolnshire.* | Flying Officer R Proudfoot | 100 | The aircraft hit high ground near Waltham airfield; the Lancaster damaged farm buildings. Proudfoot and three other crew members died. |
| 18 | *Waltham, near Grimsby, Lincolnshire.* | Flight Sergeant A J Kevis | 100 | Kevis's aircraft collided with that of another 100 Squadron member (see next row) close to the airfield. No one survived. |
| 19 | *Waltham, near Grimsby, Lincolnshire.* | Sergeant G C Denman | 100 | Denman's aircraft collided with that of another 100 Squadron member (see above) close to the airfield. The rear gunner survived. |

| | Location | Pilot | Squadron | Comments |
|---|---|---|---|---|
| 20 | Ingham, Lincolnshire. | Flying Officer Lazenby | 101 | The crew baled out and all survived. |
| 21 | Ulceby, Lincolnshire. | Flight Sergeant V Richter | 103 | Collided soon after take-off with another aircraft (see below) near the village of Ulceby, a few miles from Elsham Wolds. No survivors. |
| 22 | Sutton, Cambridgeshire. | Flight Sergeant Watkins | 156 | One survivor of this crash – the rear gunner. |
| 23 | Barrow upon Humber, Lincolnshire. | Flight Sergeant A E Brown | 166 | Crashed on return trying to locate Kirmington. No survivors. |
| 24 | Caistor, Lincolnshire. | Sergeant S F Miller | 166 | Crashed on return trying to locate Kirmington. No survivors. |
| 25 | Yelling, Cambridgeshire. | Flying Officer B A McLennan | 405 | The rear gunner was the only survivor of this crash, close to Graveley airfield, at Ingle's Farm. |
| 26 | Graveley, Cambridgeshire. | Flight Lieutenant W Allan | 405 | Three died in this crash several miles from the Graveley airfield. |
| 27 | Normenby, Lincolnshire. | Warrant Officer M Stafford | 460 | Faced with difficulties, this crew had voted to attempt to make it home because of the impending fatherhood of the rear gunner, Pilot Officer Garment. When the Lancaster crashed, he was the only crew member to die. |
| 28 | Market Stainton, Lincolnshire | Flying Officer F A Randall | 460 | No survivors from this Australian piloted crew whose aircraft hit a bomb dump in woods near Ludford Magna. |
| 29 | Binbrook, Lincolnshire | Flight Sergeant K J Godwin | 460 | Crash-landed short of the airfield. The crew all survived. |

| | Location | Pilot | Squadron | Comments |
|---|---|---|---|---|
| 30 | Ulceby, Lincolnshire | Flight Sergeant F R Scott | 576 | Collided soon after take-off with another aircraft (see above) near the village of Ulceby, a few miles from Elsham Wolds. No survivors. |
| 31 | Gayton-le-Wold, Lincolnshire | Second Lieutenant G E Woolley | 625 | Woolley and four crew members survived. |
| 32 | North Sea | Flight Sergeant T M Thomas | 138 | On SOE operations; crashed in the sea off Harwich. Four died in this Halifax. |
| 33 | Capel Green Suffolk | Flight Sergeant J G A Watson | 138 | SOE again; on return from France Watson tried to bring the Halifax down at the FIDO-lit Woodbridge aerodrome. Hit trees at 0530 on the 17th. Four deaths including the pilot. |
| 34 | North Sea | Flying Officer R W Johnson | 138 | SOE. The crew baled out of their Halifax and the aircraft crashed into the sea off Felixstowe. |
| 35 | Tangmere, Sussex | Flying Officer J McBride | 161 | Returning from France in a Lysander with two agents aboard; crashed just short of the runway. McBride was trapped in the cockpit and died. The agents survived. |
| 36 | Ford, Sussex | Flight Lieutenant S Hankey | 161 | Returning from France in a Lysander; hit a hill and crashed. Pilot and two agents died. |
| 37 | Capel St Andrew, Suffolk | Flight Lieutenant S N Gray | 161 | Early return from operations in France; tried to get down, using FIDO at Woodbridge. Hit trees at 5.05 in the morning, 17th December. |
| 38 | River Deben, Felixstowe | Flying Officer D R Harborow | 161 | Hit a wooden receiver mast on the Suffolk coast; aircraft came down in the river near the ferry at Felixstowe. One man drowned. |
| 39 | North Sea | Warrant Officer W A Caldwell | 161 | Crew baled out on early return from France over Spilsby, Lincolnshire. One injury. Aircraft hit the sea off Skegness. |

| | Location | Pilot | Squadron | Comments |
|---|---|---|---|---|
| 40 | Barton-upon-Humber | Flying Officer G M Russell-Fry | 103 | Crashed into a ploughed field near Barton. |
| 41 | Witchford, Cambridgeshire | Flying Officer W W Ryder | 115 | 'On return, collided with Stirling aircraft over base, causing considerable damage to tail, but managed to land without further damage being caused.'[1] |
| 42 | Wickenby | Warrant Officer T J Bassett | 576 | ORB refers to 'crash landing' – three injured. |
| 43 | Kelstern | Warrant Officer E S Ellis | 625 | Overshot the runway at base; hit the ground with his wing, and belly landed. |

# AVERAGE FLIGHT TIMES

This table comprises the average times for each squadron on the Berlin raid on 16 December 1943. It is based on data in the Squadron ORBs.

| Squadron | Average flight time |
|---|---|
| 7 | 7 hours 52 minutes |
| 9 | 7.11 |
| 12 | 7.49 |
| 44 | 7.39 |
| 49 | 7.46 |
| 50 | 7.45 |
| 57 | 7.26 |
| 61 | 7.38 |
| 83 | 7.29 |
| 97 | 7.32 |
| 100 | 7.19 |
| 101 | 7.46 |
| 103 | 7.19 |
| 106 | 7.34 |
| 115 | 6.50 |
| 156 | 7.06 |
| 166 | 7.22 |
| 207 | 7.25 |
| 405 | 7.45 |
| 408 | 7.14 |
| 426 | 7.21 |
| 432 | 6.54 |
| 460 | 7.25 |
| 463 | 7.30 |
| 467 | 7.22 |
| 514 | 7.14 |
| 550 | 7.41 |
| 576 | 7.21 |
| 619 | 7.49 |
| 625 | 7.32 |
| 626 | 7.56 |
| 630 | 7.26 |
| **Average for all pilots** | **7.30** |

# CRASHES ON RETURN

The table below was drawn up by the Operational Research Section during the war. It illustrates the particular difficulties associated with inexperienced pilots crashing on return. Figures are for actual crashes.

| Ops completed | 0–5 | 6–11 | 12–17 | 18–23 | 24–29 | 2nd tour: 0–10 | Over 10 |
|---|---|---|---|---|---|---|---|
| 1 Group | 20 | 10 | 4 | 3 | 2 | 1 | 0 |
| 5 Group | 2 | 3 | 1 | 0 | 0 | 0 | 0 |
| 8 Group | 8 | 2 | 5 | 1 | 0 | 0 | 1 |
| 3 Group | 4 | 1 | 0 | 0 | 1 | 0 | 1 |
| 6 Group | 2 | 2 | 1 | 1 | 0 | 0 | 0 |

# APPENDIX D

# THE REASONS FOR EARLY RETURNS, 16 DECEMBER 1943

| Number | Squadron | Reason |
|--------|----------|--------|
| 1 | 7 | 'Main planes appeared to be buckling.' |
| 2 | 12 | CSU u/s. |
| 3 | 12 | Intercom u/s. |
| 4 | 12 | Problems climbing. |
| 5 | 12 | Starboard inner engine u/s. |
| 6 | 57 | H2S and DR u/s. |
| 7 | 61 | W/T u/s. |
| 8 | 83 | Turret u/s. |
| 9 | 100 | Problems with starboard outer engine. |
| 10 | 101 | Overheating starboard outer engine. |
| 11 | 101 | Oxygen failure. |
| 12 | 103 | Leak in oxygen supply. |
| 13 | 103 | Port inner engine u/s. |
| 14 | 103 | Unable to extinguish lights. |
| 15 | 115 | Rear turret u/s. |
| 16 | 115 | Intercom failure; rear turret u/s. |
| 17 | 156 | No oxygen in mid-upper turret; gunner passed out. |
| 18 | 166 | Starboard outer engine lost oil pressure; overheating. |
| 19 | 166 | Starboard outer engine coolant leak. |
| 20 | 166 | Could not maintain height: 'no fault ascertainable.' |
| 21 | 426 | Engine failure. |
| 22 | 426 | Rear turret u/s: covered in oil. |
| 23 | 460 | Starboard inner engine u/s. |
| 24 | 463 | No explanation. |
| 25 | 467 | Intercom not operating; DR u/s. |
| 26 | 514 | Hydraulics problems: unable to raise undercarriage. |
| 27 | 550 | Coolant leak; WT/RT, DR compass and Sperry panel all u/s. |
| 28 | 550 | Rear turret u/s. |
| 29 | 576 | Low oil pressure: port engine. |
| 30 | 625 | Starboard inner engine overheated: could not climb over 8,000 feet. |
| 31 | 625 | Heavy leak in oxygen system. |
| 32 | 625 | Unable to climb. |
| 33 | 626 | Overheating outer engines. |
| 34 | 626 | Mid-upper gunner ill (short of oxygen). |
| 35 | 630 | CSU failed. |

APPENDIX E

# BLACK THURSDAY: CRASH CAUSES (DERIVED FROM FORM 1180)

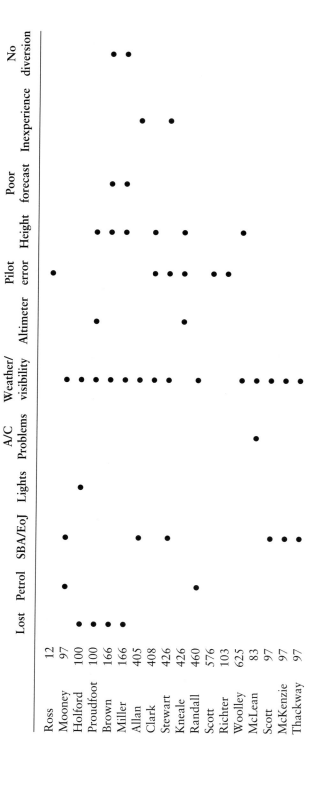

| | | Lost | Petrol | SBA/EoJ | Lights | A/C Problems | Weather/visibility | Altimeter | Pilot error | Height | Poor forecast | Inexperience | No diversion |
|---|---|---|---|---|---|---|---|---|---|---|---|---|---|
| Kirkwood | 97 | | | ● | | | ● | | | | | | |
| Deverill | 97 | | | ● | | | ● | | | | | | |
| Smith | 97 | | ● | ● | | | ● | | | | | | |
| Denman | 100 | | | | ● | | ● | | | | | | |
| Kevis | 100 | | | | ● | | ● | | | | | | |
| Lazenby | 101 | | ● | | | | ● | | | | | | |
| Cooper | 101 | ● | ● | | | | ● | ● | ● | | ● | | |
| Watkins | 156 | ● | | | ● | | ● | | | | | | |
| McLennan | 405 | | | ● | | | ● | | | | | ● | |
| Drew | 405 | | | ● | | | ● | | | | | ● | |
| Hatfield | 432 | ● | ● | | | | ● | | | ● | | | |
| Godwin | 460 | | | | | ● | ● | | | | | | |
| **TOTALS** | | 7 | 6 | 12 | 4 | 2 | 26 | 3 | 7 | 7 | 3 | 4 | 2 |

APPENDIX F

# PILOTS FLYING ON BLACK THURSDAY

| Squadron and Base | Pilot | Took off | Landed | Notes |
|---|---|---|---|---|
| **7 (Oakington)** | | | | |
| *8 Group* | Flight Lieutenant JR Petrie | 16.20 | 18.35 | **Shot down.** |
| | Flight Lieutenant DLC Thomas | 16.20 | 00.28 | **Early Return:** 'Main planes buckling.' |
| | Squadron Leader LV Harcourt | 16.15 | 00.01 | |
| | Wing Commander RE Young | 16.16 | | **Diverted:** Little Snoring, Flak damage. |
| | Pilot Officer G Tyler | 16.21 | | **Shot down.** |
| | Warrant Officer WA Watson | 16.24 | | **Shot down.** |
| | Squadron Leader PKW Patrick | 16.19 | 00.30 | **Diverted:** Marham. |
| | Flying Officer FW Rush | 16.17 | | **Shot down.** |
| | Squadron Leader AD Saunders | 16.18 | 00.32 | |
| | Flight Lieutenant JA Hegman | 16.29 | 00.25 | Flak damage. |
| | Flight Lieutenant P Williams | 16.31 | 23.55 | |
| | Flight Sergeant J Napier | 16.22 | 00.35 | **Diverted:** Waterbeach. |
| | Pilot Officer J Mee | 16.26 | 00.46 | **Diverted:** Downham Market. |
| | Flight Lieutenant D Dunlop | 16.32 | 00.45 | |
| | Flying Officer MS Evans | 16.30 | 00.40 | **Diverted:** Marham. |
| | Flight Sergeant RJ Sexton | 16.28 | 00.20 | |
| | Flying Officer RJ Croxford | 16.16 | 23.35 | |
| | Pilot Officer EA Pearman | 16.32 | 00.20 | |
| | Flight Sergeant NJ Clifford | 16.52 | 23.57 | |
| | Flight Lieutenant J Newton | 16.27 | 23.46 | |
| | Flight Lieutenant LC Kingsbury | 16.25 | 00.18 | |

| Squadron and Base | Pilot | Took off | Landed | Notes |
|---|---|---|---|---|
| **9 (Bardney)** **5 Group** | Flying Officer CP Newton | 16.39 | 23.55 | This Lancaster completed over 100 operations. |
| | Flight Sergeant AJ Jubb | 16.57 | 00.19 | |
| | Pilot Officer ICB Black | 16.47 | | Shot down. |
| | Flying Officer JV Comans | 16.44 | 00.14 | |
| | Sergeant RW Plowright | 16.59 | 23.56 | |
| | Flight Lieutenant LG Hadland | 16.51 | 23.52 | |
| | Pilot Officer FL Porter | 16.48 | 00.10 | |
| | Flight Sergeant RLC Lasham | 17.00 | 00.10 | |
| | Flight Sergeant WWW Turnbull | 16.41 | 00.24 | |
| | Flying Officer W Reid | 16.45 | 23.59 | |
| | Pilot Officer H Blow | 16.42 | 23.58 | |
| | Pilot Officer RA Bayldon | 16.43 | | Shot down. |
| | Flight Lieutenant JF Mitchell | 16.46 | 23.54 | |
| **12 (Wickenby)** **1 Group** | Sergeant A Twitchett | 16.23 | 23.56 | One combat en route. |
| | Squadron Leader H Goole | 15.51 | 23.19 | On second tour. |
| | Flying Officer D Lighton | 16.11 | 23.28 | |
| | Pilot Officer C Grannum | 15.49 | 23.49 | First aircraft to take off. |
| | Sergeant J Hawkesley-Hill | 16.24 | 23.43 | |
| | Pilot Officer KL West | 16.02 | 00.05 | |
| | Sergeant PD Wright | 16.10 | 00.10 | |
| | Sergeant DM Maxwell | 16.19 | 18.07 | **Early Return:** intercom not functioning. |
| | Warrant Officer EJ Norton | 16.07 | 18.11 | **Early Return:** starboard outer engine u/s; also CSU. |
| | Squadron Leader Woollatt | 15.56 | 00.27 | H2S u/s. |
| | Pilot Officer RS Yell | 16.08 | 00.04 | Starboard engine failed at 21.34. |
| | Sgt TC Rogers | 16.36 | 19.18 | **Early Return:** unable to maintain height. |
| | Pilot Officer K Smitheringale | 15.58 | 19.50 | **Early Return:** starboard inner engine failed. |

| Squadron and Base | Pilot | Took off | Landed | Notes |
|---|---|---|---|---|
| | Flight Lieutenant WF Snell | 15.57 | 00.18 | |
| | Flight Sergeant HR Ross | 16.14 | | **Crashed:** at Hainton, Lincolnshire. Approximate time in Form 1180: 23.45. |
| 44 (Dunholme Lodge) 1 Group | Squadron Leader A Lynch | 16.24 | 00.18 | |
| | Flight Lieutenant CH Hunter | 16.31 | 00.29 | |
| | Pilot Officer DA Rollin | 16.21 | | **Shot down.** |
| | Pilot Officer RM Higgs | 16.28 | 23.48 | 'Met accurate' – pilot's comment in the ORB. |
| | Flight Sergeant L Curatole | 16.38 | 23.59 | |
| | Flying Officer E Mercer | 16.20 | 00.05 | |
| | Pilot Officer J Bradburn | 16.55 | 00.01 | |
| | Pilot Officer C Oakley | 16.36 | 00.13 | 'Met accurate especially forecast on way back.' |
| | Pilot Officer RWG Evans | 16.33 | 00.37 | |
| | Flight Sergeant E Barton | 16.34 | 00.15 | Shot at Me 109 which blew up. |
| | Pilot Officer RTH Manning | 16.30 | 00.33 | |
| | Pilot Officer TH Knight | 16.29 | 23.38 | |
| | Pilot Officer A Wright | 16.47 | 00.14 | |
| | Pilot Officer PH Smith | 16.46 | 00.39 | |
| 49 (Fiskerton) 1 Group | Pilot Officer G Roantree | 16.22 | 00.25 | |
| | Pilot Officer GP George | 16.23 | 00.12 | |
| | Flying Officer WA Healey | 16.32 | 00.43 | |
| | Flying Officer DJ Bacon | 16.30 | 00.53 | 'Poor visibility on return.' |
| | Flying Officer R Hidderley | 16.32 | 00.22 | 'Very quiet trip.' |
| | Pilot Officer RH Ewens | 16.19 | 00.46 | Damaged by enemy fighter; GEE u/s. Pilot completed tour. |
| | Warrant Officer E Jones | 16.17 | 00.05 | |
| | Warrant Officer T Jupp | 16.01 | 23.35 | |
| | Pilot Officer GJ Young | 16.33 | 00.35 | |

| Squadron and Base | Pilot | Took off | Landed | Notes |
|---|---|---|---|---|
| | Pilot Officer GL Ratcliffe | 16.27 | | **Shot down.** First trip. |
| | Flying Officer CJ Palmer | 16.25 | 23.53 | |
| | Pilot Officer K Barnes | 16.35 | 00.06 | |
| | Flight Lieutenant AT Tancred | 16.26 | 23.44 | 'Exceptionally good route.' |
| | Pilot Officer A Blackmore | 16.29 | 00.20 | |
| | Squadron Leader D Miller | 16.28 | 23.32 | H2S u/s. 'Successful sortie.' |
| | Pilot Officer L Coxill | 16.31 | 23.40 | 'No fighters seen.' |
| 50 (Skellingthorpe) *5 Group* | Pilot Officer D Toovey | 16.49 | 00.08 | |
| | Flight Lieutenant J Edward | 16.20 | 00.01 | |
| | Flying Officer J Lees | 16.22 | 00.03 | |
| | Flying Officer W Smith | 16.27 | 00.14 | |
| | Flying Officer J Mackandler | 16.41 | 00.05 | |
| | Sergeant Lloyd | 16.48 | 00.17 | |
| | Flight Lieutenant Burtt | 16.23 | 00.13 | |
| | Flight Lieutenant McAlpine | 16.37 | 00.46 | |
| | Flight Sergeant R Leader | 16.45 | 00.30 | |
| | Sergeant R Thornton | 16.38 | 00.27 | |
| | Flying Officer M Robinson | 16.25 | 00.20 | Diverted: Spilsby. |
| | Pilot Officer JL Dobbyn | 16.45 | 00.42 | |
| | Sergeant Taylor | 16.44 | 00.36 | |
| 57 (East Kirkby) *5 Group* | Flying Officer C Lyon | 16.35 | 00.10 | |
| | Pilot Officer J Ludford | 16.30 | 00.30 | |
| | Pilot Officer AW Fearn | 16.29 | 00.09 | |
| | Flight Lieutenant RV Munday | 16.27 | 00.22 | |
| | Flying Officer N Harland | 17.02 | 00.13 | |
| | Flight Sergeant S Atcheson | 16.37 | 00.27 | |

| Squadron and Base | Pilot | Took off | Landed | Notes |
|---|---|---|---|---|
| | Flight Sergeant J McGillivray | 16.54 | 18.52 | Early Return: H2S and DR u/s. |
| | Pilot Officer KC McPhie | 16.50 | 23.39 | |
| | Pilot Officer KD Smith | 16.51 | 23.57 | |
| | Squadron Leader AW Howard | 16.24 | 23.45 | |
| | Flight Lieutenant CJ Spriggs | 16.38 | 00.38 | |
| | Pilot Officer AO Wright | 16.23 | 23.26 | |
| | Sergeant J Hinde | 16.25 | | Crashed: North Sea. Flight Sergeant Hurley rescued. |
| | Pilot Officer SG Townsend | 16.20 | 23.37 | |
| | Pilot Officer GL Grimbly | 16.47 | 23.47 | RAAF. |
| 61 (Skellingthorpe) 5 Group | Flight Lieutenant N Webb | 16.26 | 00.09 | |
| | Flight Lieutenant N Turner | 16.21 | 23.25 | |
| | Pilot Officer GA Berry | 16.24 | 23.45 | |
| | Pilot Officer H Wallis | 16.33 | 19.12 | Early Return: W/T u/s. |
| | Flight Sergeant FW Burgess | 16.39 | 00.43 | |
| | Sergeant CJ Gray | 16.19 | 00.11 | |
| | Flight Lieutenant C Harvey | 16.36 | 00.46 | |
| | Flying Officer H Scott | 16.22 | 23.39 | |
| | Flying Officer B Fitch | 16.35 | 00.19 | Diverted: Woodhall. |
| | Flying Officer RP Cunningham | 16.46 | 00.21 | Shook off fighter attacks. |
| | Flying Officer RA West | 16.42 | 00.39 | Rear gunner's oxygen mask froze. First operation. |
| | Pilot Officer JW Einarson | 16.17 | 00.05 | |
| | Pilot Officer J McLean | 16.47 | 23.56 | |
| | Pilot Officer V McConnell | 16.32 | 00.06 | |
| 83 (Wyton) 8 Group | Pilot Officer R King | 16.32 | 23.45 | |
| | Pilot Officer RA Hellier | 16.34 | 00.14 | |
| | Flight Lieutenant AC Shipway | 16.37 | 23.26 | |

| Squadron and Base | Pilot | Took off | Landed | Notes |
|---|---|---|---|---|
| | Flight Lieutenant LH Tolchard | 16.33 | 23.36 | |
| | Flight Lieutenant FC Allcroft | 16.35 | 00.20 | |
| | Flight Lieutenant MR Chick | 16.26 | 23.42 | |
| | Flight Lieutenant AHJ Sambridge | 16.30 | 00.16 | |
| | Flying Officer DH Pidding | 16.28 | 19.30 | **Early Return:** Turret u/s. |
| | Flight Lieutenant FJ Garvey | 16.36 | 23.44 | |
| | Pilot Officer TB Field | 16.29 | 23.59 | |
| | Pilot Officer G Ransom | 16.27 | 23.54 | |
| | Flying Officer WK Button | 16.40 | 00.10 | |
| | Squadron Leader J Northrop | 16.38 | 00.43 | Close encounter with Pilot Officer McLean. |
| | Pilot Officer FE McLean | 16.39 | 00.40 | **Crashed:** on landing at Wyton 'owing to nil visibility.' |
| | | | | |
| 97 (Bourn) 8 *Group* | Flight Lieutenant W Riches | 16.40 | 00.15 | |
| | Flight Lieutenant G De Wesselow | 16.40 | 00.50 | Survived fighter attack en route. |
| | Flight Lieutenant J Pelletier | 16.40 | 00.05 | |
| | Flying Officer J Nicholls | 16.55 | 00.25 | |
| | Flight Lieutenant C Wilson | 16.55 | 23.50 | Damaged on landing. |
| | Pilot Officer Billing | 17.00 | 00.35 | |
| | Pilot Officer V Flack | 17.00 | 00.35 | |
| | Flight Lieutenant D Brill | 16.55 | | **Shot down.** |
| | Squadron Leader D McKenzie | 16.45 | 00.45 | **Crashed:** on return to base. 1180 has 00.42. |
| | Squadron Leader EF Cawdery | 16.50 | 00.35 | |
| | Flight Lieutenant J Roberts | 16.55 | 00.15 | |
| | Flight Lieutenant C Owen | 16.55 | 00.05 | 'Dangerous landing.' |
| | Pilot Officer CR Snell | 16.40 | 23.25 | Low cloud down to 400 feet. |
| | Flight Lieutenant P Mansbridge | 16.50 | 00.50 | **Baled out.** |
| | Pilot Officer P Smith | 17.00 | | |

| Squadron and Base | Pilot | Took off | Landed | Notes |
|---|---|---|---|---|
| | Flight Sergeant IW Scott | 16.50 | | Crashed. |
| | Squadron Leader EA Deverill | 16.45 | 00.15 | Crashed: at Graveley. |
| | Pilot Officer J Kirkwood | 16.50 | 00.10 | Crashed: near Gransden Lodge. |
| | Flying Officer RL Mooney | 17.05 | 00.35 | Baled out. On his second tour. A/c lost at sea. |
| | Flying Officer E Thackway | 16.55 | 01.00 | Crashed. |
| | Sergeant Coates | 17.00 | 01.30 | Diverted: Downham Market. Returned on two engines. |
| 100 (Waltham) 1 Group | Flying Officer DF Gillam | 16.05 | 00.28 | |
| | Flying Officer R Richmond | 16.16 | 23.29 | |
| | Warrant Officer TV Heyes | 16.17 | 23.34 | |
| | Pilot Officer CW Henderson | 16.26 | 23.20 | |
| | Flying Officer RL Proudfoot | 16.18 | | Crashed: aircraft 'wrecked', four miles from base at Hatcliffe Top. |
| | Flight Lieutenant KA Major | 16.09 | 23.19 | |
| | Flight Sergeant PR Neale | 16.19 | 23.23 | |
| | Flying Officer GR Sidebottom | 16.30 | 23.46 | Received two small flak holes. |
| | Wing Commander DW Holford | 16.13 | | Crashed: at Kelstern, Lincolnshire. |
| | Flying Officer VLP Jones | 16.17 | 23.32 | |
| | Flight Sergeant AJ Kevis | 16.11 | | Crashed: in collision with Sergeant Denman (below) 'just south of base.' |
| | Pilot Officer LJ Stow | 16.28 | 23.27 | |
| | Sergeant JA Crabtree | 16.25 | 23.55 | |
| | Sergeant GC Denman | 16.46 | | Crashed: with Flight Sergeant Kevis (above). |
| | Flight Sergeant GJA Smith | 16.29 | 00.34 | |
| | Flight Sergeant DE Jameson | 16.31 | 18.09 | Early Return: abandoned over base – problems with the starboard outer engine. |
| | Flying Officer RM Parker | 16.33 | 00.13 | |

| Squadron and Base | Pilot | Took off | Landed | Notes |
|---|---|---|---|---|
| **101 (Ludford Magna)** *1 Group* | Flight Sergeant GA Murphy | 16.20 | 00.05 | **Diverted:** to Faldingworth; insufficient petrol so crew baled out from 2,500 feet. |
| | Flying Officer AL Lazenby | 16.17 | 00.02 | **Diverted:** to Lindholme. |
| | Pilot Officer JD Syne | 16.05 | 23.55 | |
| | Pilot Officer RA Nightingale | 16.15 | 23.55 | |
| | Flight Sergeant J Batten-Smith | 16.20 | 00.50 | |
| | Pilot Officer JW Slater | 16.10 | 23.50 | |
| | Pilot Officer DW McConnell | 16.20 | 00.05 | |
| | Flight Sergeant PF Rowe | 16.20 | 00.05 | |
| | Flight Lieutenant WR McKay | 16.05 | 23.35 | |
| | Flying Officer DH Todd | 16.25 | 00.15 | |
| | Flying Officer RR Leeder | 16.10 | 19.45 | **Early Return:** starboard outer engine overheating. |
| | Flight Lieutenant WD Austin | 16.10 | 23.25 | |
| | Pilot Officer NA Marsh | 16.10 | 23.50 | |
| | Pilot Officer BN Dickenson | 16.25 | 21.20 | **Early Return:** oxygen failure. |
| | Flight Sergeant PE Head | | | **Shot down:** 'no communication after take-off.' |
| | Flying Officer RE MacFarlane | | | **Shot down:** 'no communication after take-off' |
| | Sergeant NM Cooper | | | **Crashed:** two miles north of Eastrington, East Yorkshire. Form 1180: crash at 00.27. |
| **103 (Elsham Wolds)** *1 Group* | Flying Officer GM Russell-Fry | 16.45 | 23.34 | **Crashed:** in a ploughed field near Barton upon Humber. Fit enough to fly again on 23/12/43. |
| | Flight Sergeant HS Rathbone | 16.28 | 19.58 | **Early Return:** leak in oxygen supply. |
| | Flight Lieutenant RF Griffin | 16.40 | 00.25 | |
| | Pilot Officer J Hart | 16.47 | 00.11 | |
| | Flying Officer HD Churchill | 16.22 | 00.10 | **Diverted:** to Lindholme. |
| | Pilot Officer L Young | 16.38 | 19.35 | **Early Return:** port inner engine u/s. Bombed Texel. |

| Squadron and Base | Pilot | Took off | Landed | Notes |
|---|---|---|---|---|
| | Squadron Leader JA Whittet | 16.42 | 19.40 | **Early Return:** unable to extinguish lights. Bombed Texel. |
| | Flight Sergeant M McMahon | 17.00 | 23.47 | **Diverted:** to Kirmington. |
| | Flight Sergeant H Campbell | 16.30 | | **Shot down.** |
| | Warrant Officer BB Lydon | 16.33 | 23.37 | |
| | Flight Sergeant HT Griffin | 16.43 | 00.18 | |
| | Flight Sergeant V Richter | 16.37 | | **Crashed:** in collision with 576 a/c piloted by Flight Sergeant Scott over Ulceby, Lincolnshire. |
| | Pilot Officer JH Warren | 16.31 | 23.58 | |
| | Pilot Officer ET Jones | 16.58 | 00.10 | |
| | Warrant Officer NH Frost | | | Did not take off. |
| 106 (Metheringham) *5 Group* | Flight Lieutenant M Boyle | 16.25 | 00.20 | |
| | Flight Lieutenant TG Claridge | 16.25 | 23.55 | |
| | Pilot Officer NJ Callan | 16.25 | 23.50 | |
| | Flying Officer V Cole | 16.20 | 23.20 | 'Quiet trip.' |
| | Flight Sergeant GS Milne | 16.25 | 00.05 | 'Uneventful.' |
| | Pilot Officer D Gibbs | 16.30 | 00.25 | |
| | Pilot Officer EG Holbourne | 16.40 | 00.15 | |
| | Flight Lieutenant IR Harvey | 16.30 | 23.55 | |
| | Flying Officer RC Benfield | 16.45 | 00.15 | |
| | Pilot Officer RF Anderson | 16.30 | 00.05 | |
| | Pilot Officer R Starkey | 16.30 | 00.10 | |
| | Flight Lieutenant CJ Ginder | 16.50 | 00.25 | 'Quiet and uneventful trip with no incidents of interest.' |
| | Flight Lieutenant J Forsyth | 16.20 | 23.50 | Contact with Ju88. |
| | Flying Officer W Perry | 16.45 | 00.20 | |
| | Pilot Officer CH Storer | 16.35 | | **Shot down.** |

| Squadron and Base | Pilot | Took off | Landed | Notes |
|---|---|---|---|---|
| **115 (Witchford)** **3 Group** | Flight Sergeant R Anderson | 16.55 | 18.45 | **Early Return:** Rear turret u/s. |
| | Pilot Officer F Blackwell | 16.55 | 23.20 | **Diverted:** to Foulsham, Norfolk. |
| | Flight Lieutenant JH Christiansen | 17.00 | 23.40 | **Diverted:** to Foulsham, Norfolk. |
| | Pilot Officer N Newton | 17.12 | | **Shot down.** A new aircraft. |
| | Pilot Officer EH Boutilier | 16.30 | 00.05 | **Diverted:** to Foulsham, Norfolk. Unable to return to base until 19.12.43. |
| | Flight Lieutenant RL Barnes | 16.45 | 23.30 | **Diverted:** to Foulsham, Norfolk. |
| | Flight Sergeant R Milgate | 16.50 | 23.50 | **Diverted:** to Little Snoring. |
| | Flight Sergeant G Hammond | 16.50 | 23.30 | **Diverted:** to Coltishall. |
| | Pilot Officer AH Howell | 16.50 | 23.20 | **Diverted:** to Foulsham, Norfolk. |
| | Flight Lieutenant GD Seddon | 16.50 | 23.50 | **Diverted:** to Foulsham, Norfolk. |
| | Warrant Officer W Jolly | 17.00 | 22.25 | **Diverted:** to Little Snoring; landing time seems unlikely. |
| | Pilot Officer LJ Halley | 17.00 | 23.50 | **Diverted:** to Foulsham, Norfolk. |
| | Flying Officer WW Ryder | 18.10 | 20.30 | **Early Return/Crash:** intercom failed and rear turret u/s. Bombed Wognum. 'On return, collided with Stirling a/c over base, causing considerable damage to tail, but managed to land without further damage being caused.' |
| | Flight Sergeant S Atkin | 18.00 | 00.55 | **Diverted:** to Swanton Morley. |
| **156 (Warboys)** **8 Group** | Flight Lieutenant C Aubert | 16.28 | | **Shot down.** |
| | Squadron Leader RE Fawcett | 16.37 | 23.28 | |
| | Flight Lieutenant RGF Stewart | 16.38 | 23.14 | |
| | Pilot Officer JH Hewitt | 16.29 | 19.20 | **Early Return:** No oxygen in mid-upper turret – gunner passed out. |
| | Flight Lieutenant MA Sullivan | 16.39 | 23.40 | |
| | Pilot Officer CG Hopton | 16.30 | 23.37 | |

| Squadron and Base | Pilot | Took off | Landed | Notes |
|---|---|---|---|---|
| | Flight Lieutenant JJ Sloper | 16.43 | 23.19 | |
| | Flight Lieutenant LW Overton | 16.45 | 23.54 | |
| | Pilot Officer EC Bagot | 16.45 | 23.47 | |
| | Wing Commander NE Mansfield | 17.05 | 23.33 | |
| | Pilot Officer HF Slade | 16.47 | 00.05 | |
| | Flight Lieutenant K Kilvington | 16.48 | 23.30 | |
| | Flying Officer MC Stimpson | 16.51 | 00.07 | |
| | Flight Sergeant J Cromarty | 16.42 | 23.52 | |
| | Pilot Officer G Palmer | 16.44 | 00.19 | |
| | Pilot Officer GPR Bond | 16.46 | 23.35 | |
| | Pilot Officer J Borland | 16.50 | 00.16 | |
| | Flight Sergeant WH Watkins | 16.36 | | **Crashed:** on the Earith/Sutton road (Cambridgeshire), about 2 m. S. of Sutton – 'cause unknown.' 1180 refers to use of SBA. |
| | Flying Officer SW Little | 16.29 | 23.45 | |
| | Flying Officer DR Illingworth | 16.32 | 00.20 | |
| | Flying Officer PA Watts | 16.34 | 00.10 | |
| 166 (Kirmington) *1 Group* | Sergeant WV Butler | 16.19 | 23.27 | **Diverted:** Binbrook. |
| | Squadron Leader RA Mackie | 16.58 | 23.39 | 'Weather poor, but landed at base.' |
| | Flying Officer RE Hicks | 16.23 | 00.30 | **Diverted:** Docking. |
| | Flight Lieutenant SJ Arnfield | 16.45 | 00.16 | |
| | Warrant Officer SE Phillips | 16.11 | 00.54 | 'Difficult landing at base due to poor weather.' |
| | Warrant Officer JH Catlin | 16.12 | 00.03 | |
| | Pilot Officer L Lindley | 16.40 | 23.49 | |
| | Warrant Officer HE Jupp | 16.19 | 23.27 | |
| | Squadron Leader FS Powley | 16.09 | 23.17 | Problems with icing. |
| | Flight Sergeant B Marshall | 16.31 | 23.54 | |

| Squadron and Base | Pilot | Took off | Landed | Notes |
|---|---|---|---|---|
| | Pilot Officer J Horsley | 16.51 | 23.36 | Saw 'many combats.' |
| | Flight Sergeant RV Fransden | 16.48 | 19.42 | Early Return: starboard outer engine lost oil pressure; overheating. |
| | Pilot Officer W Stammers | 16.17 | 18.42 | Early Return: starboard outer engine coolant leak. |
| | Warrant Officer Woodcock-Stevens | 16.40 | 19.55 | Early Return: unable to maintain height – 'no fault ascertainable.' |
| | Pilot Officer CE Phelps | 16.35 | 23.40 | |
| | Sergeant SF Miller | 16.26 | | Crashed: at Caistor, Lincolnshire. 1180 – at Hundon Moor. |
| | Flying Officer PWR Pollett | 16.11 | | Shot down. |
| | Flight Sergeant AE Brown | 16.20 | | Crashed: 'near Barton on Humber.' |
| | Squadron Leader B Pape | 16.33 | 23.33 | |
| 207 (Spilsby) 5 Group | Squadron Leader DGH Pike | 16.20 | 23.43 | |
| | Flight Lieutenant JG Taylor | 16.34 | 23.52 | 'Fires taking a good hold.' |
| | Pilot Officer R Burnet | 16.23 | 00.17 | |
| | Pilot Officer A Moore | 16.36 | 13.31 | 13.31 in the ORB; more likely 23.31 (clerical error?) |
| | Pilot Officer Moulton-Barrett | 16.26 | 23.38 | |
| | Pilot Officer CW Barnett | 16.29 | 23.25 | 'Satisfactory trip.' |
| | Pilot Officer WH Benton | 16.35 | 23.28 | |
| | Flight Lieutenant RJ Allen | 16.33 | | Shot down. |
| | Pilot Officer JTH Giddens | 16.30 | 00.14 | |
| | Pilot Officer FW Gallagher | 16.27 | 23.50 | |
| | Pilot Officer JW Read | 16.32 | 23.54 | |
| | Pilot Officer DL Davies | 16.31 | 23.55 | |
| | Pilot Officer KA King | 16.21 | 23.49 | |
| | Pilot Officer KL Wright | 16.18 | 23.45 | |
| | Pilot Officer PJ Drane | 16.17 | 23.42 | |

| Squadron and Base | Pilot | Took off | Landed | Notes |
| --- | --- | --- | --- | --- |
| 405 (Gransden Lodge) 8 Group | Wing Commander RJ Lane | 16.43 | 00.14 | |
| | Squadron Leader W Weiser | 16.29 | 00.11 | |
| | Squadron Leader H Cowan | 16.31 | 01.08 | Diverted: to Marham. |
| | Squadron Leader H Sattler | 16.32 | 23.24 | |
| | Flying Officer WBB Cloutier | 16.33 | 23.36 | Diverted: to Bourn ('owing to weather conditions.') |
| | Flight Lieutenant G Bennett | 16.39 | 00.37 | Diverted: to Marham. |
| | Flying Officer AP Campbell | 16.46 | 00.35 | Diverted: to Marham. |
| | Flying Officer AD Fyfe | 16.48 | 01.29 | Diverted: to Warboys. |
| | Flight Sergeant LL McKinnon | 16.40 | 23.47 | |
| | Flying Officer BA McLennan | 16.47 | 00.50 | Crashed: 'lack of petrol and bad weather.' Pilot's seventeenth trip. Rear gunner, Warrant Officer Nutting, survived. It was his forty-fifth and last trip. |
| | Pilot Officer GR Drimmie | 16.34 | 23.45 | Crashed: near Graveley as a result of petrol shortage and bad weather. |
| | Flight Lieutenant WC Allan | 16.36 | 23.58 | |
| | Flying Officer EB Drew | 16.37 | 01.30 | Crashed: near Marham – petrol/ weather. ORB has two crash times (1.30 and 2.25). |
| 408 (Linton) 6 Group | Flying Officer JG White | 16.32 | 00.07 | |
| | Wing Commander DS Jacobs | 16.43 | 00.04 | Diverted: to Tholthorpe. |
| | Flight Lieutenant WA Russell | 16.38 | 23.54 | Diverted: to Tholthorpe. |
| | Flight Sergeant N Sutherland | 16.29 | 23.59 | Diverted: to Tholthorpe. |
| | Pilot Officer KL Bracer | 16.20 | 23.29 | |
| | Warrant Officer RT Lloyd | 16.55 | 00.35 | Abandoned: port inner engine u/s; 'avoided crossing Berlin.' |
| | Flight Lieutenant R Burns | 16.39 | 23.16 | AFI u/s on return. |
| | Second Lieutenant HR Humphrey | 16.24 | 23.45 | Diverted: to Dalton. Ceiling 500 ft. Visibility: 500 yards. 'Unable to locate base.' |
| | Pilot Officer EE Kearl | 16.26 | 23.44 | |

| Squadron and Base | Pilot | Took off | Landed | Notes |
|---|---|---|---|---|
| | Pilot Officer LH Hansen | 16.35 | 00.01 | |
| | Flight Sergeant JD Harvey | 16.40 | 23.37 | |
| | Pilot Officer WR Smith | 16.35 | 23.24 | |
| | Squadron Leader HT Miles | 16.32 | 23.55 | **Diverted:** to Sarkey. |
| | Flying Officer LC Morrison | 16.45 | 23.47 | |
| | Pilot Officer SRW Laine | 16.20 | 23.50 | |
| | Flying Officer WJ Maitland | 16.23 | | **Shot down.** |
| | Flying Officer RS Clark | 16.37 | 23.30 | **Crashed:** on the North York moors south west of Hawnby; Clark had completed eight trips. Navigator tried a GEE fix; 'misjudged their location.' |
| **426 (Linton)** *6 Group* | Squadron Leader RF Epps | 16.18 | 23.31 | |
| | Flight Sergeant RD Stewart | 16.22 | 23.45 | **Crashed:** at Hunsingore, Yorkshire. |
| | Pilot Officer EJ Stuart | 16.12 | 00.03 | |
| | Flight Lieutenant WH Stafford | 16.19 | 19.10 | **Early Return:** engine failure. |
| | Pilot Officer CA Griffiths | 16.34 | 23.41 | |
| | First Lieutenant JK Smith | 16.16 | 23.52 | |
| | Flight Lieutenant LN McCaig | 16.26 | 20.54 | **Early Return:** rear turret u/s – oil-covered. |
| | Pilot Officer S McDonald | 16.41 | 23.51 | |
| | Flying Officer LP Archibald | 16.22 | | **Shot down.** One baled out. |
| | Pilot Officer WF Griffin | 16.28 | 23.55 | **Baled out:** over Sweden and interned. |
| | Pilot Officer A Davies | 16.22 | | Returned on three engines, and with '90 × 4 incendiaries hung up and brought back.' |
| | Flight Sergeant JA Coulombe | 16.36 | 23.56 | **Crashed:** at Yearsley, Yorkshire. |
| | Squadron Leader TM Kneale | 16.30 | 23.31 | |
| **432 (East Moor)** *6 Group* | Flying Officer C Hatfield | 16.57 | 23.53 | **Baled out:** diverted to Leeming, but abandoned through 'technical failures' over North York moors. |
| | Pilot Officer W Headen | 16.56 | 23.53 | |

| Squadron and Base | Pilot | Took off | Landed | Notes |
|---|---|---|---|---|
| | Flight Sergeant W Pay | 16.51 | 23.56 | |
| | Pilot Officer T Spink | 16.58 | 00.05 | |
| | Flight Sergeant G Palmer | 16.52 | 23.44 | |
| | Flight Sergeant P Dennis | 16.55 | 23.46 | |
| | Pilot Officer L Lagace | 17.01 | 23.29 | |
| | Flight Lieutenant W Strachan | 16.54 | 23.55 | Claimed shot down aircraft. |
| | Flight Lieutenant C Wales | 16.53 | 23.38 | |
| | Flying Officer WC Fisher | 16.59 | | Shot down. The pilot's seventeenth operation. |
| 460 (Binbrook) 1 Group | Pilot Officer HG Carter | 16.14 | 23.20 | |
| | Pilot Officer JL Hills | 16.21 | 23.30 | |
| | Warrant Officer M Stafford | 16.25 | 00.17 | Crashed. |
| | Flight Sergeant RW Rowley | 16.26 | 23.54 | |
| | Flight Lieutenant ER Greenacre | 16.15 | 23.54 | Fighter contact over target: damaged. |
| | Warrant Officer DM Moore | 16.24 | 23.22 | |
| | Flight Sergeant. RAN Douglas | 16.31 | 23.57 | |
| | Flight Sergeant AJ Lynch | 16.28 | 23.59 | 'A very quiet trip, the most harassing period was over base on return.' |
| | Flight Sergeant RN Allan | 16.35 | 00.16 | |
| | Flying Officer FA Randall | 16.32 | | Crashed. 'Given permission to land at 23.04.' 'No troubles.' |
| | Pilot Officer JRE Howell | 16.34 | 23.56 | |
| | Flight Sergeant KJ Godwin | 16.22 | 23.57 | Crashed: into a field near the airfield. |
| | Flying Officer JA Cameron | 16.33 | 23.50 | |
| | Flying Officer RK McIntyre | 16.36 | 00.01 | |
| | Pilot Officer RNT Wade | 16.23 | 00.15 | Oxygen low. |
| | Flying Officer AW Wales | 16.19 | 23.09 | |
| | Warrant Officer PA Crosby | 16.37 | 23.41 | |
| | Warrant Officer JA Taggart | 16.30 | 18.30 | Early Return: starboard inner engine u/s. |
| | Flight Sergeant RM Baker | 16.29 | 00.13 | Diverted: to Ludford Magna. |

| Squadron and Base | Pilot | Took off | Landed | Notes |
|---|---|---|---|---|
| **463 (Waddington)** *5 Group* | Pilot Officer TJ Foster | 17.05 | 00.26 | |
| | Pilot Officer AR Bowman | 16.57 | 00.42 | |
| | Squadron Leader HB Locke | 16.40 | 00.21 | |
| | Pilot Officer D Dunn | 16.33 | 00.20 | Flak. |
| | Flight Lieutenant RJ Cooper | 16.46 | 23.34 | **Diverted:** to Coleby. |
| | Pilot Officer C Baker | 16.23 | 00.28 | |
| | Pilot Officer VH Trimble | 17.04 | 00.05 | Coned by searchlights. |
| | Pilot Officer EA Smith | 16.59 | 00.31 | |
| | Pilot Officer GL Messenger | 16.36 | 00.19 | |
| | Pilot Officer AR Kell | 16.32 | 00.24 | |
| | Pilot Officer AR Hart | 16.39 | 23.53 | |
| | Flying Officer AJ Leslie | 17.14 | 19.13 | **Early Return:** no explanation noted. |
| **467 (Waddington)** *5 Group* | Pilot Officer AB Simpson | 16.37 | 00.14 | 'Return to base very grim.' |
| | Pilot Officer RM Stanford | 16.38 | 23.48 | |
| | Pilot Officer NM McClelland | 16.27 | 23.45 | |
| | Flight Lieutenant DS Symonds | 16.20 | 23.32 | |
| | Flight Sergeant DL Gibbs | 16.31 | 23.58 | |
| | Pilot Officer W Mackay | 16.24 | 23.56 | 'No trouble of any kind.' |
| | Flying Officer I Durston | 17.02 | 23.42 | 4,000 lb. bomb released manually: bomb slip u/s. |
| | Pilot Officer F Morris | 16.37 | 23.56 | Broke cloud at 400 feet over sea. |
| | Pilot Officer BR Jones | 16.22 | 23.41 | |
| | Flying Officer JP Colpus | 16.29 | 18.40 | **Early Return:** WT u/s; DR compass u/s; intercom not operating efficiently. |
| | Flying Officer WD Marshall | 16.34 | 00.15 | **Diverted:** to Metheringham. |
| | Pilot Officer Riley | – | – | Did not take off: RT u/s. |
| **514 (Foulsham)** *2 Group* | Flight Sergeant RM Ashpitel | 16.52 | 23.44 | **Diverted:** to Little Snoring. |
| | Pilot Officer GS Hughes | 16.47 | 23.26 | **Diverted:** to Downham Market. 'Pretty good trip.' |

| Squadron and Base | Pilot | Took off | Landed | Notes |
|---|---|---|---|---|
| | Flight Sergeant DCC Crombie | 16.49 | 00.13 | **Diverted:** to Downham Market. |
| | Squadron Leader Reid | 16.44 | 00.49 | **Diverted:** to Downham Market. |
| | Pilot Officer EA Greenwood | 16.55 | 00.16 | **Diverted:** to Downham Market. |
| | Flying Officer GJ Chequer | 16.45 | 00.01 | **Diverted:** to Downham Market. |
| | Squadron Leader A Roberts | 16.51 | 00.28 | **Diverted:** to Downham Market. |
| | Flight Lieutenant CW Nichol | 16.50 | 00.07 | **Diverted:** to Downham Market. |
| | Flight Lieutenant C Payne | 16.45 | 18.55 | **Early Return:** problems with the hydraulics – undercarriage could not be raised. |
| | Flight Sergeant NW Thackray | 16.53 | 00.12 | **Diverted:** to Downham Market. Combat en route. |
| | Pilot Officer JK Williams | 17.07 | 23.41 | **Diverted:** to Downham Market. |
| **550 (Waltham)** *1 Group* | Flight Sergeant Bouchard | 16.08 | 23.42 | 'Landing conditions difficult.' |
| | Flying Officer Picton | 16.06 | 23.26 | |
| | Flight Sergeant Oliver | 16.41 | 23.53 | |
| | Squadron Leader GD Graham | 16.04 | 00.05 | Wing Commander JJ Bennett on board. 'Fighter flares seen from Dutch coast to targets.' |
| | Pilot Officer DC Dripps | 16.32 | 23.57 | Holed in starboard petrol tank by heavy flak just as they bombed. |
| | Sergeant HFJ Woods | 16.22 | 00.05 | 'Trip very uneventful.' |
| | Squadron Leader B Bell | 16.15 | 00.04 | |
| | Flying Officer RH Mawle | 16.16 | 23.30 | |
| | Flight Sergeant AH Jeffries | 16.14 | 00.07 | |
| | Warrant Officer GF Peasgood | 16.20 | 00.03 | |
| | Flight Sergeant WR Cooper | 16.50 | 20.19 | **Early Return:** WT/RT, DR compass and Sperry panel u/s; coolant leak. |
| | Flying Officer JO Richard | 16.25 | 01.03 | 'Difficulties on landing at base.' |
| | Flying Officer AB Craig | 16.20 | 00.09 | |
| | Flying Officer GA Morrison | 16.23 | 23.50 | |
| | Pilot Officer GB Hoddle | 16.38 | 18.40 | **Early Return:** rear turret u/s. |

| Squadron and Base | Pilot | Took off | Landed | Notes |
|---|---|---|---|---|
| **576 (Elsham Wolds)** *1 Group* | Flight Sergeant J Henningham | 16.55 | 23.25 | **Diverted:** to Waltham. Referred to as *Pilot Officer* Henningham elsewhere. |
| | Flight Sergeant FR Scott | 16.36 | | **Crashed:** in collision with 103 a/c piloted by Flight Sergeant V Richter over Ulceby, Lincs. **Shot down.** |
| | Flight Sergeant RS McAra | 16.27 | | |
| | Flight Sergeant AJ Bodger | 16.32 | 23.47 | |
| | Flying Officer GS Morgan | 16.28 | 23.39 | |
| | Flight Sergeant HR Marsden | 16.30 | 19.00 | **Early Return:** Low oil pressure - port engine. |
| | Warrant Officer TJ Bassett | 16.20 | 00.30 | **Diverted:** to Wickenby. **Crashed:** on landing – three injured. |
| | Pilot Officer RJ Edie | 16.30 | 23.20 | |
| | Warrant Officer CC Rollins | 16.20 | 00.30 | |
| | Flight Sergeant Thomas | | | Failed to take off – engine trouble. |
| **619 (Woodhall)** *5 Group* | Pilot Officer EK Williams | 16.32 | 00.07 | |
| | Lieutenant HC Knilans | 16.21 | 23.41 | |
| | Flying Officer ML Hamilton | 16.33 | 00.04 | |
| | Flying Officer JG Thompson | 16.29 | 00.01 | |
| | Flight Sergeant RW Olsen | 16.35 | 00.47 | Compass problems. |
| | Flight Lieutenant A Sandison | 16.19 | 23.47 | |
| | Flying Officer GS Stout | 16.44 | 23.52 | Monica u/s. |
| | Pilot Officer RE Knights | 16.24 | 00.14 | Died on 4 December 2004. Bombed the Tirpitz three times. |
| | Flying Officer JK Cox | 16.34 | 00.11 | API u/s. |
| | Pilot Officer FG Secker | 16.22 | 00.56 | |
| | Flight Sergeant V Langford | 16.25 | 00.21 | |
| | Flight Lieutenant AH Tomlin | 16.35 | 01.40 | **Crashed:** near base. Port outer engine problems. Engine fire over base. |
| | Pilot Officer GR Loney | 16.30 | | **Shot down.** |

| Squadron and Base | Pilot | Took off | Landed | Notes |
|---|---|---|---|---|
| | Pilot Officer GG Taylor | 16.30 | 00.25 | **Diverted:** to Binbrook. |
| | Flying Officer JA Heffernan | 16.20 | 23.59 | **Diverted:** to Blyton. |
| **625 (Kelstern)** *1 Group* | Pilot Officer GR Kroemer | 16.20 | 00.20 | **Shot down.** |
| | Wing Commander T Preston | 16.20 | 00.45 | |
| | Warrant Officer D Baker | 16.20 | | |
| | Warrant Officer ES Ellis | 17.05 | 23.30 | **Crashed:** overshot at base and hit the ground with a wing; belly-landed. |
| | Flight Sergeant RW Price | 16.35 | 18.25 | **Early Return:** starboard inner engine overheating; couldn't climb over 8,000 feet. |
| | Flight Sergeant JD Owen | 16.40 | 18.30 | **Early Return:** heavy leak in oxygen system. |
| | Flying Officer GE Woolley | 16.45 | 23.25 | **Crashed:** in bad visibility; one mile away at Gayton-le-Wold. An American. |
| | Flight Sergeant RM Etchells | 16.30 | 00.05 | **Diverted:** to Blyton. Cloud at 500 feet. |
| | Sergeant K Doyle | 16.30 | 00.30 | **Diverted:** to Ludford Magna. |
| | Flight Lieutenant JC Day | 16.30 | 23.30 | 'Landing hazardous.' |
| | Flight Lieutenant BN Dougill | 16.15 | 20.15 | **Diverted:** to Ludford. **Early Return:** on three engines after starboard outer cut out. |
| | Pilot Officer RG Bowden | 16.15 | 00.15 | **Diverted:** to Blyton. Starboard inner engine fire; navigator had leg injury. 'Tricky landing.' |
| | Sergeant GF Clark | 16.35 | 00.05 | **Diverted:** to Ludford Magna. |
| | Sergeant RJ Cook | 17.10 | 00.40 | **Diverted:** to Blyton. |
| | Flight Sergeant WS Middlemiss | 17.10 | 00.40 | **Diverted:** to Blyton. |
| | Flying Officer TM Nicholls | 16.25 | 00.15 | |
| | Sergeant R Gallop | 16.50 | 19.15 | **Early Return:** a/c would not climb. |
| **626 (Wickenby)** *1 Group* | Flight Lieutenant J Spiller | 15.53 | 00.14 | |
| | Flight Lieutenant BL McLaughlin | 15.59 | 00.02 | |
| | Flight Lieutenant AJH Wright | 16.27 | 23.55 | |

| Squadron and Base | Pilot | Took off | Landed | Notes |
|---|---|---|---|---|
| | Pilot Officer DA Sargent | 16.18 | 23.33 | |
| | Pilot Officer JAL Currie | 16.16 | 23.18 | |
| | Flight Sergeant J Butcher | 16.44 | 00.25 | |
| | Sergeant J Cuthill | 16.21 | 19.14 | Early Return: overheating outer engines. |
| | Squadron Leader JA Neilson | 15.54 | 00.15 | |
| | Pilot Officer WS Breckenridge | 16.37 | 01.10 | GEE u/s. |
| | Pilot Officer R Welham | 16.09 | 23.25 | |
| | Flight Sergeant J Torrance | 16.26 | 00.15 | |
| | Sergeant DS Jackson | 16.15 | 00.10 | |
| | Sergeant J Higgs | 16.12 | 00.35 | 'Arrived five minutes late over target through inability to climb.' |
| | Flight Sergeant NE West | 16.43 | 20.19 | Early Return: mid-upper gunner ill – possible oxygen shortage. |
| 630 (East Kirkby) 5 *Group* | Squadron Leader M Crocker | 16.44 | 18.25 | Early Return: CSU failure. |
| | Flight Lieutenant WH Kellaway | 16.45 | 23.59 | 'Fine and slightly hazy at base.' |
| | Flying Officer JH Pratt | 16.49 | 23.33 | H2S and Monica u/s. |
| | Flight Sergeant HC McIntosh | 16.52 | 00.25 | |
| | Flying Officer D Roberts | 16.54 | 00.32 | |
| | Pilot Officer A Drinkall | 16.34 | 00.04 | |
| | Flight Sergeant J White | 16.49 | 00.45 | |
| | Flying Officer J Weller | 16.41 | 00.03 | Weather 'fine at base.' |
| | Pilot Officer DH Cheney | 16.48 | 00.18 | |
| | Pilot Officer AGG Johnson | 16.43 | 00.20 | |
| | Sergeant RH Rogers | 16.57 | 00.15 | Diverted: to Spilsby. 'Low cloud.' |

# SOURCES AND BIBLIOGRAPHY

| Title | Author | Publisher | Year |
| --- | --- | --- | --- |
| We Lived to Tell | Aircrew Association | Privately published | 2001 |
| Lost Voices of the RAF | Max Arthur | Hodder | 1993 |
| One WAAF's War | Joan Beech | Costello | 1989 |
| Achieve Your Aim | Kevin Bending | Woodfield | 2005 |
| Pathfinder | Donald Bennett | Goodall | 1988 |
| The Door Marked Summer | Michael Bentine | Granada | 1981 |
| The Past is Myself | Christabel Bielenburg | Corgi | 1984 |
| The Second World War | John D Cantwell | HMSO | 1993 |
| No Moon Tonight | Don Charlwood | Goodall | 1984 |
| RAF Bomber Command Losses (various volumes) | WR Chorley | Midland | various |
| 619 The History of a Forgotten Squadron | Bryan Clark | Woodfield | 2005 |
| The Fringes of Power | John Colville | Weidenfeld & Nicholson | 2004 |
| Bombers Over Berlin | Alan W Cooper | William Kimber | 1985 |
| Lancaster Target | Jack Currie | Goodall | 1981 |
| Reap the Whirlwind | Dunmore & Carter | Crecy | 1992 |
| SOE: Special Operations Executive | MRD Foot | Pimlico | 1999 |
| Luftwaffe Night Fighter Combat Claims | Foreman et al. | Red Kite | 2004 |
| Bases of Bomber Command | Roger A Freeman | After the Battle | 2003 |
| Enemy Coast Ahead | Guy Gibson | Goodall | 1986 |
| Lancaster at War | Garbett & Goulding | Allan | 1979 |
| Fire By Night | Jennie Gray | Grub Street | 2000 |
| 1943 The Victory that Never Was | John Grigg | Eyre Methuen | 1980 |
| Selected for Aircrew | James Hampton | Air Research | 1993 |
| Despatches on War Operations | Sir Arthur Harris | Cass | 1995 |

| Title | Author | Publisher | Year |
|---|---|---|---|
| Bomber Offensive | Sir Arthur Harris | Collins | 1947 |
| 83 Squadron 1917-1969 | Low & Harper | RG Low | 1997 |
| Bomber Command | Max Hastings | Michael Joseph | 1979 |
| Torpedo Junction | Homer J Hickam | Naval Institute Press | 1989 |
| There and Back Again | James Douglas Hudson | Tucann Books | 2001 |
| The Secret Squadrons | Robert Jackson | Robson Books | 1983 |
| RAF Squadrons | CG Jefford | Airlife | 2001 |
| Most Secret War | RV Jones | Hamish Hamilton | 1978 |
| Hitler: 1936–45 Nemesis | Ian Kershaw | Penguin | 2000 |
| Call of the Goose | Diane Elaine Lazenby | | 1998 |
| The Berlin Raids | Martin Middlebrook | Viking | 1988 |
| The Bomber Command War Diaries | Middlebrook & Everitt | Midland | 1985 |
| Thunderbirds at War | Laurence Motiuk | Larmot | 1995 |
| The Bomber War | Robin Neillands | John Murray | 2001 |
| Tail-End Charlies | Nicholl and Rennell | Viking | 2004 |
| Broken Eagles | Bill Norman | Pen & Sword | 2001 |
| Joe: the Autobiography of a Trenchard Brat | Joe Northrop | Square One | 1993 |
| Maximum Effort | Patrick Otter | Archive Publications | 1990 |
| Yorkshire Airfields in the 2nd World War | Patrick Otter | Countryside Books | 1998 |
| Lincolnshire Airfields in the 2nd World War | Patrick Otter | Countryside Books | 1996 |
| Bomber Harris: His Life and Times | Henry Probert | Greenhill | 2001 |
| Training Notes for Air Navigators | RAF (HQ 21 Group) | HMSO | 1949 |
| Lancaster Operations | Ian Reid | Ashlea Thomas | 2003 |
| The Hardest Victory | Dennis Richards | Penguin | 2001 |
| Laurels for Prinz Wittgenstein | Werner Roell | Independent Books | 1994 |
| Bomber Boys | Mel Rolfe | Grub Street | 2004 |
| The Luckiest Men Alive | Mark Rowe | Privately published | 2003 |
| On the Natural History of Destruction | WG Sebald | Hamish Hamilton | 2003 |

| Title | Author | Publisher | Year |
|---|---|---|---|
| Suffolk Airfields in the 2nd World War | Graham Smith | Countryside Books | 1995 |
| An Interesting War | Arthur Spencer | Privately published | 2003 |
| Bomber Crew | John Sweetman | Little, Brown | 2004 |
| Bomber Crew | Taylor & Davidson | Hodder & Stoughton | 2004 |
| The Right of the Line | John Terraine | Hodder | 1985 |
| Edwin's Letters | David A Thomas | Cassell | 2001 |
| Lancaster to Berlin | Walter Thompson | Goodall | 1985 |
| We Landed by Moonlight | Hugh Verity | Crecy | 2005 |
| London 1945 | Maureen Waller | John Murray | 2004 |
| Beware of the Dog at War | John Ward | JOTE | |
| Flying Through Fire | Geoffrey Williams | Grange | 1995 |
| Behind the Network | Bob Wilson | Hodder & Stoughton | 2003 |
| Bomber Boys | Kevin Wilson | Weidenfeld & Nicholson | 2005 |
| On Wings of War | Jim Wright | | |
| SOE Syllabus | | National Archives | 2004 |

# NOTES

## Chapter One

1 The description is from an article for *Collier's* magazine by American journalist and writer, Martha Gellhorn, and quoted in *Martha Gellhorn* by Caroline Moorehead, page 245.

2 The average time was seven and a half hours. See Appendix B.

3 National Archives: AIR 14/3507.

4 See *Despatch on War Operations*, Sir Arthur Harris, page 20.

5 97 Squadron navigator, Arthur Spencer.

6 *Bomber Offensive*, Sir Arthur Harris, pages 186–187.

7 Telephone call with Ronald Low, ex 83 Squadron, June 2005.

8 National Archives: AIR 14/3230. See also the table at Appendix C.

9 There was a tricky balance to be struck between bombs, fuel and ammunition in terms of weight. Similarly, some gunners were resentful of any reduction in ammunition, for obvious reasons.

10 From the diary of 408 Squadron pilot Warrant Officer RT 'Skip' Lloyd (RCAF); this is held in the memorial room, RAF Linton-on-Ouse.

11 158 Squadron flew Halifaxes and so were not involved in the raid on 16 December.

12 From *We Lived to Tell*, 2001, Aircrew Association. 158 Squadron was stationed at Driffield in East Yorkshire, moving later some fifteen miles east to Lissett.

13 *The Luckiest Men Alive,* Mark Rowe, page 86.

14 *The Luckiest Men Alive,* Mark Rowe, page 65.

15 Sergeant Clark's diary can be found on the BBC's 'WW2 People's War' website.

16 Derek Giblin quoted in *The Luckiest Men Alive,* Mark Rowe, page 10.

17 Letter to the author, 25 May 2004.

18 It was an accurate, but not an original soubriquet: the German 'Black Thursday' – 15 August 1940 – had happened during the Battle of Britain, while the Americans, in losing sixty-five aircraft on 14 October 1943, had used the same term. It was even used to describe Churchill's election defeat on 26 July 1945.

## Chapter Two

1 In *An Interesting War* – privately published.
2 *Fire By Night* by Jennie Gray.
3 One over Germany and seven on return.
4 See the table at Appendix A.
5 The actual number is sixty. See Appendix F.
6 The first Halifax crew were flying out of Rufforth from 1663 Heavy Conversion Unit (HCU). See *Bomber Command Losses volume 8* by W R Chorley. Six of the crew survived.

## Chapter Three

1 The RAF had bombed Berlin thirty times in 1940, and seventeen times in 1941.
2 This story is recounted by Joe Northrop in *Lancaster at War 2* by Mike Garbett and Brian Goulding, page 127.
3 For the full horror of this, see *On the Natural History of Destruction* by WG Sebald, pages 91–93.
4 Curtis was the mid-upper gunner on Pilot Officer Billing's crew.
5 A Mosquito from 1409 Meteorological Flight.
6 Taken from the 'B' form – teleprinted briefing sheets: National Archives: AIR 14/3140.
7 Jack Currie in his book *Lancaster Target*, page 78.
8 Northrop in *Lancaster at War*, Garbett and Goulding, page 128.
9 I am indebted to the diary of Sergeant Bernard Clark, 61 Squadron for this next section. See note 15 for chapter 1 on page 223. The role of 'second dickey' is described on page 24.
10 First to take off – at 15.49 – was Pilot Officer Grannum of 12 Squadron at Wickenby, Lincolnshire. Most took off between 16.15 and 16.45. Some aircraft took off without their 'cans' – incendiaries: Skip Lloyd of 408 Squadron was one such.
11 National Archives: AIR 14/552.
12 National Archives: AIR 14/3513.
13 See *The Berlin Raids* by Martin Middlebrook page 177. Middlebrook cites as evidence the diary of a Canadian based at Linton, presumably 'Skip' Lloyd's.
14 This section draws on *The Diary of Sgt Bernard Clark* on the BBC's 'People's War' website.
15 Middlebrook makes clear that the route went straight out over Holland and returned via Denmark.
16 See *Lancaster Target*, Jack Currie, page 158.
17 Information provided by ex-115 Squadron mid-upper gunner, John H Ward.

18 '(We) estimate that with 600 aircraft bombing one aiming point in 40 minutes there (will) probably be 1 or 2 collisions.' National Archives: AIR 14/838.

19 *The Past is Myself* by Christabel Bielenburg, page 127.

20 *Bombers Over Berlin*, by Alan W Cooper, pages 108–109.

## Chapter Four

1 According to the Accident Report Form – Form 1180.

2 National Archives: AIR 27/1797.

3 See *Thunderbirds at War*, by Laurence Motiuk, page 285. I am grateful to Julian Hendy for information regarding Sergeant Jamieson.

4 I am grateful to former 426 Squadron pilot Roger Coulombe for his description of Tom Kneale.

5 I am grateful to Max Liddle of Yearsley for this information.

6 National Archives: AIR 27/1797.

7 Local resident John Thorp reported to me that the aircraft came down at Clitherbeck, and also confirmed that local children regularly turned up ammunition from the moorland.

## Chapter Five

1 Estimates of the numbers of aircraft on this operation vary slightly. 482 is the number of Lancasters according to AIR 14/905 (National Archives). That document also registers ten Mosquitoes. It indicates that 441 Lancasters pressed home the attack. 5 Group contributed the most (165) and 3 Group the fewest (twenty-five). See AIR 14/3442.

2 *One WAAF's War* by Joan Beech, page 79.

3 See *The Fringes of Power, Downing Street Diaries*, by John Colville, page 437.

4 *83 Squadron* by Ronald G Low and Frank E Harper, pages 113–114.

5 *Lancaster Target* by Jack Currie, page 86.

6 *Enemy Coast Ahead* by Guy Gibson, page 16.

7 He is describing a raid on Düsseldorf in the Ruhr.

8 *An Interesting War* by Arthur Spencer, page 9.

9 'The pilot said, 'It's about time we got out'. I got the pigeons out of the case and then threw them out...' So mid-upper gunner Sergeant Harold McLean described the moments before baling out on return from Mannheim, 9 August 1943. (See *Bomber Boys*, by Kevin Wilson, page 289).

10 National Archives: AIR 14/1405.

11 'Many of the best gunners never fired a shot in anger.' *Reaping the Whirlwind,* by Dunmore and Carter, page 65.

12 Warrant Officer Ernie Reynolds's testimony is taken from the collections of the Second World War Experience Centre, Horsforth, Leeds.

13 See Appendix B for a table showing the variation, squadron by squadron, of the journey times: lowest squadron average was 6 hours 50 minutes (115 Squadron), while the longest was 7 hours 56 minutes (626 Squadron).

## Chapter Six

1 *RAF Bomber Command Losses (1943)* by W R Chorley, page 423.

2 *Yorkshire Evening Press,* 16 December 1943. In fact, he was well enough to fly on the night of 16 December – see page 23.

3 There were no published weather reports or forecasts during the war, banned by a government determined to deny the enemy any information at all. See *London 1945* by Maureen Waller, page 76.

4 From 49 Squadron.

5 Reproduced courtesy of the Yorkshire Evening Press.

6 From Richard Allenby: his website at www.allenby.info provides interesting detail of wartime crashes on the North York Moors. The Form 1180, however, also cites high ground.

7 I am grateful to Eric 'Dick' Barton for this information.

8 Again, I am grateful to 'Dick' Barton for his valuable research.

9 Form 1180. Here, as elsewhere, extracts from the 1180s are Crown Copyright and have been reproduced with the permission of the Controller of Her Majesty's Stationery Office.

## Chapter Seven

1 Flight Lieutenant Aubrey Hall remembers a 'half moon' on return; information provided by John H Ward, 115 Squadron.

2 *One WAAF's War* by Joan Beech, pages 84–85.

3 Air Commodore Patrick Burnett died on 27 March 2004, aged ninety.

4 See *The Luckiest Men Alive* by Mark Rowe, page 44.

5 National Archives: AIR 27/687.

6 *83 Squadron 1917–1969,* by Ronald G Low and Frank E Harper, page 114.

7 Standard Beam Approach.

8 See *Joe – the Autobiography of a Trenchard Brat* by Wing Commander Joe Northrop, pages 159–161.

9 Form 1180: 'R/T failure made control instructions difficult to pass.'

10 *83 Squadron 1917–1969*, by Ronald G Low and Frank E Harper, page 114.

11 Despite his burns, he returned to flying duties with 635 Squadron. He completed thirty operations and flew with Pete De Wesselow, master-bomber on the Dresden raid, February 1945. See *Night After Night* by Max Lambert, pages 296–298.

12 Chorley notes that Tankard was the only death; however, McLean writing a letter home a month later noted: '...The rear gunner was also killed but I hardly knew him, seeing he replaced our regular gunner for that trip...'

13 National Archives: AIR 14/557 *Operational Planning of Bombs and Fuel Loads* calculated that a Lancaster 'on a normal night' would use 200 gallons per hour.

**Chapter Eight**

1 French-Canadian pilot Roger Coulombe (426 Squadron) gently reminded me of the Frenchness of swathes of Canada in an e-mail in June 2005: 'Here of course my daily language is Quebeccois – French as we speak it in Quebec'.

2 *Reap the Whirlwind* by Spencer and Dunmore, pages 278–279.

3 Crew Records, 460 Squadron: National Archives: AIR 14/2476.

4 Barometric pressure at nearby York had fallen from 1029 on the 16th to 1016 on the 17th. At Linton, it fell from 1022 at 5 pm on the 16th to 1018 by midnight.

5 See chapter 13.

6 'The 'side-slip' is a manoeuvre done by using the proper aileron to bank the aircraft on its side while using the opposite rudder' – e-mail to the author from Roger Coulombe on 26 June 2005.

7 National Archives: AIR 27/1797.

8 National Archives: AIR 27/1841.

**Chapter Nine**

1 See *The Berlin Raids* by Martin Middlebrook, pages 186–187. Buck served with both 97 and 207 Squadrons.

2 From 'Wikipedia' via Google.

3 The average height of the land where the planes came down in Yorkshire was 347 feet. This includes Sergeant Cooper's aircraft at Eastrington where I recorded a height of ten feet *below* sea level. Taking his aircraft out of the calculation alters the average to 652 feet.

4 Of the 43 crashes listed at Appendix A, five were in Yorkshire, seventeen in Lincolnshire, ten in Cambridgeshire and eleven elsewhere.

5 I am grateful to Roger Stephenson who farms locally and who sent me details concerning the fate of JB596. He has, for years, regularly turned up fragments of Proudfoot's shattered Lancaster during ploughing.

6 Form 1180.

7 Lincolnshire Archives, file Constab. 2/3/2/16/4 *Daily Situation Report, 17 December 1943 No. 32/1943*.

8 *Bomber Crew* by John Sweetman, page 147.

9 *Bomber Boys* by Mel Rolfe, pages 41–42.

10 National Archives: AIR 33/5; minute IG/973 on 22 January 1944.

11 National Archives: AIR 14/1410: from a letter from Bomber Command HQ to the Under Secretary of State for Air, dated 2 March 1944.

12 National Archives: AIR 14/364.

13 National Archives: AIR 14/364 again, referring to 'losses on mine-laying operations, May 1942–June 1943.'

14 National Archives: AIR 14/1482.

15 E-mail to the author: 31 August 2004.

## Chapter Ten

1 See *Lancaster Operations* by Ian Reid, page 77.

2 *No Moon Tonight* by Don Charlwood, pages 52–53.

3 Accident Form 1180: this judgement is based on the evidence of one of the surviving air gunners. The Form 1180 suggests Holford was lost and the 'sudden appearance of fog funnel lights distracted pilot.'

4 *Maximum Effort* by Patrick Otter, pages 91–92.

5 National Archives: AIR 27/2143.

6 *Maximum Effort* by Patrick Otter, page 92.

7 Quoted by Ian Reid in *Lancaster Operations*, page 77.

8 In a raid on Schweinfurt on 24 February 1944.

## Chapter Eleven

1 Chorley has JB373 but the ditching report in the National Archives AIR 14/1617 has JB363.

2 National Archives: AIR 14/1617.

3 AIR 14/1617 spells his name 'Hunley', but the ORB (AIR 27/538) has 'Hurley'.

4 'It is understandable that the wireless operator should make an effort to get another member of the crew out if he could, but in such circumstances as existed in this incident it is always considered very inadvisable.' Air Vice-Marshal Senior Air Staff Officer, Bomber Command 28 December 1943. National Archives: AIR 14/1617.

## Chapter Twelve

1 A typical fuel load for Berlin would be 1850 gallons.
2 He was subsequently awarded the Distinguished Flying Medal.
3 See *SOE: The Special Operations Executive 1940–1946* by MRD Foot, page 123.
4 Davies completed his tour with a new crew. However, the navigator, Pilot Officer Garriock was killed flying with 419 Squadron on 15 March 1945; while the bomb aimer, Flight Sergeant Mudry was shot down and taken prisoner on 5 March 1945.
5 National Archives: AIR 14/2476. Flight Sergeant Stafford's rank had altered to Warrant Officer by the time he flew next (to Berlin on 20 December, an operation from which he returned early with a malfunctioning compass).

## Chapter Thirteen

1 This and other extracts from Johnny Bank's journal are taken from an account written by Bill Lynn: these papers are held at the Yorkshire Air Museum archive at Elvington, North Yorkshire.
2 This raid was his ninth operation.
3 *Tail-End Charlies* by John Nichol and Tony Rennell, page 92.
4 He had lost an engine at 21,000 feet en route to Berlin.
5 Conversation with the author, 18 May 2004.
6 Presumably the tower on Foss Islands Road, in York, since destroyed.
7 See page 21.
8 *An Interesting War,* by Arthur Spencer, page 13. Arthur confirmed the remark in a subsequent e-mail: 'It was said by Bennett himself when he was talking to the 97 Squadron crews when we first arrived at Bourn.'
9 Information provided by Air Vice Marshal Jack Furner, 214 Squadron and No. 100 Group 1942–44 and quoted in the RAF Historical Society Journal 31 (2004). Furner's pilot wanted the fighter areas marked since he invariably corkscrewed throughout those dangerous sections of the night sky. This section draws on his testimony and on a copy of *Training Notes for Air Navigators (volume 1)* provided by 97 Squadron navigator, Arthur Spencer.
10 Not as high-tec as it sounds: merely a circular slide rule on one side, and on the other a mechanical device for solving a vector triangle.
11 RAF Historical Society Journal 31 (2004), page 148.
12 *Training Notes for Air Navigators.*
13 The examples are all taken from *RAF Bomber Command Losses, volume 4,* by W R Chorley. The dates/location and squadrons, in order, are: 3 January, Lakenheath, 149; 4 January, Huby, 102;

9 January, York, 158; 15 January, Pocklington, 51; 29 January, Colerne, 166; 18 March, Elvington, 77; 31 January, Fiskerton, 49; 2 March, Scampton, 57; 3 March, 98; 2 April, Topcliffe, 424; 4 May, Holme-on-Spalding-Moor, 101; 14 May, Downham Market, 218.

14 Air Vice-Marshal Thomas, commander of 3 Group, cited in *The Bomber War* by Robin Neillands, page 19.

15 *The Bomber War* by Robin Neillands, pages 19 and 67.

16 I am grateful to Ray Barker, Property Manager at Beningbrough Hall, Yorkshire whose father was the electrician concerned for this story.

17 *No Moon Tonight* by Don Charlwood, page 132.

18 One ex-navigator who survived the war commented on reading this: 'Any competent navigator ought to have been able to get an accurate fix in a matter of seconds.'

19 National Archives: AIR 14/539. The statistics also show a wide variation amongst PFF squadrons: GEE was at its most reliable during November in 405 Squadron, where just over 45 operations would be completed before GEE became u/s; for 109 Squadron, however, the figure was 11.3. The average for PFF was 20.6.

20 It should be remembered that GEE was not intended primarily as a landing device.

21 National Archives: AIR 33/5.

22 Northrop in *Lancaster at War* by Garbett and Goulding, page 134.

**Chapter Fourteen**
1 *Bomber Offensive* by Sir Arthur Harris, pages 72–73.
2 *The Right of the Line* by John Terraine, page 459.
3 Sir Charles Portal to Peirse, 23rd November 1941, quoted in *The Right of the Line* by John Terraine, page 460.
4 *The Right of the Line* by John Terraine, page 461.
5 *Bomber Offensive,* Harris, page 72.

**Chapter Fifteen**
1 He became Group Captain Spence in 1944.
2 Group Captain John Searby, quoted in *Bomber Harris: His Life and Times* by Henry Probert, page 152.
3 See *Bomber Offensive* by Arthur Harris, page 154.
4 Harris was not always so empathetic: Air Vice-Marshal Alec Coryton was removed as AOC 5 Group in early 1943 for objecting to what he saw as pointless operations in bad weather.
5 *Despatches on War Operations,* Sir Arthur Harris, page 180.

6 The data was provided by the National Meteorological Archive and Library.

7 Data for Catterick.

8 *Bomber Offensive,* by Sir Arthur Harris, page 35.

9 National Archives: AIR 33/16.

10 National Archives: AIR 33/18.

11 Para 728, clause 2. It is paradoxical, therefore, that weather observation data should include a 'Fitness for Flying' column (see chapter 18).

## Chapter Sixteen

1 I am grateful to Ron Parker and to Robin Lingard, curator of the Elsham Wolds memorial room, for bringing Marie's account of the events of that night to my attention. She died in 2005.

2 W R Chorley in *RAF Bomber Command Losses* places this crash at Ulceby near Horncastle. Confusingly there are two villages of the same name in Lincolnshire. It is clear however that the collision happened at Ulceby near Immingham. Apart from the testimony of Marie Harris, it is evident that the two Lancasters would not have covered the forty miles to the southern Ulceby in the three minutes that the aircraft were briefly aloft.

3 Lincolnshire Archives, file Constab 2/3/2/16/4. The quotation appears with the permission of Lincolnshire Archives.

4 Form 1180, RAF Museum, Hendon.

5 In *No Moon Tonight,* by Don Charlwood, page 147.

6 *No Moon Tonight,* Charlwood, page 51.

7 See *Bombers Over Berlin,* by Alan Cooper, page 103.

8 See *The Berlin Raids,* Middlebrook, page 178.

9 Schnaufer survived the war with a combat total of 121 allied aircraft shot down.

10 I am indebted to Dave Cheetham for his information on his uncle's death.

11 It is possible to correlate the downed Lancasters in *RAF Bomber Command Losses* by W R Chorley with the confirmed claims of Luftwaffe fighter pilots which are listed in *Luftwaffe Night Fighter Combat Claims 1939–1945,* by Foreman, Matthews and Parry.

12 *The Berlin Raid* by Martin Middlebrook, page 179.

13 *Behind the Network* by Bob Wilson, page 31.

14 Sayn-Wittgenstein was a friend of the Berlin diarist Marie Vassiltchikov who was taken aback at a dinner party on 25 January 1944 on discovering that he had been killed. See *Bomber Boys* by Kevin Wilson, page 422.

15 *Bomber Boys* by Kevin Wilson, pages 422–423.
16 I am grateful to Dave Cheetham for this account.
17 See *RAF Bomber Command Losses* by W R Chorley, page 420, and *Luftwaffe Night Fighter Combat Claims 1939–1945* by Foreman, Matthews and Parry, page 132.
18 It may have been the case this aircraft was shot down by a fighter: *Luftwaffe Night Fighter Claims* logs a claim by Hauptman Walter Borchers '10 kilometres NE of Berlin'.
19 Information provided to the author by Pilot Officer Norman Newton's regular mid-upper gunner, John Ward, who missed Black Thursday because of a bout of peritonitis.
20 National Archives: AIR 14/600 and AIR 14/601.
21 National Archives: AIR 14/601 – a report (no. 50) by Operational Research Section, Bomber Command, dated 8 September 1942.
22 *Most Secret War* by RV Jones, pages 389–390.

## Chapter Seventeen
1 Interview with the author. 'U' was flown by Flight Lieutenant G de Wesselow.
2 *Fire By Night* by Jennie Gray, page 79.
3 *An Interesting War*, Spencer, page 27.
4 His death is described in *Bomber Command* by Max Hastings, pages 294–295.
5 These accounts are derived from real incidents quoted by Middlebrook in *The Berlin Raids*, pages 184–187.
6 Letter to the author from the navigator, J P S Green, September 2005.
7 National Archives: AIR 27/2145.
8 From Henry Horscroft, 44 Squadron Association, dated 22 June 2005.
9 Air Commodore Clarke, as he became, was on his eighteenth operation. He was shot down over Schweinfurt in February 1944.
10 National Archives: AIR 27/833.

## Chapter Eighteen
1 National Archives: AIR 27/767.
2 I am grateful to Ian McGregor, Archive Information Manager, for his invaluable assistance.
3 Timings in the weather observation logs are in GMT, while BST+1 was the time used elsewhere. The 1600 readings then were at 6 pm BST+1. The crews were already over the North Sea.

4 *Synoptic Instruction No. 76*, National Meteorological Archive. 'When the fitness number is 0,' an Air Ministry memorandum for 15 April 1942 notes, 'the conditions are such as to prohibit landing for all types of a/c whether they are fitted with the best instrumental aids or not...'
5 Ronald Low, 83 Squadron.
6 National Archives: AIR 33/5.

**Chapter Nineteen**
1 See *Flying Through Fire* by Geoffrey Williams, page 2.
2 *Flying Through Fire* by Geoffrey Williams, pages 2–3.
3 See *Flying Through Fire* by Geoffrey Williams, page 4. Williams draws on *Bomber Command War Diaries* by Middlebrook and Everitt for this theory.
4 *Pathfinder* by Air Vice Marshal Donald Bennett, pages 214–215.
5 A total of fifteen FIDO installations were made by the end of the war. Harris in *Despatches on War Operations* page 189, notes that the first operational use of FIDO was on 19 November 1943. Thereafter, 2,500 successful landings were completed as a direct result of FIDO in the time up to the end of the war.
6 National Archives: BJ5/124 *Fog Dispersal Experiments – Meteorological Reports*.
7 *Flying Through Fire* by Geoffrey Williams, pages 106–109.
8 I am grateful to Air Vice Marshal P M S Hedgeland CB, OBE for his detailed account of the events of the night (letter to the author in July 2004). He was RDF (Radar Officer) at Graveley (with 35 Squadron) from November 1942 to April 1944.
9 *Flying Through Fire* by Geoffrey Williams, page 112.
10 *Flying Through Fire* by Geoffrey Williams, page 112.
11 This section draws on *Fire By Night* by Jennie Gray; *Flying Through Fire* by Geoffrey Williams; *RAF Bomber Command Losses* by WR Chorley.
12 The confusion is compounded by the fact that Britain was operating on double summer time during the war – but this did not necessarily find its way into official documentation. For example, RAF station weather data is logged using Greenwich Mean Time.
13 Chorley's timings appear to be one hour ahead of those used in other documentation e.g. *Flying Control Historical Record – Graveley* held at The National Archives and cited in Gray *op cit.* pages 72–73.
14 Official records time this at 00.35. The quotation is from the squadron's Operation Record Book. The accident card has the loss as being due to 'lack of petrol'.

15 Evidence of Mrs Isabelle Burton – see *Flying Through Fire* by Geoffrey Williams, page 112.

16 See *Fire by Night* by Jennie Gray, pages 72–73.

17 One pilot commented (not of the events of Black Thursday): 'I thought I was descending into hell'.


## Chapter Twenty

1 National Archives: AIR 14/557; 5 Group based their allocation of fuel on an average consumption of 200 gallons per hour.

2 *Torpedo Junction* by Homer J Hickam graphically illustrates the vulnerability of tankers in the Atlantic: a typical tanker might carry – either to port or the bottom of the ocean – a cargo of, say, 90,000 barrels of oil.

3 Doug Tritton's account is taken from *Beware the Dog at War* by John Ward. I am grateful to Tom Gatfield, Secretary of 49 Squadron Association, for drawing my attention to this description of Black Thursday.

4 National Archives: AIR 14/557; memorandum of 1 December 1943.

5 Len Whitehead in a letter to the author on 25 May 2004.

6 'Ingham had remained a sod-surface airfield, unsuitable for operation by four engine heavy bombers.' *Bases of Bomber Command Then and Now* by Roger A Freeman, page 52. Interestingly, the squadron ORB does not note this diversion.


## Chapter Twenty-One

1 In *Fire By Night*, by Jennie Gray.

2 The London Gazette for 17 November 1942 notes of Acting Flight Lieutenant Ernest Alfred Deverill DFC, DFM: '...This officer has invariably endeavoured to press home his attacks with great vigour.'


## Chapter Twenty-Two

1 See *Bomber Crew* by James Taylor & Martin Davidson, pages 340–342.

2 *Lost Voices of the RAF* by Max Arthur, page 255.

3 *Pilot's and Flight Engineer's Notes: Lancaster*, page 39.

4 American pilot, Ira Weinstein describes getting his 'chute snagged on the bombsight in *Tail-End Charlies* by John Nichol and Tony Rennell, page 257. With a massive effort he climbed back aboard the aircraft, took his 'chute off and then put it back on correctly, and jumped for a second time.

5 *Tail-End Charlies* by John Nichol and Tony Rennell, pages 292–293; Clark was flying in a Mosquito.
6 E-mail to the author on 15 June 2005.

## Chapter Twenty-Three
1 The telling phrase is Jennie Gray's in *Fire By Night*, page 75. I am very grateful to her for her account of the events surrounding JB531 Y-York and her crew that night.
2 For this extract from the *Suffolk Chronicle*, and for other invaluable research concerning the exact location of the crash site, I am deeply indebted to Brian Boulton. Pauleen Balls from Sudbourne also contributed background information.
3 From Flying Officer Mooney's aircraft over Wyton.

## Chapter Twenty-Four
1 Not all accommodation was so spartan. An intruding German had attacked Linton-on-Ouse in May 1941 and, as a result, a number of aircrew were billeted away from the main base. Beningbrough Hall (see pages 36–37) was used, while others were lodged at Aldwark Manor. Roger Coulombe was one such: 'I remember that having slept in once and missed the transportation bus, I walked to the station taking a short cut through the bomb dump which was situated under trees in a small wood.' (E-mail to the author on 25 June 2005).
2 *Reap The Whirlwind* by Spencer Dunmore and William Carter, page 14.
3 In fact the citation noted the 'difficult time in achieving the amalgamation of units and personnel moves... He has done well in trying circumstances.' He retired in November 1944 and died in Toronto in 1982. He was also awarded the Queen's Coronation Medal (1953); the Chevalier of the Legion of Honour (France) in 1947, and Croix de Guerre avec Palme in the same year; as well as the King's Cross of Liberation in Norway in 1948. Information gathered from the website of *The London Gazette*.

## Chapter Twenty-Five
1 Letter to the author from Len Whitehead, 22 June 2004.
2 On return they were diverted to Woodhall Spa where they waited for the fog to disperse before flying the thirty-five miles back to base.
3 97 Squadron navigator.
4 *Bomber Offensive* by Sir Arthur Harris, page 98.
5 *Selected for Aircrew*, James Hampton, page 135.

6 *Edwin's Letters*, David A Thomas, page 42. Edwin Thomas died in action on 16/17 April 1943.
7 'Pop' Walker, 12 Squadron. See chapter 26.
8 *There and Back Again, A Navigator's Story*, Flying Officer James Douglas Hudson, page 21.
9 National Archives: AIR 14/508.
10 Information provided to the author on 26 November 2004.
11 Operational Training Unit.
12 E-mail to author on 23 November 2004.
13 Report 312 (dated 23 November 1943 to 8 December), National Archives AIR 33/5.
14 National Archives: AIR 33/5.

## Chapter Twenty-Six
1 There is some uncertainty about the exact location: Form 1180 has the location as '1 mile SW of Barton on Humber', but the village of Thornton Curtis has been crossed out. That village is two miles south east of *Barrow* upon Humber, as opposed to Barton-upon-Humber.
2 Form 1180.
3 National Archives: AIR 27/1089.
4 The incident is described in *On Wings of War* by Jim Wright. It was brought to my attention by Peter Parnham.
5 The location indicated on the Form 1180 is Hundon Moor, half a mile north of Caistor.
6 *RAF Bomber Command Losses* by W R Chorley, page 428.
7 National Archives: AIR 27/1908.
8 Form 1180 has 'Feltwalk Farm'.
9 Form 1180: '. . . maybe caused by shortage of petrol.'
10 National Archives: AIR 14/2476.
11 Letter from the Air Historical Branch, Ministry of Defence dated 12 March 1990.
12 In *The Door Marked Summer* by Michael Bentine. The account of Walker's ghost is taken from an article by Bentine in *The Sunday Times*.

## Chapter Twenty-Seven
1 Until 15 December 1943, the Commanding Officer of 97 Squadron was Group Captain Fresson; predictably he was known as 'Press On Fresson'.
2 *Reap the Whirlwind* by Dunmore and Carter, page 107.
3 *Tail-End Charlies* by Nicholl and Rennell, page 161.
4 *Tail-End Charlies* by Nicholl and Rennell.

5  See Appendix D.

6  For Sergeant Rogers (12 Squadron); Rogers brought some of his bombs home. National Archives: AIR 27/167.

## Chapter Twenty-Eight

1  Not including the eight man crew of Flying Officer D Brill, a Wiltshire man, whose aircraft was shot down over enemy territory.

2  Thirty-six men from 97 Squadron died: just under 25 per cent of the 151 flying that night.

3  The ORB has a constant theme from returning pilots that 'cloud obscured results' or 'no results – cloud'.

4  *Fire By Night* by Jennie Gray, page 65.

5  The average was seven and a half hours.

6  Gray, *op. cit.* page 65.

7  Chorley has them crashing at 01.45 am. The ORB entry states: 'Crashed on landing on returning from raid on BERLIN owing to bad visibility and low cloud...'

8  National Archives: AIR 27/767.

9  In 97 Squadron, Deverill, Thackway and Scott were posted on 5 December; 19 November; and 14 November respectively.

10  The aircraft came down in the North Sea.

11  97 Squadron ORB.

12  *Fire By Night,* Jennie Gray, page 80.

## Chapter Twenty-Nine

1  See page 106.

2  See page 5 for an indication that this clay pigeon shoot was used by 405 Squadron's gunners the day before Black Thursday.

## Chapter Thirty

1  Flixton is the home of the Norfolk and Suffolk Aviation Museum. The Rebecca aerial was salvaged from the River Deben in 1982.

2  422 Squadron, 305th Group, 1st Bombardment Division (National Archives: AIR 40/509).

3  Squadron Leader James Wagland died on 2 April 2005, aged 91.

4  See *SOE Syllabus: Lessons in Ungentlemanly Warfare,* published by the National Archives, pages 147–148.

5  *SOE: the Special Operations Executive 1940–46* by MRD Foot, pages 142–143.

6  *The Secret Squadrons* by Robert Jackson, page 88.

7  A Lysander's range was about 700 miles.

8  *The Secret Squadrons* by Robert Jackson, page 88.

### Chapter Thirty-One

1 *Thunderbirds At War* by Laurence Motiuk, page 166.
2 *Call of the Goose,* by Diane Elaine Lazenby.
3 Letter to the author, 11 December 2004.
4 Lincolnshire Archives, File: Constab. 2/3/2/16/4.
5 See page 74.
6 The pre-war and wartime method of pinpointing location.
7 See page 17.

### Chapter Thirty-Two

1 *Maximum Effort* by Patrick Otter.
2 National Archives: AIR14/1410.
3 See Appendix E for an analysis of the reasons for each crash.

### Chapter Thirty-Three

1 Written by *Oberleutnant* Karl von Manowada and quoted in *Broken Eagles:* Luftwaffe *Losses Over Yorkshire 1939–1945* by Bill Norman.
2 Both 83 and 97 Squadrons returned to 5 Group in April 1944.
3 See *RAF Bomber Command Losses (volume 6)* by W R Chorley, page 157.

### Chapter Thirty-Four

1 National Archives: AIR 19/557.
2 National Archives: CAB 66 includes the 'weekly résumé'.
3 *Fire By Night*, Jennie Gray, page 93.
4 See Appendix A for a full list of all crashes on Black Thursday.
5 National Archives: AIR 14/1410.
6 National Archives: AIR 14/1410.
7 *Flying Through Fire* by Geoffrey Williams, page 113.
8 The Director of Aircraft Safety has written to the Commander-in-Chief Bomber Command along these lines. National Archives: AIR 14/1410.
9 The AOC i/c noted on the 1180 that 'the station has Sandra lights but no personnel to operate them'. Sandra lights were designed to assist pilots in gauging height when approaching the runway.
10 *Maximum Effort* by Patrick Otter, page 93.
11 The wording which follows is taken verbatim from a letter from the Director of Air Safety to Sir Arthur Harris on 14 February, 1944. It can be found in AIR 14/1410, National Archives.

### Appendix A

1 National Archives: AIR 27/890.

# INDEX